This clear and comprehensive introduction to the films of Spain's most popular director gives a fascinating insight into the influences and ideas behind his inimitable mix of melodrama, farce and social satire.

A Spanish Labyrinth ranges from the international success of *Women on the Verge of a Nervous Breakdown*, the critically acclaimed *Live Flesh* and 2000 Oscar-winning *All About My Mother* to early works previously unheard of outside Almodóvar's home country. Mark Allinson sheds light on the conditions surrounding production of the films and places them in the cultural context of a newly Democratic Spain, with Almodóvar as 'agent provocateur' and icon of this new-found freedom.

Highlighting Almodóvar's playful attitude to cinematic genre, his use of parody and satire and his distinctive visual style, Allinson also explores the director's controversial characterization of gender roles and the importance of social and national identity in his films. High-profile relationships with actors, actresses and the popular press – as well as his love of his adopted city Madrid – are also revealed as major influences on Almodóvar's unique cinematic vision.

An indispensable work for enthusiasts of Almodóvar's films and students of cinema and Hispanic studies alike.

Mark Allinson lectures in the Department of Hispanic Studies, Royal Holloway College, University of London.

A Spanish Labyrinth

The Films of
Pedro Almodóvar

Mark Allinson

I.B. Tauris *Publishers*
LONDON • NEW YORK

Published in 2001 by I.B.Tauris & Co Ltd,
6 Salem Road, London W2 4BU
175 Fifth Avenue, New York NY 10010
www.ibtauris.com

In the United States of America and in Canada distributed by
St. Martin's Press, 175 Fifth Avenue, New York NY 10010

ISBN 1 86064 507 0

A full CIP record for this book is available from the British Library
A full CIP record for this book is available from the Library of Congress

Library of Congress catalog card: available

Set in Monotype Garamond by Ewan Smith, London
Printed and bound in Great Britain by MPG Books Ltd, Bodmin, Cornwall

Contents

Illustrations

Preface and Acknowledgements

Lauren Bacall was recently asked in an interview when she was going to star in another great film. Modestly, she replied that she had never appeared in a great movie, her first would be – she hoped – the first English-language film by Pedro Almodóvar.[1] Looking the world over for a great director, Bacall set her sights firmly on Spain's new man from La Mancha; she could yet have the chance if Almodóvar is tempted to make a film in the USA, as has long been speculated.[2] If the director does begin an 'American phase', then this book will prove timely, for it deals with twenty years of films made in Spain, very Spanish films which have nevertheless earned Almodóvar an international reputation, culminating in the Oscar for *All About My Mother* in March 2000.

The increasing interest in Almodóvar in the English-speaking world is my main reason for writing this book. Until now the only monograph available in English has been Paul Julian Smith's excellent *Desire Unlimited* (1994) which focuses on the themes of gender, nationality and homosexuality. My aim is to provide an introductory guide for anyone interested in Almodóvar's cinema, whether it be film specialists who want to read about the cultural context of the films, Hispanists who want to read about the films as cinematic texts, or the general film-goer eager simply to read more about Almodóvar. Part One contextualizes the films with a brief survey of their cultural background, including changing production conditions and the effects of Almodóvar's own media-friendly persona. Part Two concentrates on the thematic 'content' of the films, covering questions of national identity, gender, sexuality and the less frequently addressed question of social structures. Part Three focuses on construction, with chapters on the use of Madrid as cinematic space, on Almodóvar's original use of genre, as well as on visual style and music. The conclusion analyses Almodóvar's relationship to the postmodern concepts of performance and parody. Short summaries of the plots of the films are provided in Appendix 2, for those who have not seen certain films or whose memories need jogging. I have also included a glossary of Spanish terms (Appendix 1). And as the chapters are not organized film by film, a degree of cross-referencing is included.

A number of people have helped to make this book possible and so deserve thanks. Kirsty Dunseath gave initial encouragement. Paz Sufrategui at El Deseo was enormously helpful with photographic material, Press Books and her well-kept archives. Esther García generously answered my questions on production. A special thank you goes to Jesús Robles of the 8½ bookshop (Alphaville cinema) in Madrid for locating (and donating) what even the Biblioteca Nacional could not find. Friends in Spain, among them Enrique, Merche, Alicia and Vincenç, Isabel, Javier, sent me articles and videos. Deborah Shaw kindly sent me a copy of her unpublished article. Antonio Sánchez shared his thoughts on postmodernism. Colleagues and friends read early drafts and gave helpful advice: Sarah Wykes, the Introduction, Penny Noble on Visual Style, Jill Hobson on Social Structures, Santi Fouz on Gender and Sexuality, Ian Biddle on Music, and Richard Pym on National Identity (as well as countless questions on bullfighting!). Chris Perriam and Stella Bruzzi each read the whole manuscript and gave expert advice about shaping the final book to meet the needs of both Hispanists and film specialists/enthusiasts. Finally, I thank my parents for relieving pressures elsewhere, and for taking me to Spain twenty years ago – the year in which Almodóvar made his first film.

All translations, both of dialogue from the films and of secondary material originally in Spanish, are my own. All stills are courtesy of El Desco SA. The image on page ii reproduced with kind permission of Juan Gatti.

For Gejo,
for understanding Almodóvar when I didn't
and for sharing my passion for the films.

Part One
Context

Introduction: Almodóvar – the *Auteur* of a Free Spain

In 1942, Gerald Brenan used the metaphor of the labyrinth to explain the complexities of Spanish history that led to one of the twentieth century's most bloody and bitter civil wars and, subsequently, to Western Europe's longest-surviving dictatorship.[1] Forty years later, Almodóvar's second feature, *Labyrinth of Passions*, uses the same metaphor to describe life in a Spanish capital suddenly liberated from decades of dictatorship, suddenly freed from the weight of recent Spanish history. That the name 'Almodóvar' should mean 'place of freedom' or 'freeing of slaves' is a happy coincidence.[2] For in 1999, Pedro Almodóvar symbolized free and democratic Spain – as its chronicler and as its *agent provocateur* – to the extent that Spain's most prominent national newspaper asked in its main editorial why Almodóvar had become the symbol of Spain's rupture with Francoism (Vidal-Beneyto 1999: 17). The director's clear identification with Spain's *movida* (the explosion of pop culture which followed Franco's death in 1975) partly explains his iconic status. The nature of Spain's transition to democracy – a gradual process of constitutional reform rather than a radical break with the past – necessitated a cultural revolution to compensate for the absence of a political one. Almodóvar was present in the right place at the right time, capturing with his films the excitement of a liberated nation. His films' disavowal of Francoism provided not only an image of Spain consistent with the national will towards collective memory loss ('*desmemoria*'), but also a colourful, festive image of Spain which appealed to foreign audiences.

Almodóvar's adoption as national symbol combines with his status as the 'one true auteur to emerge in the 1980s' (Smith 1994: 5). More than most directors, he can lay claim to *auteur* status because he not only directs, but also controls the production and pre-sales of his work. Almodóvar's relationship with the people who work with him – both actors and his staff at El Deseo, the production company he runs with his brother Agustín – is central to his status as an *auteur*. Coinciding with the Spanish release of *All About My Mother* in the spring of 1999, El Deseo's press officer, Paz Sufrategui, wrote a short piece about the Almodóvar 'factory': 'an old family with parents, children, grandparents and lots of friends'. The accompanying photograph shows Pedro sitting in the middle of his factory/family. In the offices of El Deseo the impression given is certainly one of dedication to the films made by Almodóvar and others which El Deseo produces.[3] Among the 'friends' of the family are the many actors who have worked in the films: the Spanish press call them '*chicos* Almodóvar' (more often, *chicas* Almodóvar). Where Almodóvar's reception outside Spain is much the same as for other venerated *auteurs*, at home, his high-profile relationships with the actors and actresses of the moment provoke media coverage akin to that afforded royalty. This, in turn, reflects Almodóvar's personal estimation of the importance of actors. Initially, the actors came from Almodóvar's entourage: Fabio McNamara, Eva Siva, Alaska, Agustín. These were joined increasingly by professional actors, one of whom encouraged Almodóvar to make his first film and went on to become his first 'muse' and the actress most closely associated with him even twenty years later: Carmen Maura. Maura has been singled out by Almodóvar as exceptional among the other great performers in his films. The field of star studies is largely undeveloped in relation to Spain, nor is it within the scope of this book to engage with it. Nevertheless, the importance of actors and directing them is central to Almodóvar:

> I don't know if I have a method when directing; my directing is more and more precise, I give the actors so many details that I think they begin to fear that they can't do what I'm asking. But actors are the life of the cinema, everything is transmitted by them; lighting, mise-en-scène, all the rest, though important, are nothing compared to the actors. (García de León and Maldonado 1989: 221)

Almodóvar's adoration of his actors explains (and is explained by) his attitude to story-telling and to film genres. Narrative, the telling of stories, is what first attracted Almodóvar to the film medium. While working on short Super-8 films (all of them narrative, unlike much marginal film-making), he was also contributing stories to magazines. Almodóvar's prose and, unsurprisingly, his dialogue in the novel *Patty Diphusa* (1991) are engaging in style and enhance an entertaining story. His relationship with his characters is strong: he claims to know everything about them, and that he could write a complete novel about each one (Cobos and Marías 1995: 119).[4] And the importance of stories also relates to his distinctive use of genre.

Where many European *auteurs* have shunned genre films, Almodóvar is acutely aware of their potential, both to attract audiences and to provide narrative or visual frames of reference. Often, awareness of genre conventions becomes parody. Conscious of the multiple perspectives and interrelations of contemporary, postmodern culture, Almodóvar reworks and recontextualizes not only genres but also popular culture, especially music and television. Parodic recontextualization is not exclusively a source of humour: parodying television, advertising or folkoric music is one way of investigating and challenging gender or sexual roles, social or national identities. Marsha Kinder (1997: 3) describes how Almodóvar was able 'to perform a radical sex change on Spain's national stereotype'. Far from the *machista* men and passive women of Spain's mythical, reactionary past, Almodóvar, for better or for worse, places strong females centre-stage and brutally demolishes weak male characters. Almodóvar's deconstruction of Spanish national identity has ironically become a *re*-construction in that his films are now the most accessible (and most accessed) depiction of contemporary Spain for most of the world. The director frequently described as the *enfant terrible* of Spanish cinema is accused of superficiality when he eschews questions about Spain's political past. At the same time, he is accused of being politically incorrect in representing sexual difference, violence, even rape, in an off-hand or humorous manner. Part Two of this book revisits the themes of gender, sexual, social and national identities, contextualizing and summarizing their place in Almodóvar's films.

In spite of all the polemic, Almodóvar is increasingly recognized for his skill as a director (universally acclaimed in the case of *All About My Mother*). The construction of the films themselves has received far less attention, which is why this book is weighted more heavily to the *how* rather than the *what* of the films, with extensive chapters on visual style, genre, urban space and music in Part Three. The colourful, glossy images of the 'high comedies' and the design-conscious world of the later films both stem from Almodóvar's background in theatre and amateur film-making. His career is an exercise in the art of the possible, from low-quality DIY to Oscar-winning mastery. The early conditions of production have clearly influenced all the films. These financial, technical and cultural contexts are the subject of Part One.

1

Cultural Context

From La Mancha to Madrid

Almodóvar's origins in backward, rural La Mancha – the desolate flatlands which drove Don Quijote to madness – and his migration to Madrid in time to witness both the later years of the Franco dictatorship and the new freedoms of democratic Spain, have clearly left their mark on his films. An overwhelming enthusiasm for urban life is tempered by nostalgia for a rural past which he often represents through the elderly in his films. His humble background stands in contrast to the middle-class origins of many film-makers, and his incorporation into the cultural life of his adopted city was a determining factor in his education and personality. Both affect his film-making: with no formal training at his disposal, his film trajectory represents the visible learning curve of the autodidact; and the changing cultural scene in Madrid determined the production conditions and values of the films, as well as Almodóvar's own status as entertaining eccentric in the 1970s, or increasingly respected celebrity in the 1990s.

Born in Calzada de Calatrava in the province of Ciudad Real at the start of the 1950s, Pedro Almodóvar's biography is split unevenly between the village of his birth, his schooling from the age of eight to sixteen in Cáceres and his entire adult life in the Spanish capital. While Calzada did not even have a cinema, the street where he lived in Cáceres contained not only the school, but also a movie theatre. Thus, for Almodóvar, his entire education took place in one street. He sang in the choir and believed his desire to see the films of Tennessee Williams's plays was truly sinful (Cobos and Marías 1995: 76). He was taught by Salesian brothers whose abuse was one autobiographical element which he incorporated into *Law of Desire*, where Tina has been abused as a boy by the priests (Vidal 1988: 196). The films Almodóvar watched as a child were US comedies with Doris Day and 'very clean kitchens' (Cobos and Marías 1995: 83), but Spanish singer Lola Flores was equally significant to him, as were English and American pop music. In his late teens, Almodóvar went to Madrid, by now firmly under the spell of US pop culture and the British 'swinging sixties'. He travelled to Ibiza, London and Paris, and worked as an extra in films and television (Boquerini 1989: 16).

Almodóvar secured a permanent job in Telefónica (the Spanish national phone company) where he worked until three in the afternoon, leaving the rest of the day free for other pursuits. During his time at Telefónica, Almodóvar also began to write for the alternative magazines *Star*, *Vibraciones* and *El Víbora*. His Telefónica job brought him into contact with the lower middle class later depicted in his cinema, and, though he was very much the eccentric at work, at night he was among his own kind (Cobos and Marías 1995: 77). Madrid's nightlife provided a forum for Almodóvar's social talents, and brought him into contact with a range of artists, groups and individuals, including the members of Spain's first punk band Kaka de Luxe, which included the teenage Alaska who would star in his first film and figure among the foremost personalities of Spain's pop culture for more than twenty years. Through the well-connected director Félix Rotaeta, he began collaborating with the theatre group Los Goliardos (Boquerini 1989: 17). These last years of the Franco regime (the early 1970s) were marked by the final violent throes of cultural censorship, including battles with the press leading to newspaper closures (Boquerini 1989: 19). After the death of the dictator in November 1975, the limits of the censor were pushed back with the release of films and books prohibited under Franco, some of which held mythical status (Kattán-Ibarra 1989: 273). On 1 December 1977, film censorship was abolished altogether (Torres 1995: 369). Predictably, this led to a veritable avalanche of films with themes hitherto unimaginable. As Peter Evans (1995: 326) puts it, 'for the first time in thirty years, questions of history, politics and government, religion, ethnicity, regionalism, family, and sexuality could all be discussed openly and directly'. Almodóvar would be one of the first to make the most of this new freedom.

When Almodóvar arrived in Madrid in the late 1960s he already knew he wanted to make films. The Madrid film school (the only one in Spain) had been closed by Franco, so a formal training was out of the question. As soon as funds allowed, he bought a Super-8 camera and started to make short films with his increasing circle of friends. The Super-8 shorts gave him the freedom to film what he wanted, cheaply, and they also provided his only training in technique. Almodóvar describes his apprenticeship in the 1970s:

> If I wanted to make films I had to invent a means of distributing them [...] I showed them in bars, in parties [...] I couldn't add a soundtrack because it was very difficult. The magnetic strip was very poor, very thin. I remember that I became very famous in Madrid because, as the films had no sound, I took a cassette with music while I personally did the voices of all the characters, songs and dialogues. (Cobos and Marías 1995: 76–8)

This self-reliant *modus operandi* conditions all Almodóvar's work. Twenty years later, newcomer Candela Peña records that in pre-rehearsal discussions with his actresses, he explains all the parts by improvising their dialogues himself.[1]

Another feature of Almodóvar's Super-8 work which marks him out at this early stage is the primacy of narrative. The production of Super-8 films was largely based in Barcelona, where conceptual films were the norm. Almodóvar, though well-received because of the humour in his films, was anathema to Catalan abstract film-makers because he wanted to tell stories (Albaladejo et al. 1988: 31–2). For Almodóvar, these films clearly indicate the direction he was to take: 'I think the little Super-8 camera already contains elements of the narrative. If you want to move the action, you move with the camera or you climb onto a wheelchair. I have been a believer in the art of the possible' (Cobos and Marías 1995: 78).

After four years of working with short films in Super-8 format, in 1978 Almodóvar made both his first full-length film and his first 16mm short. A magazine-style melodrama, *Folle ... folle ... fólleme, Tim (Fuck, Fuck, Fuck Me, Tim)* is described by Almodóvar as the 'great success of all my Super-8 projects' and he even considered expanding it to 35mm format (Albaladejo et al. 1988: 35). While this film provided a further learning experience, *Salomé* was his first contact with the professional world of cinema (Boquerini 1989: 26). Carmen Maura and, through her,

Félix Rotaeta were the contacts who encouraged Almodóvar to seek funding for a script *Erecciones generales* (*General Erections*) which, with the new title *Pepi, Luci, Bom and Other Girls on the Heap*, was to be Almodóvar's break into commercial cinema. The story of its production is now part of the Almodóvar mythology.

Almodóvar recalls that his flatmate kept a marijuana plant in the window of their apartment, and he worried that it might be discovered by the police. From this came the story of Pepi and the policeman (Cobos and Marías 1995: 122). Initially the money (half a million pesetas or £2,000) came from a variety of supportive friends and colleagues. Neither Almodóvar nor any of the actors received any payment. Even with the stretching of the film to 35mm, the total cost was between 3 and 5 million pesetas (£13,000–20,000), making *Pepi, Luci, Bom* by far Almodóvar's cheapest film. Shooting began in 1978 and finished in June 1980. The resulting problems of continuity also form part of the film's mythology. Almodóvar recounts the filming of the first scene: it began where Pepi (Carmen Maura) gets up from her Superman scrapbook to open the door in June 1979; in December 1979 she opens the door; but the close-up of Pepi with the policeman was not filmed until June 1980 (Albaladejo et al. 1988: 40). When the money ran out, Almodóvar, desperate to finish the film, considered standing in front of the camera and describing to the audience how he would have filmed the rest had he acquired the funding (Cobos and Marías 1995: 79). This meta-cinematic monologue of production problems was avoided. Producer Pepón Corominas saw the film's potential and found the funds to finish it. The film's many imperfections (such as the scene where Almodóvar himself appears with his head out of frame) were seized upon by commentators as part of a radical innovative technique. Almodóvar says his purpose was not to 'introduce a new cinematic language, but to convey immediacy and freshness' (Cobos and Marías 1995: 79). While the film is technically the most imperfect of all Almodóvar's output, it is also, in his words, 'the one which most clearly demonstrates my vocation as a film-maker' (Cobos and Marías 1995: 124).

During the shooting of the film, Almodóvar kept his job at the Spanish telephone company. The scripts for both *Pepi, Luci, Bom* and *Labyrinth of Passions* were written there, and Almodóvar took advantage of the Spanish state sector's unpaid leave scheme on five occasions, but he had to return when the money ran out (Cobos and Marías 1995: 78). The success of *Pepi, Luci, Bom* meant that his next film, *Labyrinth of*

Passions, would be properly produced. Madrid cinema Alphaville was looking to venture into production and their decision to produce Almodóvar allowed him to ask for leave of absence from his job. He never returned. *Pepi, Luci, Bom* took him eighteen months to shoot and cost less than 5 million pesetas (£20,000). Its production conditions are unique in Almodóvar's career. Twenty years later, his thirteenth film, *All About My Mother*, was filmed in ten weeks and cost about 600 million pesetas (£2.3 million including publicity). By 1999, Almodóvar's films were selling more in France and Italy than in Spain, providing excellent returns for the Almodóvar brothers' own production company El Deseo, and for their French co-producers (Renn Productions and France 2 Cinema). Although the cost and box-office returns of the films do not concern me directly here, money clearly affects production values and the finished film product.

Almodóvar's production manager, Esther García, identifies three stages in his film production: the films up to *Law of Desire*, which sought outside producers; the films from *Law of Desire* until *All About My Mother* in 1999 produced by El Deseo; and a potential new era, an 'American stage' which will probably begin with the US-filmed *The Paperboy*.[2] The films which comprise these stages are part of an upward trajectory in terms of budgets and box-office receipts. Almodóvar films become progressively more expensive and make more and more money. In Spain, box-office figures show a steady improvement until *Law of Desire*, which made twice as much as its predecessor, but *Women on the Verge of a Nervous Breakdown* represents the big breakthrough, making five times as much money as the previous film, and, critically, taking more than twice the domestic box office in international receipts. As Angus Finney (1996: 248) puts it, 'The film allowed Almodóvar to break completely from a domestic market, and win an international following.' The conditions of production of Almodóvar's films clearly impact on the finished films themselves, affecting working conditions, schedules, technology, marketing and, crucially, 'author' freedom.

Labyrinth of Passions was made with 21 million pesetas and filmed over five weeks. This is no small achievement for a film with some fifty locations, but Almodóvar's focus is still very much on narrative. In *Dark Habits* Almodóvar began to experiment more widely with the technology now at his disposal and dispensed with the proliferation of characters used in the previous film. Despite the improved technical conditions of the films made for the producers Tesauro (*Dark Habits* and *What Have I Done to Deserve This?*) and Andrés Vicente Gómez (*Matador*), certain 'unfavourable obligations'[3] left Almodóvar unhappy with producers controlling the finance of his films. A new director of cinema at the Ministry of Culture, film-maker and former Spanish Television chief Pilar Miró, was to provide the solution. For the director's brother, Agustín, the introduction of the so-called Miró Law in 1983 effectively 'allowed directors to become producers' (Vidal 1988: 245). The measure, inspired by French models of subsidy, offered planning investment grants and a range of subsidies to Spanish film-makers (Gubern et al. 1995: 400–3).[4] This new opportunity, coupled with the problems Almodóvar encountered searching for finance for *Law of Desire*, propelled him and Agustín into setting up their own production company, El Deseo, in 1986.

For Almodóvar, El Deseo represents freedom to write and film what he chooses. One of Spain's top five productions companies, its resources mean that he can shoot many more takes before editing, and film as near as possible to the order of the script. This would be most directors' preference, and Almodóvar can permit himself this luxury. Relative freedom from the demands of producers also allows modifications to the script during filming, consecutive editing while shooting, which enables extra takes to be filmed if the editing requires it, and even the filming of completely different versions (Cobos and Marías 1995: 118, 84). Almodóvar often shoots the same scene in two distinct tones, usually one realistic and the other as a gag. In *Matador*, for example, having Carmen Maura kiss Banderas awake was a gag which worked and was kept in the final version. However, in a film like *The Flower of My Secret*, all the 'amusing options' were removed in the final version (Cobos and Marías 1995: 85).

Production clearly affects *where* as well as *how* films are made. El Deseo is currently investigating the possible construction of their own studios.[5] While this would be principally a new venture for the company – not dictated by Almodóvar's needs as director – it would certainly offer him even greater artistic freedom. In Spain, the practice of studio set filming is not common. Almodóvar's early films make use of real interior locations until *What Have I Done*, the interiors of which were filmed in a studio. *Law of Desire* was filmed in two real apartments and in the Lara theatre in Madrid. Almodóvar's 'studio period' begins with *Women on the Verge*, where the artificiality of the décor is central to the film's aesthetic. *Tie Me Up! Tie Me Down!*, which foregrounds the film production medium itself, was shot entirely in two different studios. *Kika*'s interiors were entirely shot in the aptly-named Los Ángeles studios in the Madrid suburb of Getafe. These strongly codified and stylized genre films are suited to studio filming unlike the more sober *Flower*, *Live Flesh* and *All About My Mother* which combine studio and location interiors with inspired exterior filming. Leo's house in *Flower* is a real flat. In *All About My Mother*, Manuela's home in Madrid is a real flat, as is Rosa's *eixample* apartment in Barcelona, and Agrado's flat opposite the Palau de la Música. Manuela's Barcelona flat is more hybrid: after much location hunting, Almodóvar combined elements of several flats and re-created them in the Los Ángeles studio in Madrid. Just as important for both the social context and the aesthetic of Almodóvar's films – the early films especially – is the transformation of the streets and plazas of the then unfashionable Madrid into a great studio. (See Chapter 6.) By taking his films out on to the streets of the Spanish capital, Almodóvar reflected, starred in and arguably directed the most exciting period in Spain's cultural history after Franco.

The *Movida*

> The cultural pluralism of contemporary Spain owes much to the accelerated change of the last two decades which has obliged Spaniards to live in different time frames at once: that is, to ex-perience simultaneously what in the rest of Europe have been successive stages of development. (Graham and Labanyi 1995: 312)

In 1978 Spain's new constitution was adopted after a referendum officially ending nearly forty years of dictatorship. In the same year, Almodóvar began filming his first commercial feature, *Pepi, Luci, Bom*. The director's first two decades of film-making correspond to Spain's first twenty years as a democratic nation. During this period, Spain was transformed from being 'the pariah of the West, the last great bastion of the dictatorial days', to 'one of the most liberal states in the world' (Elms 1992: 2). Although the political transformation was a gradual one – transition rather than revolution – the change in the cultural environment was rapid and, at times, excessive. Thus, while for many adults Spain's new democracy represented the achievement of radical political ambition through peaceful means, for the younger generation it meant an instan-taneous break with repressive social norms and regulations. The high profile of social and cultural transformation contrasted with the gradual changes in the political process. This had two effects: first, it ascribed what is arguably an over-determined role to youth cultures as the ambassadors of the new Spain; second, the cultural legacy of liberated Spain originated mainly with a youth which would inevitably grow up.[6] The second point accounts for the demise of Spain's post-Franco, postmodern 'end of history' carnival (Fuentes 1995: 157). The first point accounts for its genesis.

Almodóvar was nearly thirty when he began to shoot his first commercial feature, though both he and his early films are none the less closely associated with youth culture. What distinguishes the Spanish youth culture of the late 1970s from other youth cultures or subcultures is its reception in a newly-liberated society as acceptable and even desirable, where youth is usually inscribed as resistant or deviant (Allinson 2000: 265). Rather than counter-hegemonic, Spain's youth subculture was eventually welcomed by Spain's political elite as 'the official image of Spain' (Graham and Labanyi 1995: 312). The social and cultural context for Almodóvar's early films – and arguably for the shaping of his persona and the future direction of his career – was, principally, the *movida madrileña* (the Madrid 'scene').[7] This explosion of new trends in music, fashion, design, art and film which centred on the Spanish capital took its name from the drugs subculture. The height of the *movida* is agreed by the majority of its protagonists to be between the years 1981 and 1985, though the energy released in those years was a build-up of social and cultural trends dating from the end of the Franco period. Those who lived through it argue about most aspects of the *movida*, but there is a clear perception that something exciting was happening in Madrid. José Luis Gallero (1991: 9), meticulous chronicler of the *movida*, recalls that 'from one day to the next, a worn-out city became the maximum emblem of modernity'. Music subculture led the way in the city with scores of new groups and artists taking up residence and guitars in the do-it-yourself spirit of British punk.[8] As in the UK and the USA, Spain's 'new wave' was in part a reaction against the perceived stagnation of rock music in the 1970s. Venues and record labels suddenly opened their doors to these new bands and the city became a magnet for aspiring talent. Almodóvar, who had served his musical apprenticeship providing a running soundtrack for his Super-8 films, took to the stage with his friend Fabio McNamara in performances which have become part of the *movida*'s folklore. Pedro, usually clad in a dressing-gown, hair curlers and stockings at half-mast, was joined by Fabio, whose unpredictability made any rehearsal a pointless exercise (Holguín 1999: 306).

But the *movida* was not limited to pop music, as the contents of its emblematic magazine *La Luna de Madrid* demonstrate. Its first issue in November 1983 led with a piece about Madrid as a symbol of post-modernity. Its eclectic mix of articles and features included the first appearance of Almodóvar's fictional porn star Patty Diphusa,[9] articles on punk, pop music, painting, photography, film (new and old), theatre, free radio, football, poetry, as well as a month-planner, an advert for Almodóvar's second film, *Labyrinth of Passions*, cardboard cut-outs of Madrid buildings and lyrics for songs like 'Sexo chungo' (Bad Sex) by punk group Siniestro Total (Write Off). The editor of *La Luna*, Borja Casani, identified the Rastro, Madrid's fleamarket, as the site of the burgeoning subculture that would become the *movida* (Gallero 1991: 8). This market, the scene of the opening of Almodóvar's second film, *Labyrinth of Passions*, is a fitting place for a cultural phenomenon based largely on what Lévi-Strauss called 'bricolage', that is the 're-ordering and recontextualization of objects to communicate fresh meanings'.[10] The artists of the *movida* used whatever they could find in the market-place to create something new. Almodóvar's own part in this DIY culture included work on *fotonovelas*, comics, writing and performing music, even art. He claims his film-making was in this sense 'the sum of a lot of artistic frustrations' (Cobos and Marías 1995: 80).

Artists and designers were as much at the centre of the *movida* as musicians. Maldonado writes that the habitual introductory question 'Do you study or work?' became, during the period, 'Do you design or work?' (García de León and Maldonado 1989: 139). Almodóvar's films contain many plastic elements which contribute to their aesthetic. The artists Ouka Lele, Guillermo Pérez Villalta, Las Costus and Pablo Pérez Mínguez all feature in *Labyrinth of Passions* alongside Javier Pérez Grueso, Carlos Berlanga and Fabio de Miguel (alias McNamara). Ceesepe de-signed the titles and posters for *Pepi, Luci, Bom* and *Law of Desire*. Poster artist (and director) Iván Zulueta undertook the posters for *Labyrinth of Passions*, *Dark Habits* and *What Have I Done*.[11] This close link with the world of artists survived well into the 'post-*movida*' films of the late 1980s and after. Juan Gatti and his studio designed many of the films' title sequences and interiors. The work of Dis Berlin is featured from *Law of Desire* onwards, and that of Antonio de Felipe in *Live Flesh*.

Photographer Pablo Pérez Mínguez appears in *Labyrinth of Passions* photographing the pornographic *fotonovela* starring Fabio McNamara (Holguín 1999: 218). The influence of the comic on both the aesthetic of the early Almodóvar and its transgressive attitude is considerable. The catalyst for the film *Pepi, Luci, Bom* was the game-show parody *Erecciones generales*, which was originally destined for the comic *El Víbora* (Strauss 1996: 11).

Almodóvar's first two films, *Pepi, Luci, Bom* and *Labyrinth of Passions*, are the greatest cultural legacy of the *movida*. In their almost carnivalesque depiction of the lifestyles of young *madrileños* they represent a 'utopian rendering of Madrid as locus amoenus, a space of infinite possibilities' (Vernon and Morris 1995: 8). *Pepi, Luci, Bom* is a testimony to the success of the *movida*'s opportunist bricolage culture, where neither actors nor director receive any financial gain for their efforts, but can look back on the venture as a launch-pad to greater success. Almodóvar describes *Labyrinth of Passions* as 'a catalogue of modernities' (Vidal 1988: 39). Although this testimonial aspect recedes after the first two films, elements of Madrid's subculture (in post-*movida* manifestations) survive into later films. In *High Heels* the drag parody group Diabéticas aceleradas appears as fan club to singing transvestite Letal (Miguel Bosé) [fig. 1] complete with a dressing-room wall poster of the colourfully queer Paco Clavel. The link between Spain's popular culture and both gay and transvestite communities is acknowledged by Borja Casani (Gallero 1991: 248). Almodóvar includes these groups in his early *movida* films as part of his surroundings. But Yarza (1999: 17) makes the point that the culture of camp (whether an aesthetic or a more general attitude) serves to liberate the pop culture of the Franco period from fascist ideology, using parody to reappropriate traditional Spanish iconography. Even the name, *la movida*, is, in Triana Toribio's (2000: 275) words, 'a defiant, slangish pun on the Francoist *Movimiento*', the term used to describe collectively the different strands of Franco's regime.

The ambivalence of *movida* culture towards Spain's history – halfway between 'make it new' and the parodic rebranding of Spanish cultural heritage – was not shared by Spain's political establishment. In search of a new image for Spain, the political class seized upon the *movida* as an opportunity to suggest a complete break with the past.[12] Thus, Madrid's first democratic mayor, Tierno Galván (who had been imprisoned by Franco when a professor at Madrid University), opened an exhibition in 1984 entitled 'Madrid, Madrid, Madrid' with Fabio

1. *High Heels*. Femme Letal (Miguel Bosé) with his fan
club Diabéticas aceleradas.

McNamara at his side proclaiming, '*Soy una asquerosa, soy una marrana por
la mañana*' ('I'm disgusting, I'm a pig in the mornings' – all in the
feminine gender) (Vallina 1984: 8). The exhibition featured the plastic
marijuana plant from *Pepi, Luci, Bom*. Even the 1992 World Exposition
in Seville included works by Almodóvar and Ouka Lele in the Madrid
pavilion, while early punk star (now pop and television personality)
Alaska looked after the music.

Borja Casani has suggested that the explanation for the cultural
effervescence which was the *movida* lay in the need for producing new
candidates for mythical status in a post-Franco society where past myths
were unacceptable (García de León and Maldonado 1989: 131). Did the

movida come up with the goods? It proved to be relatively short-lived. At the start of the 1990s, the former editor of *La Luna de Madrid* predicted that Spain would 'be diluted in an international world', and claimed that the last cultural explosion was the 1980s (Gallero 1991: 1). His prediction was already reality. Spain from the late 1980s became increasingly integrated into Europe and into Western (Americanized) culture. The cultural conditions in which Almodóvar has worked throughout the 1990s are much the same as those of most other European nations. Though Almodóvar's style has been appropriated by the rest of the world as emblematic of post-Franco Spain, his later films have more universal themes, and even non-Spanish origins (*Live Flesh* is from a novel by Ruth Rendell; *The Paperboy*, possibly Almodóvar's first film of the new century, will be set in Florida). Gallero (1991: 9) lists the forces ranged against the survival of the *movida*: the scepticism of the intellectual old guard, propagandistic use by political institutions, the voracity of the press and of commercial enterprise, and lastly, the *movida*'s own iconoclasm. Perhaps just as important is the fact that the protagonists have grown up; much of their work is now mainstream and commercially successful. The production values may be better (certainly the case with Almodóvar), but 'Rastro bricolage' has become pure commerce. Aware that his brother Pedro would be unable to find the time to write a book on the *movida*, Agustín Almodóvar suggested that Luis Antonio de Villena should write a fictionalized account, the result of which was published in 1999. The subtitle (over illustrations inevitably by Ceesepe), is 'Esplendor y caos en una ciudad feliz de los ochenta' ('Splendour and Chaos in a Happy City of the 1980s') which contrasts with the novel's title: *Madrid ha muerto* (*Madrid is Dead*). What survives of the defunct *movida madrileña*, the only real candidate for mythical status, is Pedro Almodóvar.

Persona: Art not Life

One must always improve on reality.[13]

One of the offers of work that Pedro Almodóvar has received since his emergence as a veritable star director was an invitation to direct opera. Almodóvar, with his characteristic iconoclasm, replied that he would be willing to direct an opera only if actors replaced the singers and the voices were dubbed on later. He also feigned surprise that this idea was seen as little short of sacrilegious by the opera establishment (Cobos and Marías 1995: 101). Almodóvar's career is characterized both by a refusal to make art imitate life, and by a refusal to accept his own work and persona as controversial.

Albaladejo (1988: 20) refers to the 'daily ordinariness of the extraordinary' in Almodóvar's work. From his earliest short films, Almodóvar portrays the sensational and the taboo-breaking with absolute naturalness; for example, a newsreader in *High Heels* confesses on live television to the murder of her husband as if it is an everyday occurrence. An early draft script of *Labyrinth of Passions* 'had Dalí and the Pope meeting and falling passionately in love' (Strauss 1996: 23). Examples of such extraordinary occurrences accepted as natural abound in Almodóvar, but there is no suggestion that they reflect 'reality', perceived as too dull by Almodóvar's standards. Indeed, far from using the film medium as a mirror to nature, he prefers to turn life into art. At the very beginning of the film *What Have I Done*, we hear Almodóvar as director giving instructions to actress Carmen Maura. A crane shot records another camera and crew below, Almodóvar himself visible among them. This meta-cinematic reference seems like a homage to the authentic location shooting used by neorealist film-makers. The meta-cinema is confirmed when we then see Gloria (Carmen Maura) as filmed by the lower camera previously in frame itself. Almodóvar explains this self-reference in simple terms: 'this shot is a good example of how I work, making the most of everything around me' (Vidal 1988: 136). Thus immersed in the world of cinema, it is only natural that the environment of films is included in the films themselves. Almodóvar's self-reference is not studied or theoretical (like that of Godard, for example), but a natural result of the author's interest.

The blurring of the frontier between art and life is most transparent in Almodóvar's utilization of advertising, as demonstrated in his eighteen-minute *Trailer para los amantes de lo prohibido* (*Trailer for Lovers of the Forbidden*, 1984). Asked to do a television publicity trailer for *What Have I Done*, Almodóvar did not produce merely a self-referenced publicity product for its own sake, but introduced, irresistibly, a new narrative, which itself parodies other genres. *Trailer* takes the form of a series of set-piece songs performed at appropriate moments by actors (karaoke fashion) in a melodrama which very definitely crosses the line into parody. Any narrative which at intervals breaks into song to move forward is close to parody because of the incongruity of spontaneous singing. The first number (an Olga Guillot *bolero*), for example, is parodically deflated by the character's domestic clothing (an apron), and by the flowers which droop instantaneously when the song lines indicate so. Where musicals try to integrate the songs, which ostensibly remain subservient to the narrative, this film subverts the story to the role of keeping together the parodic set-piece numbers. And the characters are quite evidently miming rather than singing, which increases the parodic deflation. At various points the incipient drama is halted by recourse to comic effects. When the mother hijacks a woman in the market, she instructs the woman to take off her knickers before stealing her bags of food. There are references to the film he is supposedly publicizing in the form of the film's poster, the painting of which is seen in *Trailer*. The gigantic poster is later seen over the entrance to the Proyecciones cinema in Madrid, many times the cinema chosen for the premières of Almodóvar's films. Later, a television set shows the opening night of the film with all the stars arriving at the usual première party. Here, for the first time, Almodóvar uses real footage of his own actors at his own première, in pure self-reference. And to coincide with the launch of *High Heels*, Almodóvar arranged for posters of fictional singing star Becky del Páramo to be put up all over Madrid, as a way of promoting the film (Strauss 1996: 50–1). And for *Flower*, a gigantic poster of an anthology of fictitious novelist Amanda Gris was erected on the wall of a huge Madrid record and bookshop. Almodóvar premières are staged media events. Boquerini (1989: 63) recalls that on the première of *What Have I Done*, Almodóvar distributed fake boxes of washing powder and aprons to the waiting press.

Such skill with the whole range of publicity devices has generated media interest in Almodóvar unparalleled in Spain. As well as the flurry of interviews (including self-interviews), photo-montage synopses and usual reviews, Almodóvar's star quality makes him, uniquely, more famous than his actors. As García de León et al. (1989: 15) put it, 'the personality of Almodóvar is one of his best works'. But this show-manship, which has its origins in Almodóvar's early days as a high-profile figure in the still marginal *movida*, represents more than the pursuit of publicity. Almodóvar is genuinely interested in the public reaction to his films. Speaking at the London Film Festival première of *Flower*, he began by asking the audience for their opinions about the film. In television interviews he frequently refers to the great pressure he feels under before each première and insists that 'not being misunderstood' is a constant worry. Though he presents characters in extreme situations (which is, after all, the stuff of drama and comedy), his intention is not provocation, but rather naturalness and reciprocity with the viewer. He even offers the premise of social documentary as a justification for the extreme situations of his films, suggesting that Spanish cinema has not evolved as quickly as Spanish society and that his films try to capture the reality of contemporary Spain rather than harking back to the past.[14] Clearly, Almodóvar himself sees his work as in some way emblematic of a new Spain. The reconstruction of Spanish national identity is the subject of the next chapter.

Part Two
Content

2

National Identity

Almodóvar's emergence on to the international stage of film directors
marks a change in cinematic representations of Spanish national
identity from the hitherto introspective, sombre and often solipsistic
creations of other art-house directors such as Carlos Saura or Víctor
Erice (both masters of the 'indirect' style of allusions and metaphor) to
a more confident, direct engagement with what makes Spain different
and what it shares with the rest of the world. By both playing to the
commonly held and stereotypical conceptions of Spanish identity, and
also challenging them, Almodóvar has achieved something none of his
predecessors has: where many films attempt to reflect national identity,
Almodóvar's films, for better or worse, have appropriated it. No other
Spanish cultural product has been as instrumental in the 1980s and
1990s in shaping the world's impressions of Spanish national identity.

What, exactly, does 'national identity' mean in general and in the
context of contemporary Spain? And how is it mapped on to cinema?
Anthony Smith (1991: 14) defines the nation as 'a named human
population sharing an historic territory, common myths and historical
memories, a mass, public culture, a common economy and common
legal rights and duties for all members'. Some of the categories in this
definition are distinctly problematic for the nationhood of contemporary
Spain. Its territory is the site of intra-national disputes between the
central state and the so-called 'historical nations' of Catalonia and the
Basque country. Historical memory is no less problematic in a state

which spent nearly forty years of the twentieth century denying the validity of the memory of virtually half the population, imposing a regressive and monolithic version of its history. The direct and proportionate consequence of this for contemporary (post-Franco) Spain is *desmemoria* (self-imposed amnesia), and a contemporary Spanish mass culture based on dehistoricized spectacle and consumption (Moreiras 2000: 135). Where territorial integrity and collective historical memory are awkward sites on which to construct national identity for Spain, Benedict Anderson's concept of 'imagined communities' is more helpful. For him, national identity becomes a 'cultural artefact' which is '*imagined* because the members of even the smallest nation will never know most of their fellow-members, [...] yet in the minds of each lives the image of their communion' (Anderson 1991: 9). Anderson explains how nationalism replaced religious community and dynastic realm as 'taken-for-granted frames of reference' (p. 11). He also cites the importance of shared language in the formation of imagined communities (pp. 37–46). In the case of Spain – and indeed reflected in Almodóvar's films – both religion and language are especially important national marks of identity, as this chapter will illustrate.

The reconstruction of national identity through film has a special resonance in a state ruled by a military dictatorship for nearly four decades. Early Francoist film sought obsessively to validate the victors (the military, the Church, the aristocracy) and demonize the losers (workers, separatists, 'reds'). This gave way to the so-called *españolada*, stylized folkloric musicals and priest dramas (Higginbotham 1988: 18). Later film-makers faced a choice: either opt for a European *auteur* cinema which is firmly grounded in national preoccupations, and consequently has limited appeal outside Spain (the route of Luis García Berlanga and Carlos Saura);[1] or look far wider than national boundaries, as was the case with Luis Buñuel, the only truly international figure in Spanish cinema before the 1980s, and largely the product of a film career which took him away from his native Spain for much of his life. Spain's culturally-specific genres either affirmed the nationalistic discourse of the regime, or carefully avoided vexed questions of nationality. Spanish cinema relentlessly pursued such culturally-specific genres while, at the same time, Hollywood movies continued to dominate the national market. Almodóvar breaks with that division: he does depict, whether affectionately or satirically, the *national-cultural specific*, but not in a monolithic, *nationalistic* way. And he makes much use of the conventions of

Hollywood, often used as the model against which to define 'national' cinemas (Crofts 2000: 1).

Hollywood is the classic example of a national (and often subtly nationalistic) film tradition which attempts to subsume national identity under an appearance of universality, and to reach a much wider world audience. Spanish film, on the other hand, has a tendency towards an insular, almost narcissistic, national specificity. Its earliest films show scenes of particular interest to Spanish audiences (worshippers at Zaragoza's El Pilar, the Spanish royal family's visit to Barcelona in 1898, bullfights).[2] A century later, the engagement with national identity in Almodóvar's films runs the whole gamut of Spanish characteristics: the peculiarities of the Spanish language, the stereotypical – but none the less profound – obsession with religion, death and sexuality, the nation's history and politics, national icons and stereotypes.

Death, Desire and Religion

'to stop killing would be to stop living' (dialogue from *Matador*)

The Spanish poet and playwright Federico García Lorca, who was one of the first victims of Spain's civil war in 1936, wrote that 'a dead man in Spain is more alive when dead than is the case anywhere else' (García Lorca 1960: 133). The paradox of this fascination with death is explained by Marsha Kinder at the beginning of her excellent volume on national identity in Spanish film, in which she describes

> a nation whose history is marked by a fratricidal civil war with bloody repercussions, by a long period of Francoism that glamorized death, by a deep immersion in the conventions of the Counter-Reformation that fetishized the bleeding wounds of Christ and other martyrs, and by a 'Black legend' of cruelty and violence dating back to the Inquisition and the Conquest. (Kinder 1993: 1)

Unlike many of the other national-cultural specific themes which Almodóvar explores throughout his film-making, the subject of death – and its peculiar relationship with desire, and with religion – is heavily concentrated in one film, *Matador*.[3] This exceptional film is Almodóvar's most artistically wrought piece of cinema. Its stylization and abstraction befit an investigation of the highly ritualized *corrida de toros* which may itself be seen as an expression of humankind's more discomforting coupling of death and desire. Eroticism, no more than a subtle under-current in bullfighting, is brought to the fore in the film, with clear implications for constructions of gender/power relations.

The grounding of murderers Diego and María in the very Spanish world of the *corrida* is constant. The fable of the two lovers becomes an extended metaphor for the *corrida* itself. Almodóvar has stated that 'the authentic *corrida* is theirs with each other' (Cobos and Marías 1995: 137).[4] The word '*corrida*' in fact means 'running' (as in the running of the bulls in Pamplona); hence, the idea of being carried away by some-thing uncontrollable, and this characterizes Diego and María's violent destiny. The transposition of the ritualized killing of the bull into the criminalized killing of human victims becomes apparent from the second sequence of the film, which shows Diego (Nacho Martínez) giving a class on the different ways to kill a bull. This is intercut with shots of María (Assumpta Serna) who is seen inciting and then killing a young man with the same technique (see Chapter 8). The meetings of the death-obsessed lovers resemble the carefully choreographed *tercios* (stages) of the *corrida* in which the bullfighter attempts progressively to dominate the bull. On their first encounter, María attempts to seduce and then murder Diego with an exquisitely phallic hairpin. As she hesitates, Diego reminds María of 'one of the golden rules of bull-fighting': 'When it comes to the kill we must not hesitate.' Diego's insistence that he keep the offending hairpin ('I think I deserve it') recalls the practice of the *matador*'s compensation for a good *faena*, usually the gift of the bull's ear (Edwards 1995: 173). Round one to Diego. Later, it is he who pursues María to the Segovia viaduct, the traditional site for suicides in the Spanish capital. Bathed in the golden light of the setting sun, María rapturously recalls seeing a suicide there. Diego tells her they have in common an obsession with death. María replies, 'Everyone is obsessed with death' [fig. 2]. Diego has escaped María's *estocada* and now has further proof of her obsession. Hemmed in, María escapes and the final kill is postponed.

Of course, when the moment comes, it is María who first kills Diego (stabbing him in the neck like a bull) before taking her own life (with a gun in her mouth). The shifting of power between the two through the film parallels that of the *corrida*, but with one difference: in the bullring, the male matador takes on the male animal, but in the film, this becomes a battle between a man and a woman. Here Almodóvar picks up on an irony relating to gender relations in the bullring. As he explains:

2. *Matador*. Diego (Nacho Martínez) and María (Assumpta Serna).

Even though bullfighting is a very masculine world, the *torero* takes on the female role in the *corrida*. When he puts on his shining costume, hard like armour, he resembles a gladiator. But the costume is also very tight-fitting, the way he moves in it isn't entirely masculine, he hops about like a ballerina. During the first stage of the *corrida*, the *torero* represents temptation. He teases the bull, seduces it. It's a typically feminine role. (Strauss 1996: 57)

Focusing thus on the flux in power relations between the sexes, this film contributes to the reassessment of gender, and its relationship to national identity. Where other films contest gender stereotyping through what Kinder (1997: 3) refers to as 'an outrageous libertarian array of transgressive sexualities', *Matador* challenges the masculine supremacy of the *torero*, depicting an active, predatory female.[5] The fine balance of power between Diego and María is replicated in their donning of the colours and costumes of the bullfight. We see Diego in full *traje de luces* twice: once in the video-recorded footage of the goring which ended his career, and once for the final scene where he is killed by María. The inversion is reinforced by María's appropriation of the suit of lights.

She dresses in an outfit which copies the colours of the *corrida* and, eventually, Diego gives her his own suit.

The visual style of the film as a whole gives primacy to pinks, yellows and reds – the colours of the *capote* and the *muleta*, respectively. Spanish music reinforces the cultural specificity, as does the explicit linguistic connection with religious expression. (Diego recites, 'a *torero* who doesn't make the sign of the cross is taken by the devil'.)[6] But, ultimately, the nationally-coded context may be incidental. Georges Bataille believed all human sexuality to be irrational, excessive and even murderous, qualities which depend not on historical or geographical-cultural contexts, but on a timeless need for taboos and for their transgression (Bataille 1962: 69). For Bataille, taboos such as murder or rape are maintained only through their occasional transgression. In pagan cultures this transgression is ritualized through sacrificial offerings. There is evidence to suggest that the bullfight may be related to such pre-Christian rituals.[7] Yarza sees the death scene in *Matador* as a 'ritualized transgression which sacrilizes the sexual union and death of the lovers'. He continues, 'As in any ritual transgression of a taboo, this sequence is highly codified.' He cites the purifying bath, the demarcation of an arena and the *corrida* repertoire as elements of this codified ritual (Yarza 1999: 177). Bataille (1962: 170) states that 'pleasure is so close to ruinous waste that we refer to the moment of climax as a "little death"'. In *Matador*, this symbolic or 'little' death inscribes María and Diego as the extreme human incarnation of the excess which is common to all desire. At the other end of the scale, Ángel – an unlikely *torero* – represents the absolute repression of desire through a religious inculcation which offers an excess of restraint and guilt as an alternative to excessive sensuality. In fact, the young trainee *toreros* and *toreras* are depicted as far less eccentric than the religious zealots in the film. Religion is thus brought into a triangular relationship with death and desire, a conflation which forms another trope of Spanish cultural history.[8] Another example of institutionalized ritual, religion is none the less both determinant and ubiquitous in Spanish history and culture.

Spain's birth as a nation is inextricably linked to the defence of Catholicism against Islam in the South and the heretic Protestantism of the North. The home of the Jesuits and of the Inquisition has afforded institutionalized religion (the Catholic Church) a special place in society and in relation to the state.[9] Franco's victory in the civil war ensured for the Catholic Church in Spain the full backing of the state in return for the Church's unquestioning support of the regime, and for its contribution to the unifying, nation-building project of the administration. This arrangement was known as National Catholicism (Shubert 1990: 233). Hooper (1995: 126) remarks that, in Spain, 'saying that you are a Christian could, until very recently, be as much a claim to national identity as a profession of religious belief'. While personal spirituality features very little in Almodóvar's films, references to the institutions and to the morality associated with religion abound. Almodóvar's religious references are entirely Spanish, extravagantly Spanish, many of them involving gentle, or occasionally savage, satire.

Dark Habits is a comedy melodrama which transfers the locus of melodramatic action from the family to the convent, allowing an exploration of the anachronistic situation of institutionalized religion in contemporary Spanish society. The convent's degeneration into excess and caricature is the result of the discrepancy between the social role of religion under Franco and its redundancy in the 'anything goes' culture of democratic Spain. Cabaret singer and heroin addict Yolanda (Cristina Pascual) seeks refuge in the convent, along with drug dealers and police fugitives, just as the dishonoured young ladies of Spain's traditional honour plays inevitably ended their days in nunneries. But the worldly misdemeanours of contemporary Spanish women clash violently with the values of the established church. None of the girls the nuns refer to as *redimidas* is redeemed: Lola is a drug dealer, while Merche is on the run from the police. This is an ironic reversal of the role of the clergy from the 1960s onwards in opposing Franco, the so-called *curas rojos* ('red' priests) who allowed political meetings in the safe haven of their churches (Hooper 1995: 137). Here, the convent acts as a haven for immorality, a site of opposition to the morality of institutionalized religion. The numbers of young women seeking 'redemption' in the convent – never more than two – testifies to the social redundancy of the order as much as to any spiritual deficit in society. This parallels a marked drop in church-going in Spain over the last thirty years. While 64 per cent of Spaniards considered themselves practising Catholics in 1970, the number had fallen to 27 per cent by the late 1980s (Longhurst 2000: 21). When the Mother Superior (Julieta Serrano) tells the Marquesa (Mari Carrillo) 'the young need us', the response is, 'What young? The young only want us to leave them alone.' In fact, the Mother Superior is a heroin addict and a lesbian, whose charitable work is only a means of meeting needy young women. She admits, 'from admiring them so much I have become one of them'. As the engine of the convent's dubious project, she explains how their mission has adapted to the times: 'Soon this convent will be full of assassins, drug addicts and prostitutes, just like in times gone by', and her companion Sister Rat responds, 'May God hear you', the adulatory tones registering the incongruity of this mutated social role.

From the moment the nuns appear in the nightclub dressing-room in search of Yolanda's autograph, framed by a 1970s poster of Mick Jagger, the juxtaposition between religion and society is marked by irony and often absurdity. Yolanda gives the nuns a signed photograph and when she sees their home-made handbags, exclaims '*hostias*', a common swear-word but the most sacrilegious in the Spanish language.[10] The nuns belong to the Community of Humiliated Redeemers, a grotesque caricature of religious orders. Their eccentricity is confirmed by their names, Sister Damned (Carmen Maura), Sister Rat of the Sewers (Chus Lampreave), Sister Snake (Lina Canalejas) and Sister Manure (Marisa Paredes). The Mother Superior explains the rationale of their excessive humility: 'Man will not be saved until he realizes he is the worst being in all creation.' For her, sinners are worthy of gratitude because they are the reason God died and is resurrected. This position – a paradox exposed by the exaggerated veneration the Mother Superior shows towards the women – is only just outside the normal tenets of religion. Similarly, Sister Manure's market cry, 'Miracle pies made with the blood and flesh of Christ', is a ridiculous conceit, a literal objectification of the symbolic rituals of communion. The convent's versions of these rituals are shown to be in continuous conflict with reality. Sister Manure's visions are drug-induced not mystical, and she is motivated by excessive self-hate and unquestioning gratitude to the Mother Superior. Almodóvar shows religion as the sublimation of desire for all the nuns: Sister Snake's piety is a cover for her romantic love of the Chaplain; Sister Damned satisfies frustrated maternal instincts through attentions to her hens [fig. 3] and to her tiger called El Niño (the Child). Obsessed with housework and domesticity, when the Marquesa gives her a present of a box of detergent, she reads the label ('Multi-use detergent, biodegradable, open here') as if it were the gift of her dreams. Sister Rat seeks no more than diversion and entertainment. In reality, she turns out to be a romantic novelist. The fetishization of the Marquesa's daughter Virginia's room (sumptuously decorated as a replica of her room at home) indicates the decadence of a religious order dependent on such whims.

3. *Dark Habits.* Sister Manure (Marisa Paredes), Sister Damned
(Carmen Maura) and one of her hens.

At best, the rituals of the Church are shown to be empty, such as the
mechanical vacuous repetition of phrases like '*Ave María Purísima / sin
pecado concebida*' ('Hail Purest Virgin / Conceived without sin'), or the
exuberantly sensual lesson on kisses (from a religious manual entitled
La doncella cristiana), which demonstrates a fixation on religious morality
that only sharpens the palpable human desires of the women. At other
times, religion is associated with a more reactionary social attitude. The
Mother Superior burns Sister Rat's romantic novels, as Yolanda puts it,
'as in the Inquisition'. It should be remembered that one of the Church's
main roles during the Franco regime was to censor the cinema, publishing and the media against its criteria, the 'norms of Christian decency'
(Hooper 1995: 152). The Marquesa refers at one point to the other main
role of the Church in Franco's Spain, the connection between piety and
fascism. While for the Mother Superior the Marquesa's dead husband
was 'a good servant of God', his wife refers to him as a fascist.

Almodóvar's next film, *Matador*, is no kinder in its portrayal of the
repressive effects of religion. Ángel (Antonio Banderas), the victim of
the film, is the guilt-ridden product of an over-zealous religious up-
bringing.[11] He tells Diego, 'My family belong to Opus Dei. I've spent

my whole life praying and doing physical exercise.' Opus Dei is a religious organization (consisting of both lay people and the ordained) founded in Spain in 1928 with a mission to place its members in positions where ultra-right religious values can be upheld at the highest levels.[12] Ángel's mother, Berta (Julieta Serrano), is a caricature of an Opus mother and one of the most dislikeable of all Almodóvar's characters. Evans (1993: 328) describes her as a 'monstrous, self-mortifying, pre-democratic fascist ideal', and Almodóvar simply calls her 'bad, bad, bad' (Albaladejo et al. 1988: 80). She spies on Ángel and wears a *cilicio* (a spiked chain worn on the upper thigh to inflict pain while keeping the scars from view). While her outward religiosity is clear, she shows no signs of Christian charity: her dinnertime prayers are said automatically, and when she says (of her dead, mad husband) 'may he rest in peace', she spits it out venomously. Asked by her son's defence lawyer about the case, she can only respond, 'My son must take whatever punishment God imposes upon him.' Ángel's guilt complex is so powerful that it leads to his accusing himself of murders he did not commit. He tells the lawyer, 'I'm much more guilty than you imagine, if you don't believe me ask my mother.' Ángel is even oppressed by the religious imagery of the Church: the horror-like music helps to make his flight from the church one of the most fearsome moments in the film.

The more sinister, superstitious form of religion is part of the biting satire of *Kika*. One of the more morbid episodes of the television programme *The Worst of the Day* features La procesión de los Picados in Villaverde de los Ojos, a macabre religious procession which includes public self-flagellation. (The procession really exists and takes place in a village in La Rioja, San Vicente de la Sonsierra.) *The Worst of the Day* also includes among its headlines the story of 'a member of the Archbishopric of Seville [...] charged with dishonest abuse', implicating the clergy in abusive criminal activity. And in *Law of Desire* the 'spiritual director' of former pupil Tina, her choirmaster Padre Constantino, has clearly sexually abused Tina as a child. Even where references to religion are not directly an indictment of immoral practices, Almodóvar depicts religion as a ritual whose value lies only in the solace it can provide for the weak, and in the pleasure which can be derived from its iconography. In *Law of Desire*, Tina, looking for something to fill a vacuum, turns to religion, but in its folkloric, popular Spanish manifestation. When she and Ada (Manuela Velasco) make a Cruz de Mayo – a religious altar or domestic shrine common in Spain[13] – to keep them company, Pablo tells her, 'You should find yourself a man, it would be more hygienic.' In *Flower* Leo's mother expresses the need for religion as a soothing influence. She says women need to pray even if they don't believe, its benefit being the company of others. In *What Have I Done* religion is an empty tradition: there is a virgin on the door of Gloria's flat, but religious values do not shape their lives at all. Hopewell (1986: 55) contrasts the Francoist myth of the 'Catholic stereotype of woman as [the] mainstay of the family' with the reality of a 'heroine housewife who maintains [her] family at [the] cost of personal drug addiction and [the] sale of a son'. Religion's role in the film is virtually reduced to superstition: the grandmother (Chus Lampreave) asks San Antonio to find things and recites prayers against the storm.

In the later films, there is some softening of the attitude to religion. In *High Heels* the chaplain who confesses Becky is understanding of her situation. In *Live Flesh*, Víctor's Bible has real applications in his life experience, though his naïve interpretation of its content offers an opportunity for gentle comedy. In *All About My Mother*, Sister Rosa (Penélope Cruz) is genuinely compassionate but all too human as well. Here, the nuns who are tempted by what the outside world offers in *Dark Habits* have ventured out into a sordid world of prostitution, drug addiction and AIDS, and the HIV-positive Rosa has paid the price for her social intervention.

Where Almodóvar really values religion is for its aesthetic potential.[14] This is comically interpreted in *Dark Habits* where Sister Snake designs costumes for the religious statuary based on the latest fashions. This eccentricity is 'only a slight grotesque exaggeration of a Spanish reality' as García de León puts it (García de León and Maldonado 1989: 96). Statues of the virgin are dressed up by local *beatas* in many churches. Almodóvar cites, as his most extravagant representation of religious iconography, the sequence in *Dark Habits*, where the Mother Superior places a handkerchief over Yolanda's face and her make-up leaves a perfect image of her face. The Mother Superior, in raptures, says, 'God forgive me if I feel like a new Veronica.' For Almodóvar, this preposterous idea is on a par with others the Catholic Church expects people to believe (Albaladejo et al. 1988: 71). *Law of Desire* also appropriates religious imagery in the final shot of Pablo (Eusebio Poncela) cradling Antonio (Antonio Banderas) which is a visual reference to the Pietà.[15] This scene is played out in front of the Cruz de Mayo Tina and Ada have constructed as a locus of their prayers for happy relationships.

Almodóvar comments on the way Spanish culture has exploited religion's practical uses, its role as an emotional support (Albaladejo et al. 1988: 70). Elsewhere the references are more ironic. In *Tie Me Up!* a painting of a Christ figure hangs above the bed in ironic juxtaposition with the criminal captivity and violent sex taking place under it. A similar image adorns voyeur Ramón's bedroom in *Kika*. Navajas sees Almodóvar's use of iconographic reference to religion as an aesthetic deflation: 'This minimization is one of the most effective in Almodóvar's aesthetic mode and it fulfils a useful function in Spain's cultural model, which traditionally has conferred too much importance on certain ideological categories, the defence of which Spain has over-prioritized' (Navajas 1991: 71).

The iconography of religion affords an opportunity for kitsch which Almodóvar cannot resist.[16] That Almodóvar should take this element, above all, from religion, says much about his personal style – a mixture of iconoclasm and aesthetic bricolage – and about the aesthetic mode of the postmodern age, which dilutes the deeper meanings of objects and delights in their superficial qualities. This, in turn, reflects Almodóvar's ambivalence towards ideology; depleting the ideological content of religion is itself a political statement.[17]

History and Politics

Almodóvar is a political film-maker. Making films at all was a gesture of cultural politics for an independent film-maker in the years when Spain had no national film school, and when figures like Pilar Miró (one-time head of Spanish state television) was threatened with a military court for her 1979 film *El crimen de Cuenca*, merely because it depicted the torture of prisoners by the Guardia Civil (Gubern et al. 1995: 369–70). Much of Almodóvar's first commercial feature was filmed in 1979, amid a fever of democratic activity, the first in a generation for Spain. Almodóvar chose to entitle this first film *Erecciones generales* (*General Erections*) as a parodic gesture towards the new political obsessions, though the title later became *Pepi, Luci, Bom*. A line of young men take part in a competition which offers a prize to the man with the best erection. Almodóvar picks up on the excitement of the new-found democratic process in Spain and, with an irreverence typical of the *movida*, turns the game of politics into a satire on public life, an alternative culture to the extravaganza of Spain's new democracy, a parallel show in the Spanish capital. The film concentrates heavily on a youth culture largely too young to be involved in the first general election in Spain since 1936. Much of the politics depicted is of political apathy (*pasotismo*), reflecting accurately the huge turn-off that politics represented for many younger Spaniards. Almodóvar attributes the cultural success of the period (the *movida*, though he dislikes the term) to the lack of government by the UCD (Unión del Centro Democrático) in the years 1977–82 (Vidal 1988: 39–40). There are, nevertheless, vignettes of political commentary. The (unnamed) policeman is politically far right, reading the reactionary newspaper *El Imparcial*. Disgusted at what he sees as the degeneracy of the 'New Spain', he remarks, 'This country: with so much democracy I don't know where we'll end up.' He holds similarly conservative views on the role of women, telling his wife, 'You shut up! This isn't women's business' when she makes a suggestion about their domestic arrangements. Much of the conflict in the film revolves around the differing political and social attitudes of enemies Pepi and the policeman, and the latter's tactics seem to indicate a throwback to the time of Franco's police state. References to the military are not made in Almodóvar's films until much later, and then only in passing. In *Kika* the sensation-seeking Andrea (Victoria Abril) reports that an artillery commander killed his wife and then himself (but the man's name is not revealed, which is not the case in all the other crimes). In the same film, dim-witted porno actor Paul Bazzo is also described as 'ex-boxer and ex-legionnaire' in another passing reference to the military. And in *Flower* Paco (Imanol Arias) is an officer with the international forces in Bosnia (his job coming first and used as a pretext 'to run away from the war' at home).

Elsewhere specific political insights are limited. In *Law of Desire* Antonio's father is a politician and his mother is worried about her husband finding out about Antonio's sexuality and possible involvement in the death of Juan (Miguel Molina). In *What Have I Done* there is a short appearance of a *portera* (caretaker and, during the Franco period, unofficial spy for the regime), an impertinent old woman who calls writers Patricia and Lucás drunkards. In *Women on the Verge* Almodóvar further satirizes the *portera* played by Chus Lampreave. She is a Jehovah's Witness and unable to tell lies, thus an extremely unhelpful character to have around when discretion is required.

References to Spain's traumatic twentieth-century history are rare and Almodóvar has consistently created his cinematic world in a post-

Franco, democratic Spain, almost as a denial of the country's tragic past. In *High Heels* Marga, secretary to singer Becky (Marisa Paredes), is the daughter of a Catalan doctor who went into exile during the civil war, the only mention of Spain's civil war in all Almodóvar's films. In *Kika* the sponsor of the macabre reality show *The Worst of the Day*, Leche La Real (Royal Milk), has a logo which is strongly reminiscent of the falangist arrows and yolk sign. There is only one reference to Franco: in *High Heels* a television newsreader reports that 'the health of the Head of State is excellent and you are authorized to say so'.

Only in *Live Flesh* does Almodóvar truly engage (though not at length) with Spain's recent political history: the Franco regime. The first sequence – Víctor's birth in 1970 – is one of only two sequences in all Almodóvar's films set during the Franco years,[18] significantly beginning on the night when interior minister Manuel Fraga announced on the radio a 'state of exception' (a curfew and the suspension of personal liberties). The following words appear on the screen in the first shot of the film:

> A state of exception is declared in all national territories. The defence of peace, Spain's progress and the rights of Spaniards oblige the government to suspend the articles of the Spaniards' charter affecting freedom of reunion and association, as well as article 18, according to which no Spaniard can be detained without reference to prescribed laws.

For audiences who had come to associate Almodóvar with the very freedoms which created the conditions for his cinema (and for his Spain – the Spain portrayed elsewhere in his *oeuvre*), this must have represented something of a shock. The tone of the remaining scene depicting Víctor's birth in a city bus, and the newsreel which narrates the event, is decidedly comic, though the wall behind is full of slogans such as 'freedom' or 'down with the state of exception'. But the political gesture is confirmed and completed at the end of the film. Víctor, stuck in traffic in the busy streets of the capital, speaks to his unborn son:

> I know exactly how you feel... twenty-six years ago I was in the same position as you, about to be born..., but you have better luck than I had, you little bugger...You wouldn't believe how all this has changed [...] look at the pavement, full of people. When I was born there wasn't a soul on the streets. Everyone was in

their houses, scared to death. Luckily for you, my son, we stopped being afraid a long time ago in Spain.

The 1970 section of *Live Flesh* also features the NoDo, the Franco regime's movie theatre newsreels, the compulsory, state-controlled news programme which preceded all film screenings and was associated with Spanish life and national identity for thirty-eight years. The narrator's clipped voice in the typical enthusiastic style of NoDo, with the hospital scene including the nuns who occupied social care roles everywhere at that time, captures the forced formality of the period.

The latter part of the film, though, represents a truly transformed Spain, as emotively expressed by Víctor (Liberto Rabal) to his son at the end of the film. Yarza (1999: 187–8) points to the traditional Spanish couple, *machista* Sancho (Pepe Sancho) and victim Clara (Ángela Molina), as signifying Spain's past: they are 'condemned to disappear' as Clara herself puts it. The new Spain is clearly the child about to be born to Elena and Víctor. This new Spain is reflected in the Barcelona Special Olympics, the inclining towers of the imposing Torres Kio building, or the liberal newspaper *El País* (in *Flower*). The appearance of extremely positive images of Spain, such as the AVE (high-speed train) in *Kika*, led to some commentators suggesting that Almodóvar had adopted a complacent, pro-government attitude in his films. But the contemporary politics in *Flower* suggests otherwise. Leo (Marisa Paredes) stumbles on a demonstration by unemployed medical students, chanting 'Now Felipe can cure flu too'.[19] Certainly the tone in Almodóvar's later films is much less iconoclastic, his satire more affectionate and less caricatured than in the earlier ones.

Idiosyncrasies: National Cultural Specificity

Almodóvar's films contain vignettes of Spanish peculiarities, portrayed with varying degrees of self-consciousness but none the less consistent with verisimilitude. Apart from the repeated references to religion and to the gypsy culture of the bullfight in *Matador*, other culturally-specific allusions include the appearance of flamenco stars Joaquín Cortés and Manuela Vargas in the performance of a *soleá* in *Flower*. Vargas plays Blanca, a gypsy. A more stereotypical gypsy role is given to Bibi Anderson, a fortune-teller in *Matador*. Another, less internationally recognized but equally Spanish performance genre, the *zarzuela*, is parodied in *Pepi,*

Luci, Bom. Spain's other national obsession, football, is mentioned on only two occasions in Almodóvar, both in *Live Flesh*. In the first, a critical moment in a game featuring one of the Madrid teams, Atlético, even unites the enemies Víctor and David. At the end of the film, the international match between Spain and Malta means less traffic on streets and a quicker journey to the hospital.

The national obsession with food features in *Pepi, Luci, Bom* where Pepi prepares Bom's favourite dish, the famously difficult *bacalao al pil-pil*. Gazpacho features in both *Matador* and *Women on the Verge*. In *Law of Desire* Pablo, Ada and Tina are seen eating in the Manila restaurant after a performance. In *Flower* Rosa represents the typical Spanish housewife, obsessed with food: she prepares very Spanish dishes (flan, squid, Spanish omelette) and insists in saving them all for her sister. In the same film, Leo is left in charge of a paella but cannot manage to keep it warm, a sure indication of wifely dereliction of duty in Spain.

A recent cultural preoccupation, the much-discussed lack of reading in Spanish society, is satirized in the television programme *Hay que leer más* (*We Must Read More*) in *Kika*. The elderly presenter (played by Almodóvar's mother) reads badly and without spontaneity and doesn't read her literary guests' books at all because of her bad eyesight. Furthermore, she is uncertain about foreign names or, indeed, foreign authors, but sure of the delights of Spanish food (*choricillo*) and good women. They sit at a round table which, one suspects, will have the typical *brasero* (an under-the-table electric, formerly wood-burning, heater) underneath it.

Comparisons with other countries, though based on stereotypes, tend to reinforce the national-cultural specificity of Spain. Perhaps the most explicit example of stereotypical national identities is the comparison made in *Tie Me Up!* between Germans and Spaniards. The television advert asks, 'Why do retired Germans holiday in Benidorm while poor retired Spaniards have to beg outside the metro?' with shots of revelling Germans cut with a shot of an old woman begging outside the main Madrid bullring. The answer is unsurprising: 'Because the Germans think about their future when they are eighteen' (shots of blonde Aryans with swastikas filling in forms), 'and the Spanish ... the Spanish only think about their retirement when it's too late' (shots of young Spaniards dancing the tango followed by the elderly in social security queues).[20] This self-critical attitude to Spanish national identity extends to its literature. In *Flower* writer Leo explains to the literary editor of Spanish daily *El País* that she prefers to avoid Spanish literature in her writings for the newspaper.

Almodóvar's sardonic allusion to what could be described as a national inferiority complex is matched by a range of characters and characteristics which suggest that a Spanish temperament really does exist (whatever it may be). Interfering caretakers, over-talkative taxi drivers, domineering grandmothers always speaking in proverbs and pining for their villages, all form part of Spain's tapestry of popular myths. The no-nonsense activism of Spanish farmers is represented in the briefest of mentions, by the newsreader in *High Heels* who describes how farmers dumped hundreds of kilos of corn outside the US embassy – a typically Spanish headline. Protesting and the sheer aggressive strength of vocality is another stereotype, doubtless based on some reality. Spain is said to be the second noisiest country on earth (after Japan) and in *Pepi, Luci, Bom* noise levels on the street almost impede conversation. *Flower* features the local customs of Colmenar de Oreja's *concurso de gritos* (an annual shouting competition which takes place in a small town south of Madrid). Another custom (though less quaint) is the typically unhelpful attitude of those meant to serve the public in Spain, a good example being the airport receptionist Alicia, played by Eva Siva in *Labyrinth of Passions*. The line of bad-tempered characters is particularly well-served by the actress Kiti Manver, who had to wait until her fourth film appearance before she was offered a sympathetic character to play. In *Pepi, Luci, Bom* she plays an Andalusian singer drawn to Madrid in search of fame, but constantly shocked and irritated by men's attempts to take advantage of her sexually. In *What Have I Done* she plays the bitter and vindictive Juani who mistreats her daughter Vanesa and has no patience with any of her neighbours. In *Women on the Verge* she plays Paulina Morales, the obnoxious and unprincipled feminist who threatens Pepa, 'I'm going to give you a lawsuit for the Shiite terrorists that will make you shit yourself.' The allusion to bodily functions is apt, for scatological references are another recurrent feature in Almodóvar.

The willingness of the Spanish to talk about bodily functions makes Anglo-Saxons grimace. Examples are everywhere: in *Pepi, Luci, Bom*, Bom (Alaska) obliges Luci (Eva Siva) to eat the contents of her nose and Pepi creates anti-fart underwear; Angustias in *Labyrinth of Passions* also has a flatulence problem and the female caretaker fails to reach the toilet after taking a laxative; in *High Heels* Becky steps in dogdirt; in *Flower* Leo's mother is obsessed with bowels, telling her daughter, 'If I don't use a glycerine suppository, I don't shit.' The Spanish language exhibits the same frankness when it comes to reference to body parts and functions, as will be shown in the following section.

Language

It is difficult to overestimate the importance of the Spanish language to the characterization of both individuals and the national socio-cultural context of contemporary Spain. For anyone familiar with both Spanish and English, a random check on the subtitles in any of the films reveals how much is lost in translation, how difficult it is to find equivalents in English for the many colourful phrases which abound in Almodóvar's films. To find an equivalent in English in an appropriate register for many phrases is to dampen the impact of an often crude Spanish utterance. To translate literally into English produces phrases which are far beyond the levels of tolerance of Anglo-Saxon audiences. Subtitle translations frequently fail miserably to render the original Spanish into satisfactory English. For example, in *Dark Habits* Yolanda's boyfriend Jorge shouts 'joder' – quite normal for Spaniards and equal to 'damn' in English. It is translated as 'fuck off' in the subtitles.

The fact that Spaniards have no qualms about graphically sexual or scatological expressions is apparent from Almodóvar's films, which tend to use a naturalistic mode of dialogue. Insults are especially colourful. An angry Juani in *What Have I Done* tells Cristal '¿Por qué no te metes la lengua en el culo?' translated in the subtitles as 'jump in the lake', when the literal translation is 'Why don't you stick your tongue up your arse'. In the same film, when writer Lucas asks his wife to put on some make-up, she responds '¿Por qué no te maquillas tú la polla?' ('Why don't you make up your prick?'). In *Women on the Verge* Lucía (Julieta Serrano) shouts at Pepa, 'Váyase a la mierda' ('Go to hell') and Pepa responds in kind, 'Váyase a la mierda usted también' ('You go to hell' – but using the polite form 'usted'). In the same film an incredulous Pepa tells lawyer Paulina, 'Y usted tampoco es una abogada. Usted es una hija de perra' ('You're no lawyer. You're a fucking bitch'). Later, under attack from the objects Pepa throws out of her apartment window, Paulina shouts 'Me cago en la puta madre de esta señora' (roughly translatable as 'I shit on the whore that bore that woman'). Even the mature landlady Doña Centro (Pilar Bardem) in *Live Flesh* shouts 'hijo-puta' ('son of a bitch') at a driver who does not stop to help them.

Many set phrases in Spanish make allusions to sexual or bodily functions. In *What Have I Done* the exhibitionist refers to 'pollón' ('big dick'), 'leche' ('semen'), 'coño' ('pussy') as he tells the women of his supposed sexual prowess. In keeping with its transgressive role, pushing back the boundaries of acceptability, *Pepi, Luci, Bom* is, unsurprisingly, the most excessive. The lyrics of the song 'Murciana marrana' (see Chapter 9) are both sexually explicit and distasteful, and they are made hilarious by the juxtaposition with the incomprehensible English introduction by Roxy (Fabio de Miguel). In the same film, timid housewife Luci tells her husband, 'Ese decreto me lo paso yo por la brinca del coño' ('You can stick your decree ...'). Earthy and direct Lola in *Tie Me Up!* tells her sexy sister, Marina (Victoria Abril), who is intent on taking off her knickers for the shooting of a scene, 'No sé qué es peor, que se te noten las bragas o que se te note el cocho' ('I don't know what's worse, seeing your panty line or seeing your pussy'). And in *All About My Mother* the women drink *cava* and discuss penises and blow-jobs. In *Tie Me Up!* Lola complains that the producer's wife wants the sofa they are using on set 'porque se le ponga la pipa el coño que quiere el sofá...' ('just because she fancies the sofa' – but in the Spanish this untranslatable phrase alludes to the producer's wife's 'pussy'). In *Kika* the protagonist (Verónica Forqué) rails against publicity: 'me toca el coño la publicidad' ('I don't give a fuck about publicity', but literally, 'publicity gets on my pussy'). Similarly, in *Live Flesh* David tells Víctor, 'me toca los cojones' (again, 'I don't give a fuck', but literally, 'it gets on my balls'). Elsewhere such earthy phrases are tied to rural life, such as the phrase used by Leo's mother in *Flower*. She calls her other daughter, 'cara de ladilla' ('crabface'), and says that women alone are 'como vacas sin cencerro' ('like cows without cowbells'). In *Matador* a character like Eva's mother Pilar (Chus Lampreave) is characterized as more down-to-earth than the rest of the characters who speak an unreal, heightened language. She uses phrases like 'todo el tufo de esto no me gusta nada' ('this all smells fishy to me') and 'le puedo meter un paquete' ('I'll lay one on him').

Swearing is much more common in Spain than in many other Western nations, and this is also reflected in Almodóvar. The relatively light sexual swearwords are everywhere: words such as 'cojones' ('balls'), even uttered by an elderly mother in *Tie Me Up!*, 'coño' ('damn', literally 'pussy' – or even 'cunt' – and the most common swearword in Spain) and 'joder' (fuck). More transgressive in Spanish are swearwords which misuse religious terms. The link between language and religion is explained by Stanton (1999: 2): 'Only a people with an intimate sense of religion, like the Spaniards, could blaspheme so much and so well.' 'Hostias' ('the Host') is both one of the strongest expletives and one of the most common. It appears in *Kika*, *What Have I Done* and *Women on the Verge* among others. Most significantly it is used in the presence of the religious orders in *Dark Habits* where it truly could offend. A postman uses the word 'hostias' when he hears that one of the girls in the convent has taken the veil.

Slang is also quite common in Almodóvar, with words like 'pelas' for pesetas or 'pajote' ('wank') both in *Tie Me Up!* In *What Have I Done* Toni uses the slang associated with the city's subculture: 'guay' ('fantastic'), 'de puta madre' ('excellent'), 'chaval' ('guy'), 'talego' for a 1,000-peseta note, and 'chinorri' ('little kid'). In *Dark Habits* Lola speaks in a *pasota* drug street language: 'lo ha palmao' ('he snuffed it') 'se ha tirado' ('he went AWOL') 'su tronca' ('his girl') 'business' ('drug dealing') 'la pasma' ('the cops/pigs') 'pelas' ('pesetas') 'estar tirao' ('easy') 'guay del paraguay' ('fab'). And in the same film, Sofía asks whether there are many delinquents in the convent, 'En el convento ¿qué? ¿mucha choriza?' ('In the convent, what? Lots of criminals?') using the feminine version of the slang term *chorizo* (criminals but also sausage!). At times, the combination of slang words begins to sound like another language. In *Pepi, Luci, Bom*, Bom tells Pepi that the boys have got money from prostitution, using the expression 'chuleando un carroza' ('pimping an old man').

Finally, accent plays an important part in the identification of Spanish national identity and, in particular, of regional identity, a highly prominent political and cultural subject in Spain. Argentinian accents testify in *Pepi, Luci, Bom* to a time when Latin Americans were highly visible in Madrid. Elsewhere, most common is the Andalusian accent, considered the most humorous accent in Spain for reasons too complex to investigate here. In *Law of Desire* Antonio's mother speaks with an Andalusian accent but with hint of a foreigner. Kiti Manver plays Andalusians with notable accents in *Pepi, Luci, Bom* and *What Have I Done*. In *Women on the Verge* Candela's Malaga accent adds to the comic effect of her hilarious dialogue, as is the case with transsexual prostitute Agrado (Antonia San Juan) in *All About My Mother*. In the same film, Rosa's mother has a Catalan accent, though Catalan itself is not heard in the film despite the Barcelona setting. Almodóvar chooses not to represent the pluralities of national identities and languages which is contemporary Spain. The overwhelming predominance of an unproblematically Spanish Madrid (see Chapter 6) elides prominent national preoccupations with regionalism and separatism. Also absent are the military, and Spain's rising anxiety about increasing numbers of immigrants. But the focus on recuperating and recycling the cultural legacy of the Spanish language, idiosyncrasies, and national mythology (such as the elevation of death through the *corrida*), does not exclude exploring more socially inscribed questions, as will be seen in the following chapter.

3

Social Structures

Power, Ethics and Corruption

> This country has always been divided in two [...] on the one hand there are the envious and on the other, the intolerant.[1]

Despite Almodóvar's association with a postmodern world, as a director of surfaces and playful parody, his films do bear fruit when approached, in an old-fashioned, humanistic way, as social histories of their times. The highly manipulated and sometimes self-conscious processes of mediation which operate in the films do not deny a social reading. Apart from omnipresent gender and sexual relationships (discussed in Chapters 4 and 5), the films reflect a contemporary society which encompasses economic relationships, education, television and the media, crime, law enforcement and friendship. Much of Almodóvar's cinema shows dysfunctional relationships in the process of breaking down. Clearly, neither proper and fair societal relationships, nor well-adjusted happy families make for good drama or good comedy; some form of conflict is required in both. Beyond this narrative-driven context, however, Almodóvar does use the film medium to make critical points about Spanish society and about the contemporary world.

The first power relationship in Almodóvar's first film, *Pepi, Luci, Bom*, is shown to be corrupt. The policeman who discovers Pepi's marijuana plants is prepared to enter into a sordid agreement with her, accepting Pepi's sexual favours in return for his silence. Moreover, she takes his compliance for granted, lifting her skirt to provoke his response. The deficit in professional integrity is not peculiar to *Pepi, Luci, Bom*. The Mother Superior in *Dark Habits* abuses her position of authority to feed her sexual and drug habits, resorting first to blackmail, then eventually to drug trafficking. The hierarchies of the convent create a tension that mimics the power relations of a family structure, complete with the usual jealousy and personal animosity. The Mother Superior and Sister Rat were novices together but the Mother Superior is now the senior of the two, and is envious of Sister Rat's friendly relations with the girls. Sister Manure is most faithful to the Mother Superior, but then we learn the reason: Manure had murdered a man and the Mother Superior had lied under oath to save her. Manure spends much time spying on the other nuns to report back to the Mother Superior. Above her is the senior nun of the order, the Senior Mother Superior who represents the oppression of the hierarchical structure, threatening to close down the Madrid convent.

Figures of authority and professionals (police officers, psychiatrists, doctors, priests, lawyers) do not fare better in other films. In *Matador*, both the gay police inspector (Eusebio Poncela) and his unfortunate girlfriend exceed the limits of professional acceptability: he is sexually attracted to Ángel and she is romantically inclined towards the young man. In *Tie Me Up!*, the female director of the mental institution abuses her position of power over Ricky (Antonio Banderas) (Navajas 1991: 68). Marina's dope-smoking doctor fulfils the function of her dealer, while a pharmacist – somewhat annoyed that her commercial duties have interrupted sex – suggests they buy drugs in the street. In *Law of Desire*, the doctor advises Tina to dispose of any incriminating evidence before the police arrive, and attempts to protect Pablo from the police despite suspecting that Pablo knows about Juan's murder. In the same film, it is evident that the school chaplain Padre Constantino has sexually abused young boys under his care. The abuse of power characterizes many professionals in the films. In *Women on the Verge*, feminist lawyer Paulina Morales takes advantage of her client Lucía's mental illness to steal her husband, Iván. She gives extremely unsympathetic advice to Pepa. In *High Heels*, Judge Domínguez is motivated entirely by his attraction to Rebeca (Victoria Abril) and he is quite prepared to see a murderer freed. When he asks Rebeca why she is not more grateful to him, she responds, 'I'm sorry if I didn't buy you a leg of ham, but I thought that if you freed me it was because you believed I was innocent.' Clearly, if Domínguez has behaved according to his professional duty to justice, the indication of gratitude should not be necessary at all. (A token culinary delicacy always goes down well in Spain as a gesture of thanks for services rendered.) Shaw makes the point that the judge serves not the law of the land (patriarchal justice) but 'Almodóvar's law, the law belonging to the moral system of the film'.[2]

The portrayal of social and professional relationships in the films of the late 1990s is altogether more positive. In *Flower*, Leo has a long-standing relationship of trust with her employee Blanca. Only the desperation of Blanca's son Antonio (Joaquín Cortés) allows corruption to creep in. He steals a script from Leo's wastebin. From a film-maker who rarely feels an obligation to political correctness, there is never-theless a careful balance here between the entirely honest gypsy Blanca, and her less-than-honest gypsy son, Antonio. In any case, the end result, the investment in the flamenco performance, justifies the means, for Leo at least. Leo's best friend Betty (Carmen Elías) also works in a field with a progressive sense of social reform: she coaches doctors on how to break the news of a death to a relative, and then broach the difficult topic of organ donations. (In her capacity as a psychologist, however, Betty does go beyond the call of duty, becoming romantically involved with Paco.) There is a marked social conscience in *Live Flesh* too. Unlike in earlier films where characters are passive victims, here they have aspirations and work towards them: Víctor is determined to learn what he can and make the most of his life, even in prison; David (Javier Bardem) triumphs even against the adversity of his disability, a feature of the film that was seized upon as a welcome positive representation of the disabled;[3] and Elena (Francesca Neri) has an acute social conscience, using her inherited wealth to finance a shelter for homeless children, and paying her debt of guilt for her part in the personal disaster of David and Víctor. Elena has moved on from the early 1990s, paralleling a change in Spanish society from the aftermath of the hedonistic 1980s. In *All About My Mother*, Rosa works with the genuinely poor and with prostitutes, and Manuela (Cecilia Roth) is a nurse who, apart from her intensive care job, helps with training doctors in handling organ dona-tions. Moreover, effective support relations between middle-class social workers, prostitutes, nurses and actresses suggest a society which is functioning, quite unlike the dysfunctional and corrupt world of the earlier films. Either Almodóvar's view of society has lost the acerbic, critical edge of rebellious youth, or Spanish society has begun to escape from the ethical vacuum of dictatorship.

Money and Class

Contemporary Spanish society could make reasonable claims to being 'classless', in the sense that an individual's social ranking in Spain is largely based on material wealth and education, advantages equally accessible, in principle, across the population. This is not to suggest that Spain is free from economic class divisions or that there begins a perfect meritocracy south of the Pyrenees, but rather that the legacy of one's class as established at birth is not so powerful as fully to segregate the classes. The concept of being born into a class, though associated with the British empire, was quite as much a national obsession in Spain for much of its imperial history. Franco's dictatorship only served to perpetuate social divisions, but contemporary Spain is much less concerned about class. A 1995 survey revealed that only 23 per cent of Spaniards believed a class system existed (Lawlor and Rigby 1998: 314). Though Almodóvar's films say considerably less about class than many British films, social relationships in the films are marked by economic class differences. Most particularly, individuals or groups are divided by material wealth and by education. Almodóvar depicts a wide range of social classes, often within a single film.

The homes of characters tell the viewers much about their inhabitants and, in Almodóvar, the details of interiors are socially inscribed as well as aesthetically striking. In *Pepi, Luci, Bom*, the very first shot of the building where the policeman lives suggests a poor area, and Pepi's flat has the appearance associated with rented accommodation. She has little time to spend indoors and a beautiful home is not a priority in Pepi's life. In *Live Flesh*, the division of rich and poor is reflected in the homes of characters Elena, Víctor and David. Elena first lives in a luxurious ambassador's residence, and later, with David, in a hyper-modern loft apartment with very expensive furnishings, described in the script as 'ample, comfortable, classics of modern design'. The script mentions the designers Hoffman, Eileen Gray, Corbusier and Donald Judd, not as an index for set designers, but simply to indicate wealth. This is in stark contrast with Víctor's home in La Ventilla, an expropriated estate of prefabricated homes which Clara likens to war-torn Sarajevo. The more subtle distinction between affluent and intellectual Leo's apartment and her working-class, poor but respectable sister's flat (in *Flower*) is created by realistic interiors which reflect their lifestyles: Leo's home is stylish, full of books and plants and functional but attractive furniture, whereas Rosa's flat is furnished with mass-produced consumer items, all with a patina of cheap ostentation. Moreover, Rosa lives in the unfashionably remote Parla district. In *What Have I Done*, Gloria's minuscule flat is frequently linked visually to the monstrous block of which it is a part, and Gloria herself similarly associated visually with its constraining domestic items: we see shots of her from inside the washing machine or the oven (see Chapter 8). But the interiors of some of her clients are quite different: the sex therapist boasts a spacious modern apartment; the writer Lucas and his wife live in a suitably messy yet decidedly bourgeois intellectual home. And Gloria's prostitute neighbour Cristal (Verónica Forqué) lives in an apartment which looks rather like the inside of a theatre dressing-room, complete with costumes and showbusiness paraphernalia, but which is full of plastic and shiny vulgarity. Pepa's flat in *Women on the Verge* is a well-designed, luxury penthouse, reflecting her financial status. She decides to rent it without any hesitation over financial arrangements; moreover, she knows its exact size, including the all-important roof terrace, a reflection of the values of fashionable Madrid society at the time.

Most of Almodóvar's characters are identified in terms of financial standing (though this is rarely a primary mark of identity). Pepi refers to herself as 'a rich heiress' in *Pepi, Luci, Bom*, and remarks that her father gives her the money she needs. When this flow of cash is interrupted, Pepi confronts the question of useful employment for the first time. When she goes to see a potential client about one of her publicity adverts, she tells Bom 'my capitalist lives around here', referring to the client as if to another species. Sexi (Cecilia Roth), protagonist of *Labyrinth of Passions*, is also supported by her father (a renowned doctor) and thus has ample time for music, drugs and sex. Her father can afford holidays on the Costa del Sol (a luxury in the late 1960s), a psychoanalyst for his daughter and a Cuban maid. Her friend Queti (Marta Fernández Muro) escapes the family business to occupy Sexi's social position, indicating an easy, almost carnivalesque social fluidity (though this is, of course, a comic film). In *Flower*, Leo buys clothes for her sister Rosa, loans her money and also gives her mother money for the village local taxes. Rosa's husband is out of work and has a drink problem. Though Leo is not accustomed to financial problems, she is threatened by her publisher Alicia, who tells her to think about her chalet, her trips to the Caribbean and her cosmetics bill. When characters have no financial worries this is indicated both by their surroundings

4. *Matador.* Diego (Nacho Martínez) questions Ángel
(Antonio Banderas).

and by the absence of references to money or the lack of it. Even the
titles of films like *Kika* or *High Heels* suggest a world of expensive
fashion and design. In *Women on the Verge*, relationships are very much
the focus of the film; there are no social problems for this class, and
they are thus free to pursue emotional goals rather than material ones.
This is also true in *Matador*. María visits Diego's secluded mansion and
asks him if it was very expensive; he replies, 'money doesn't worry me.
I have earned enough in the past.' Diego's profession is associated with
young people from poorer backgrounds trying to make their fortunes
as bullfighters, much as youths take up boxing in the Anglo-Saxon world.
Here Ángel is an exception – middle-class and out of place. Diego
himself remarks on this: 'you're not like the other kids' [fig. 4].

Although main characters tend to be sympathetically depicted whatever their social standing, Almodóvar is more critical of the way in
which money perverts relationships in society. He is much more bitingly
satirical, for instance, in his depiction of the *nouveaux riche*s. The most
comically grotesque example is the sister of nun-cum-writer Sister Rat
in *Dark Habits*, Antonia, who is a shallow materialist. She has exploited
her sister's situation in the convent to pass off as her own the nun's

romantic novels, and she tries to persuade Rat to stay inside the convent in order to continue to benefit. But her motives are discovered when Rat and Yolanda pay her a visit at home. Antonia is being interviewed by a journalist, and, unable to answer questions about her writing (she cannot as she is not the author), she prefers to direct the conversation towards the spectacularly kitsch transformation of her flat. For her, a home is 'the mirror of the soul', and she boasts a recently installed 100,000-peseta illuminated fountain. But the volumes of classic literary works on her bookshelves are hollow boxes, just like her own authorship. The more aristocratic Marquesa fares little better in *Dark Habits*. She plunges the convent into a financial crisis by refusing to continue the allowance that her husband had set up, preferring to spend her money on her new-found lifestyle as a widow. When the Mother Superior points out that she is a millionaire, she responds, 'To survive these days you have to be.'

From the earliest films, money is portrayed as the great social and *sexual* lubricant: Pepi (*Pepi, Luci, Bom*) is prepared to sell her virginity for 60,000 pesetas and Toni and Moncho (both apparently heterosexual) have no problems prostituting themselves with older men for money. By the time of *Live Flesh*, a film made almost twenty years later, Víctor tries to work out how many tricks his mother must have done to save 150,000 pesetas: at least a thousand tricks, he calculates. In *Flower*, Antonio thinks he can repay Leo (whose script financed his flamenco show) with sexual favours, and earlier, his mother Blanca asks her son if the producer is asking for something in return for his money, she too assuming that nobody gives money for nothing. The first relationship depicted in *Law of Desire* is a commercial one between the young porn actor and the director/dubber whose money (we see him give it) buys the performance and, with it, sexual obedience. In the same film, a model accompanies Pablo home and is prepared to sleep with him for a part in his next film.

But it is in *What Have I Done*, where characters are truly mired in poverty, that money will buy almost anything. Ironically, the most negatively portrayed character, Gloria's husband Antonio (Ángel de Andrés López), claims that 'there are things which are much more important than money ... decency, for example', but he himself is unable to provide for his family and his moral stance is no consolation for Gloria. She has to watch her son contemplate a solitary tin of stale tomatoes and sends him to the neighbour to be fed. Her sons are survivors, their cynicism exaggerated to almost absurd levels. Toni sells drugs while younger brother Miguel is experienced in the sordid commerce of sex with older men. Gloria comes to a financial arrangement with the child-molester dentist (she 'sells' Miguel to him as she cannot pay the dentist's bills). Miguel accepts once certain material conditions are met. In this context, the traditional sex-worker Cristal seems almost respectable. She acts as a substitute girlfriend for the impotent police inspector when he has an appointment with the sex therapist. And her session with the exhibitionist is further testimony to the extent of the commodification of social and sexual relations. The pathetically scrawny exhibitionist can buy self-esteem and delude himself about his sexual prowess simply by paying Cristal to have sex. Cristal feigns orgasm as Gloria sits beside her on the couch, the sole spectator of the client's exhibition fantasy, in her hands her own symbol of commodity worship – a pair of new curling tongs. In *Flower*, the power of money to filter out social problems is eloquently (though innocently) revealed by Leo's publisher. Angry over a change in style from romantic novel to black social realism, Alicia reveals the true social function of pulp romantic fiction: people want to forget 'their sordid surroundings'. She describes how the miserable district portrayed in Leo's latest work is inappropriate for such novels, but what she is in fact complaining about is Leo's penchant for writing about real life. Leo sincerely remarks, 'reality is like that, Alicia'. The publisher's response is unequivocal: 'Reality! We all have enough reality in our homes. Reality is for the newspapers and television ... and look at the result. Because of so much reality the country is about to explode. Reality should be banned!' Leo's contract includes the unambiguous clause, 'absence of social conscience'.

In a 'post-caste' society, education can act as a leveller. In a country where illiteracy was a common problem until relatively recently, differing levels of education effectively separate people into classes, and this is frequently portrayed in Almodóvar's films. It clearly applies to the sequence in *Live Flesh* set during the Franco period: the young Isabel who in 1970 is about to give birth is at the bottom of the social scale. An unmarried mother and prostitute, Isabel is not even capable of calculating the due date of her baby: 'I can't count.' Hotel-owner Centro responds, 'illiteracy is so terrible!' Twenty years later, her son Víctor is still at the lower end of the social scale, but he is working for a living, a beneficiary of the increased investment in and access to secondary education (a sevenfold increase from 1960 to 1975).[4] Later, when Víctor is wrongfully imprisoned, he makes the most of his time there, studying education, Bulgarian and the Bible. His desire for self-improvement pays off and he is able to make the most of the more fluid class structure at the end of the film. Hooper (1995: 258) remarks that 'there is nothing which separates the generations in Spain as pitilessly as their differing levels of education', and this is also borne out in *What Have I Done*: Gloria is unable to help her son Toni with his homework, telling him, 'You know I'm illiterate.' Gloria is also separated from her employer Patricia who remarks, 'cleaning depresses me so much'. Of course she can afford to think like that, her intellectual class showing her a way out of poverty. Even prostitute Cristal is educating herself in English (through an eccentrically British English 1960s LP record course) in preparation for her big career move to America. In *Flower*, the maid Blanca doesn't know what 'aphrodisiac' means and Leo explains her literary talent as a result of helping illiterate neighbours to write letters: 'for economic reasons, we emigrated to Extremadura. We lived in a street full of illiterate people.'

Television and Advertising

The Spanish have the second highest television viewing figures in Europe,[5] making television – and not bullfighting or even football – the most popular national pastime. Almodóvar reflects this obsession: in thirteen films only one does not include characters watching television. The appearance may be no more than domestic contextualization, as in *Pepi, Luci, Bom* where the policeman typically has the set switched on but is not watching the black and white transmission of a chat show; or a television programme may feature as a prelude to a film (more often accorded metaphorical or narrative importance in Almodóvar, see Chapter 7). In *Live Flesh*, Elena watches a documentary on the subject of hospital waiting lists before the Buñuel film commences.

By far the most frequent television form to appear in the films, though, is advertising. Almodóvar admits there is much to admire in its technique: 'Advertising is the best thing on television. Moreover, the best Spanish cinema is advertising cinema, with the highest standards in originality and technical innovation.'[6] Nevertheless, he shows little respect for this medium in his many parodies of adverts. Even before his first commercially released film, Almodóvar was making parodies of adverts in Super-8 film. From the beginning, they were a feature of his films.[7]

In *Pepi, Luci, Bom*, Pepi sets up her own advertising agency and the advert for Bragas Ponte (a spoof Almodóvar had already completed) is inserted as the first of many in Almodóvar's films. The commercial for anti-flatulence knickers conforms to the standard television advert: the use of a narrator (the omniscient voice of authority), the mood music, the champagne cork popping which masks the offending bodily sound. But the incongruity of such an obscene product following the romanticized formula of these conventions is clear. This is followed by the revelation of another usage of the product, as urine-absorbing knickers, complete with the usual pseudo-technical diagram. Once again, the deflation of the norms of advertising is apparent: the girl makes noises of delight and surprise at the miraculous properties of the knickers even before the narrator has got to the main selling points. Then comes the final twist: Bragas Ponte can also be used, rolled up, as the perfect dildo. This conforms to the idea of parody as a comic exaggeration of a style, deflation through ridicule, the exaggerated claims more ridiculous in each of the three sections. The final slogan completes the perfect send-up: '*Hagas lo que hagas, Ponte bragas*' ('Whatever you do, put your *Knickers* on'). At the end of the screening of Pepi's new advert, Bom remarks that she wishes the urine-absorbing underwear were real, drawing attention to the vacuity of adverts and their extravagant claims.

In *What Have I Done*, the advert for coffee watched by Antonio again constitutes true parody of the genre with exaggeration and incongruity, for pure send-up value. The sensuous tone of the female first-person narrator, the romantic music and the slow-motion shot of the falling coffee granules, are all the stuff of conventional adverts, but details like 'we made love a dozen times, very satisfactorily, by the way' ruptures the credibility before the final accident (the girl receives the scalding coffee full in the face) which turns the advert into a horror sequence. In *Women on the Verge*, Pepa plays the mother of a serial killer whose washing powder is so thorough as to make it impossible for the police to detect even the slightest mark of blood, or 'entrails', as one of the inspectors adds. The advert mimics the style of countless others which claim to have the recipe for the whiter than white wash, exposing the excesses of these claims and their formulaic repetitiveness.

Television presenters are also a recurrent feature in the films. In *Kika*, the literary chat show is parodied. The title *Hay que leer más* (*We Must Read More*) appears in a hand-made tapestry far removed from the chic, cosmopolitan sets normally used for cultural programming. Almodóvar's elderly mother plays the hostess in an affectionate critique of ill-qualified presenters. The title alludes to the much-discussed problem of Spain's low reading figures (for both newspapers and fiction), but this elderly matron is the antithesis of the sharp intellectual. We hear her ask if the cameras are rolling at the start; far from a conversation, she has to read every question from cue cards and seems more preoccupied with selling her native Spain and La Mancha than inquiring about the American author's book. She urges him, 'Have a *choricillo*', and later confirms the insular stereotype: 'There's nothing like Spain.' She admits that she has not read the book, nor will she, as her eyesight is poor. Towards the end she veers off into an explanation of why she is doing the programme: her son, the director (a characteristically self-reflexive gesture on Almodóvar's part) has given her the job of presenting the programme so that mother and son can spend time together. In *Women on the Verge*, Almodóvar's mother plays a newscaster, her performance slow and faltering, once again contrasting with the usual newsreader in Spain, typically, an attractive young woman or an authoritative-looking middle-aged man in a suit. Elsewhere, gentle parody becomes more aggressively satirical. In *Matador*, a newscaster not only relates Ángel's alleged murders, but offers her own opinion, referring to María Cardenal's decision to represent Ángel as 'truly dreadful cynicism'. This opinionated newsreading, taken to idiosyncratic extremes by the Antena 3 newsreader José Antonio Carrascal, reflects the frequent adoption by Spanish television news of what in the printed press would be called an editorial line.

The sensationalist world of television news is revealed in *High Heels* where Rebeca works as a newsreader, the smaller screen reflecting her lesser achievement when compared to her large-screen mother Becky. When Rebeca first appears reading the news – the dumb blonde signer next to her – she giggles nervously, aware that her mother is watching. On Rebeca's second appearance, we see also the workings of the television studio: make-up room, studio, monitors and auto-cue, production team. But by now Rebeca's husband Manuel (Feodor Atkine) has been murdered. Knowing she will have to read this news item, the director of the show warns his colleagues, 'Be careful about what could happen here.' This is followed by the news introduction, as both Rebeca's colleagues and her mother watching at home ask how Rebeca can read the news in such circumstances. The answer is revealed soon enough: she confesses live on television to the murder of her husband. After briefly considering cutting the broadcast in favour of 'the gardens of Spain', the director decides to take full advantage of the scoop: 'Don't cut whatever happens.' Her live confession is the central dramatic event of the narrative and was Almodóvar's starting point in the conception of the film (Strauss 1996: 105). The police arrive to detain Rebeca with the cameras still rolling. The sensationalism of this scene prefigures the excesses of the media ferociously satirized in Almodóvar's next film, *Kika*.

The television programme *The Worst of the Day* (*Lo peor del día*), as presented by Andrea Caracortada (Cutface), is Almodóvar's most corrosive comic conceit and perhaps the most grotesque of all his cinema. Andrea herself is a former psychologist turned morbidly melodramatic television presenter. The extreme sensationalism of the content is only one step beyond the reality shows which filled Spanish screens in the early 1990s and which still form a staple of world television. Andrea's stylized delivery strips all humanity from the horrific details of the litany of crime and violence.

> A woman sets herself on fire in the BVB bank; [...] charged with dishonest abuses; [...] kills his wife and then himself; [...] the Orcasitas rapist committed suicide yesterday in prison unable to face up to being repeatedly raped himself by several inmates ... Ángel Moya condemned to four years in prison for prostituting the physically disabled ... uncovered in Madrid a network of child prostitution and the recording of porno videos in the Prosperity nursery.

After this breathless preamble, Andrea finds a smile to greet the audience, 'Good evening, ladies and gentlemen, you are watching Andrea Caracortada, with, exclusively, the Worst of the Day.' The applause which greets this is false, as the studio audience seats are empty. The optical trick is later revealed as Caracortada sits alone and pretends to talk to guests; presumably they will be added on later, the simulation of verisimilitude easier than filming real people on set. Before screening the programme's first 'reality' clip, Andrea tells the public: 'Oh, I should warn you that the following might offend your sensibility, if you have any left.' During the clip, which Andrea has shot with her personal camcorder, the murderous husband appears and shoots his wife dead on camera. Andrea – embodying the entire show as journalist, camerawoman, editor and presenter – pursues him but is shot at herself. The interview with the murderer's mother only exaggerates the inherent sensationalism of the genre: the mother cannot believe her son committed murder although she has witnessed it recorded on film. When she admits to being nervous about the interview, Andrea replies 'good', relishing the manipulative power of the medium. In a further grotesquely ironic revelation, the sponsor of the programme is, incongruously, a milk company.

The second episode of *The Worst of the Day* contains what Andrea refers to as 'our popular section "bloody ceremonies"'. This week's feature comes from Villaverde de los Ojos, where local residents parade through the streets flogging themselves until they bleed. The so-called '*procesión de los picaos*' is integrated into the story, as it is revealed that rapist porn star Paul Bazzo has escaped prison during day release for the event, and subsequently turns up at Kika's house. The last episode portrays Paul Bazzo's rape of Kika, and, for Andrea, it represents 'a real scoop'. As she explains what happened she runs her fingers provocatively up her body from between her legs to her breasts, savouring the prospect of the televised rape. She reminds the viewers, 'Be optimistic: this, or even something worse, could have happened to you: this is a message from our sponsor, Royal Milk.' Apart from the co-operation of whole-some sponsors, Andrea has the police working for her. Angry at their ineptitude she tells them, 'We don't pay you to think but to act': she is not talking about tax-payers' money here, for she has these policemen on her personal payroll. She calls them *gilipollas* (dickheads) and *maderos* (a derogatory term meaning 'wooden' and connoting 'thick') and com-plains that they cannot even get Paul Bazzo's description right. And when Andrea describes the cases to appear in the show, she dismisses the *policía* and Guardia Civil with a shake of the hand and head. Crime and commercial exploitation are hand in hand in the media-crazed world of *Kika*. But the portrayal of tainted or inept law enforcers in Almodóvar is a constant.

Police, Crime and Drugs

Of all the social institutions portrayed in Almodóvar's films, the police are most consistently depicted in a critical or derisory tone. Gentle satire is used for minor, often incompetent officers. Police inspectors who figure more prominently are often characterized by more serious professional and personal flaws. For forty years the agencies of law and order, Franco's *Policía Armada* (armed police) and the long-established rural Guardia Civil, had been the most feared and hated groups in

society. While the actual repression they represented during the dictatorship was much diminished in 1980s Spain, the police are a still a negative
force in Almodóvar.

The policeman in *Pepi, Luci, Bom* is the most objectionable incarnation
of the profession in all the films. He rapes Pepi, does not investigate his
brother's attack through proper police channels, tries to enact revenge
on Pepi for his wife's transformation, and wonders why there is no law
that he can invoke to force his errant wife to return home. He is also
sexually predatory: apart from the initial encounter with Pepi, he tries
to seduce his wife's best friend Charo. Among the policemen under
him, one calmly steals Pepi's magazines in full view of his boss. The
police do not feature at all in *Labyrinth of Passions*, an absence that is not
by chance. Hooper (1995: 208) explains that 'the degree of lawlessness
which the police […] are willing to tolerate' is a consequence of a law-
making generation with a deep suspicion of the forces of law and order
still associated with the dictatorship. The invisibility of the police in
Labyrinth of Passions, and the permissiveness of early-1980s Spanish
society in general, are in direct proportion to the severity of police
repression under Franco. In *Dark Habits*, the police reappear, though
with minimal success as law enforcers. At the beginning of the film
when the police come to talk to Yolanda about boyfriend Jorge's death,
she is able to fool them that she is someone else and then calmly walk
out of the club under their noses. Later, Sister Manure tells nuns from
another convent that 'the police are the natural enemy of nuns', and the
Mother Superior attempts to thwart the police search for Merche. The
mission of the convent, to provide a safe haven for females fleeing
justice, reflects the antagonistic relationship between nuns and the police.
All the former inmates of the convent are criminals: Sofía is now a
diamond smuggler and tells the nuns that the police are also involved
in the trade. Lola is a drug trafficker. In *What Have I Done*, police
inspector Polo behaves with little sense of professional discretion. He
attempts to have sex with Gloria in the showers of the martial arts club
where she cleans. He goes to the prostitute Cristal to act as his girlfriend
for sex therapy sessions. In her flat he discovers heroin, and, after
trying it himself, is willing to turn a blind eye if she doesn't charge him
for sex. He never discovers that Antonio's killer was his wife Gloria,
despite her angry attempt to confess. His inept colleagues blunder
around the tiny flat getting in the inspector's way and acting as if they
have learnt police procedure from Hollywood films.

In *Law of Desire*, the police are a caricature of corruption, sarcasm and ineptitude. Father and son, the investigating inspectors, are respectively at the end and the beginning of their careers. The cynical father tells his son 'to be a policeman it isn't enough not to have any scruples. You also need a sense of humour.' He tries the cocaine they find in Pablo's flat and admits he would have sex with Tina right there given the chance. The son is earnest and eager to impress, but he still has much to learn. When Antonio takes hostages and demands an hour to negotiate with Pablo, the young policeman infuriates him with threats while the father tries to appease the desperate Antonio. When the young man asks for a gun his father tells him, 'first learn how to use it'. The lawyer comments, 'What a disgrace! To think that's what tax-payers' money is spent on', a throwaway comment but surprisingly political in the midst of what is, after all, a melodrama. Paradoxically, even the depiction of the police in a positive light contributes none the less to a contestation of their social role. While the senior of the two local policemen who question Pablo over Juan's death is cold and suspicious, the younger man surprisingly tells Pablo, 'Juan loved you'. Focusing on the film's final scene, D'Lugo (1991: 49) comments on the irony that it is the police who are 'the dramatized audience and presumably the authenticators of th[e] new demarginalization' of this gay romance, where formerly they would be among the most reactionary forces in society.[8]

As the focus shifts away from crime in the remaining films, the police figure less and their portrayal is largely humorously stereotyped. In *Women on the Verge* the two men who come to Pepa's penthouse in search of information about the Shiite terrorists are the typical comic policemen duo, the sarcastic boss and the earnest but inexperienced sidekick. They are easily dispensed with by the famously spiked gazpacho, as Edwards (1995: 194) puts it, 'a spectacle of authority completely undermined and made to look ridiculous'. The inspector states that in the airport there are 'more policemen than passengers' but the first shot of the airport reveals policemen asleep. In *Kika* the police are as comically incompetent as ever. When Ramón (Alex Casanovas) telephones the police station to report Kika's rape, the two duty policemen do not take him seriously. But after a lengthy discussion about dimples and Hollywood film actors, they decide to investigate the alleged rape only because they are bored. Once again they are a contrasting pair: one adventurous, desperate for some action and quite happy to break through the door with a hail of bullets, the other cowardly. Once they are inside the flat they are grotesquely unsympathetic, and, despite an attempt lasting nearly five minutes, they fail to capture escaped rapist Paul Bazzo. The police in *Live Flesh* at first appear to follow in the line of almodovarian comic duos. Sancho drinks whisky in his squad car and he is foolishly keen to take on the reported rapist, whereas his companion David is frightened. They argue about whether to call for back-up just like the pair in *Kika*. In fact, this comically prepared episode ends in disaster, with David receiving a paralysing bullet in the spine. Alcoholic wife-beater Sancho is finally discovered to be guilty of David's injury.

Crime pervades the narratives of Almodóvar's films. In *High Heels*, Manuel describes Madrid as a dangerous city: 'For example, in the place we're going tonight a transvestite was killed a few months ago.' In fact, this perception is due to Manuel's subtly portrayed reactionary social attitude (carrying a gun to a Madrid nightclub, feeling threatened by a transvestite). Neither Madrid nor Spain as a whole are, statistically speaking, dangerous places.[9] Of course, the dramatic nature of fictional narrative film focuses more on the unusual than the usual, on conflict rather than stasis, hence the high levels of violence in Almodóvar's films (in comparison, say, with those of other less narratively-driven auteurs). All the films feature criminal activity of some sort, be it the complicated deceit of Judge Domínguez in *High Heels* (who should be a legal figure of authority but, in fact, betrays his profession because of feelings for Rebeca), or the multiple murders in *Matador*. In that film, Ángel's hallucinatory visions include actual crimes which he witnesses, and later he mentions the crimes committed in Madrid. And in *Live Flesh*, Sancho describes how he sees his role in a crime-ridden society: 'dogs, that's how they treat us'; he refers to society as a 'sick flock' while we see a tracking shot of groups of criminals doing deals.

Spain's truly spiralling crime problem is drugs; it has the worst drugs problem in Europe, comparable only to that of the USA (Hooper 1995: 204). Drugs appear in all Almodóvar's films. In *Pepi, Luci, Bom*, first Fabio and then Pepi bring drugs to the painters' house where Bom is staying. In *Labyrinth of Passions*, Sexi has drugs at her party, but, she points out, 'only stimulants'. In both these films drugs are seen as recreational, but in *Dark Habits* the action of the film is driven by drugs. Yolanda brings her boyfriend Jorge heroin which, unbeknown to her, is mixed with strychnine. Jorge dies immediately and Yolanda flees to the relative sanctuary of the convent. But the Mother Superior is also a heroin addict and Sister Manure takes acid. Despite the surreal comedy of the film, drug taking is portrayed with some realism. When Yolanda and the Mother Superior come off heroin there is a montage sequence which vividly reflects the hallucinations and sufferings of withdrawal. Eventually the Mother Superior resorts to drug trafficking to rescue her beloved convent. Adolescent Toni in *What Have I Done* sells drugs for a living, though he tells the cashier at the bank, 'I have no vices'. His mother Gloria tries to escape from her world with drugs, but she is forced to resort to substances which are part of her daily routine as a housewife, such as washing-up liquid or glue. Her most desperate point comes when she has been refused drugs by an unsympathetic pharmacist. In many of the films drug taking is portrayed simply as part of the lifestyle of the rich, the famous or the young. In *Law of Desire*, Pablo, Juan and Tina all take cocaine. Pepa in *Women on the Verge* is addicted to sleeping pills, as is Rebeca in *High Heels*, tablets finding their way into the prison via her friend Paula. In *Live Flesh*, Elena is an addict in the 1990 section of the film. Her anger over missing her dealer sparks the scuffle which eventually lands Víctor in prison. In *Flower*, Alicia's son is a drug addict, the first time drugs are not viewed positively (Escudero 1998: 160).

In two films the consequences of drugs are more fully shown. In *Tie Me Up!*, Marina's drug habit obliges Ricky to go out in search of drugs. He finds his way to Chueca, an area now famous for its gay scene but infamous for drugs in the 1980s and early '90s. The drugs market there is buzzing with business, but Ricky's rough tactics with the dealer (played as hyper-aggressive by Rossy de Palma) are not well received. She later catches up with him and, along with two thugs, beats him up and leaves him bleeding and unconscious in a gutter. The consequences of drug taking depicted in *All About My Mother* are still more serious. Transsexual Lola is a drug addict who is dying of AIDS. Drug use is the prime cause of AIDS in Spain and the country has the highest infection rate in the EU (Truscott and García 1998: 266). But this is the first time AIDS affects any character in an Almodóvar film. More significant, perhaps, is the fact that, despite the sexual risks of prostitution, drug use rather than sex is the transmission route, which testifies to the reality of contemporary Spain's drug problem. But in a film which compels the viewer to confront a pregnant young girl who is HIV-positive and then, after her death in childbirth, the prospect of a baby with AIDS, the ending (like the film overall) is uplifting, with the young toddler being one of the first in Spain to shake off the virus.

Family and Friendship

Families are ubiquitous in Almodóvar's films, whether they be the conventional nuclear family (often including elderly grandparents), highly unconventional families or groups of friends who function as families. The dichotomy between family and friendship is a constant in the films. The standard family is portrayed as oppressive, uncaring and frequently in the process of breaking down. This disintegration of the family is literal in *What Have I Done* where Gloria loses her family members one by one. Her unloving and chauvinist husband Antonio is accidentally killed by Gloria. She virtually sells her younger son to a paedophile dentist, though Miguel seems more than willing to go. Then her elder son and mother-in-law leave for the village. Gloria is happy to get rid of the burden of her family, but once alone she feels redundant. She has been brought up entirely in the city, and the village means nothing to her. She meets Paquita, an old woman from the *pueblo* who knows Gloria's family history, but the *pueblo* which the woman still inhabits emotionally is unknown to Gloria, whose life in Madrid has little of the social cohesion of village life in Spain. Only at the very end, when Miguel returns announcing 'this house needs a man', is Gloria's role reinstated.

Fathers fare particularly badly in the films. They tend to be either repressive patriarchs or absentees. In *Pepi, Luci, Bom*, the faceless figure of Pepi's father serves only to limit her lifestyle and to remind her of her responsibility. Once she secures employment her life moves entirely away from family.[10] In *Labyrinth of Passions*, Queti's father (Luis Ciges) has sexual relations with her in lieu of her mother, who has left them. And the sex-phobic doctor discovers true sexual passion only when he sleeps with his daughter Sexi (though in fact, it is Queti who has swapped places with Sexi). In *Dark Habits*, a tyrannical father is the cause of Virginia becoming a nun and subsequently dying in Africa; he prevents his daughter from seeing her lover and she enters the convent on the young man's suicide. Ángel's father in *Matador* has gone mad, where Rosa's father in *All About My Mother* is in the late stages of Alzheimer's disease and is unable to recognize her.

Almodóvar's depiction of mothers is more revealing and more varied. Motherhood is not idealized. In the early films mothers are absent. In *Labyrinth of Passions*, the mother of the test-tube child played by Eva Siva has an attitude to children which is far from conventional, openly remarking that in retrospect she would have preferred to remain childless. Other bad mothers include Juani (mother of telekinetic Vanesa in *What Have I Done*) and, notably, Ángel's mother, a castrating Catholic bigot whose legacy to her son is a disturbing guilt complex (see Chapter 2). In complete contrast, Eva's mother (played by Chus Lampreave) is a modern, liberal-minded companion and confidante for her daughter. Almodóvar has commented that the two mothers in *Matador* represent the two Spains: 'one is tolerant, a friend to her child, which symbolizes a Spain that has changed, become humanized and lost some of its prejudices, and the other is the eternally intolerant' (Vidal 1988: 177). Ada's mother in *Law of Desire* is not a good parent. She spends long periods abroad, leaving Ada with ex-partner Tina. After rowing with and then hitting her daughter, she can only comment to herself 'that girl makes me hysterical ... she has broken two of my nails'. In *All About My Mother*, Rosa's mother is a cynical pragmatist who does not understand her daughter's vocation, interpreting it as an act of rebellion. She says her child was always like an extraterrestrial to her, echoing Almodóvar's own choice of word to describe how he felt during his village childhood (Strauss 1996: 5). *Women on the Verge* offers further examples of good and bad mothers. Lucía's psychotic obsession with her husband Iván makes her resent their son Carlos as representing the years she spent away from Iván. Pepa (Carmen Maura) discovers she is pregnant at the start of the film (by the departing Iván) but what begins as her problem turns out to be her salvation once she has discovered her self-sufficiency through the course of the drama around her.

In *High Heels*, the mother–daughter relationship provides the main narrative conflict, a generational conflict which has a socially inscribed dimension despite the melodramatic excess. The early 1970s flashbacks at the start of the film, which correspond to Rebeca's most poignant memories of her mother, show how Becky puts both the men in her life and her career before her daughter. Rebeca as a young child causes the death of her stepfather in an attempt to free her mother from his tyranny. (Under Franco a married woman could not work without the permission of her husband.) Becky repays her by leaving for Mexico and Rebeca's adoration for her mother continues from afar, dangerously mixed with bitterness and hate. On Becky's return to Spain, they clash on everything despite, or perhaps because of, their acute desire for reconciliation. The film's dialogue obsessively returns to this delicate and painful attempt at emotional conciliation [fig. 5]. Even when she is

5. *High Heels*. Becky (Marisa Paredes) and Rebeca (Victoria Abril).

being interrogated by Judge Domínguez, Becky finds it impossible not to justify her actions to Rebeca [fig. 6]. In a reckless and defiant gesture of self-affirmation, Rebeca has attempted to better her mother by marrying one of her former lovers. Even here, Becky wins through, returning and restarting the affair with the man who is now her son-in-law. The courtroom scene where Rebeca confronts her mother with this history of competition and her desperate desire for acceptance is the dramatic climax of the film [fig.7 and 8]. Whether construed as egocentricity or as a reaction to the impasse of the ambitious woman trying to reconcile work and motherhood in a reactionary patriarchal society, the gulf which separates the two women is Becky's inability to see beyond herself. When, in the metaphorical theatre of conflict represented by the courtroom, Rebeca narrates a scene from *Autumn Sonata* (Ingmar Bergman, 1978), the obvious parallel in the destructive, competitive mother–daughter relationship is missed by Becky. As her daughter's identity crisis becomes clearer to her, Becky asks what she can do to right the wrong. Rebeca replies that she can only listen. All Rebeca's efforts (murder, marriage, confession of murder) strive only to make her voice heard to a deaf maternal love-object. The rupture of

6. *High Heels*. Rebeca (Victoria Abril), Becky (Marisa Paredes) and Isabel
(Miriam Díaz Aroca) interrogated.

such a deep familial link can be healed only by Becky's sacrifice at the
end of the film, taking the blame for her daughter's act of murder.

There are, however, two examples of loving mothers. In *Live Flesh*,
though Víctor is never seen with his mother and admits that he hardly
knew her, it is clear that, despite her life as a prostitute, she has instilled
in her son both a moral decency and a constant desire for self-
betterment. When his own son is born at the end of the film, there is
much optimism for this new little family. In *All About My Mother*,
Manuela's relationship with her son Esteban is excellent. She cares for
him economically (their home appears comfortable) and responds to
his burgeoning adult intellect, buying him a Capote novel and taking
him to the theatre for his birthday. At the end of the film, she is seen
equally natural as a mother to the substitute Esteban, Rosa's baby. (Before
Rosa's death in childbirth, Manuela says to Rosa: 'If only I had you and
your child all to myself.') Both these 'model' mothers are single mothers,
Almodóvar presenting the alternative family in a positive light.

Elsewhere, non-standard families often provide equal if not better
support for adults and children alike. *Law of Desire* brother and sister,
Pablo and Tina, are an extremely unconventional family but they do

7. *High Heels*. Rebeca (Victoria Abril) confesses to her mother
in the courtroom.

provide support, and little Ada is happy with Tina, whose background
(sexually abused, incest victim, transsexual) does not pose a problem
for the child. Ada wants to stay with Tina always [fig. 9]. Marsha Kinder
interprets this alternative family as parodic:

> All of these complex erotic relations seem designed to parody the
> Oedipal triangle and to rupture its reproductive chain. For ex-
> ample, Ada not only rejects her bisexual mother both as an object
> of desire and as a model of identification but she also falls in
> love with the homosexual Pablo and yearns to adopt both him
> and his transsexual brother Tina as idyllic parents – a familial
> fantasy that restores her faith in the Virgin. (Kinder 1993: 247)

Similarly, in *High Heels*, Rebeca, who loses both her husband and her
mother, is carrying the child she conceived with her transvestite friend
in a one-night stand. The Judge (who is simultaneously Hugo, Femme
Letal and the Investigator) tells Rebeca, 'You and I have formed a
family.' Despite Rebeca's insecurity about her baby's father's fickle
identity, she none the less is heading towards a relationship with him at
the close of the film. In *Tie Me Up!*, Ricky's goal in life is 'to work and

8. *High Heels*. Becky (Marisa Paredes) hears her daughter's courtroom
confession.

form a family, like a normal person', though the director of the mental
establishment reminds him, 'You're not a normal person.' Certainly,
Ricky's chosen programme for finding the mother of his children
(abducting Marina and using physical force to restrain her until such
time as she realizes she loves him) is unorthodox. But, once again, the
unconventional triumphs and Marina duly falls in love with Ricky,
fulfilling his plan. Marina's sister even promises to find work for him in
their village, thereby entirely satisfying his ambitions. Ricky frequently
indulges in the fantasy that he and Marina are already a couple, such as
when they are together in the bathroom, in his words, 'like a couple
getting ready to go out', or when he returns to the tied-up Marina
calling, 'It's only me!' in cheery domesticated tones.

Undoubtedly Almodóvar's favoured form of social relationship in
his films (above both familial and romantic love) is friendship.[11] Indeed,
friendship is often strongest where family relations have broken down
or are non-existent. *Pepi, Luci, Bom* is a film about friendship. Pepi's
friendship with Bom is the central relationship of the film (and not the
sexual relationship between Bom and Luci). Two scenes in particular
demonstrate this. In the first, Pepi cooks Bom's favourite dish (*bacalao*

9. *Law of Desire*. Tina (Camen Maura) with Ada
(Manuela Velasco).

al pil-pil) and they talk about Bom's relationship with Luci and about
Pepi's project to film it. In contrast to the cold domestic atmosphere in
Luci's home with the policeman, this scene is shot in a manner which
emphasizes intimacy, the giggling Pepi and Bom filmed through a
window framing them in medium close-up. The second scene is at the
end of the film, where Pepi offers Bom a room in her flat, their
strengthened friendship corresponding to the optimism of the film's
ending as they cross the footbridge over the motorway arm-in-arm.
Families are largely absent (in the case of Pepi and Bom) or a negative
institution (in the case of Luci), so that characters look to support from
friends. This corresponds to the historical period beginning with the

1960s economic boom in Spain, when the children of comfortable families came to Madrid seeking independence, fun and possibly fame or notoriety. This same social phenomenon applies to *Labyrinth of Passions* where friendship is depicted as a strong social link and where families are seen to be dysfunctional. Queti, raped by her father and abandoned by her mother, is immediately able to strike up a strong friendship with Sexi despite class difference and the fact that they meet largely through Queti's secret borrowing of Sexi's skirt.

In *All About My Mother* Manuela is forced to substitute friends for family when her son dies. She returns to Barcelona and immediately takes up where she left off with her old friend Agrado. Through this old friend, Manuela meets Rosa, who comes to depend on her as a substitute mother. Here, the substitution of family with friendship is more than metaphoric: after helping Rosa through her difficult pregnancy, Manuela adopts the baby when Rosa dies in childbirth. The generosity of Manuela – played wonderfully by veteran actress Cecilia Roth after a fifteen-year absence from Almodóvar's films – corresponds to her need to fill the role of carer. Manuela's positive influence as a friend helps Huma (Marisa Paredes) cope with the difficult Nina (Candela Peña) and eventually to move on. In a similar role, Pepa in *Women on the Verge* realizes at the end of the film that friendship is stronger than romantic love. After prioritizing the problems of her friends (Candela's terrorists) over her own worries, Pepa is better off at the end of the film, and has apparently gained a friend in Marisa (Rossy de Palma). And in *Live Flesh*, Doña Centro acts like a true friend – and, to a certain extent, another substitute mother – to Isabel.

On occasions, jealousy threatens friendship, with different outcomes. In *Flower*, Leo's friend Betty betrays her only to realize their friendship is more important to her than Paco. Kika's friend Amparo lets her down, but she discovers the friendship of Juana which she had had all along, though their relationship had been subject to economically imposed social rules. In *Live Flesh*, David's friendship with Sancho is ruined by jealousy, and the effects produce disastrous results. Sancho's rage over his companion's illicit relationship with his wife leads him to shoot David, making it look like the work of the innocent Víctor. When David finds out he starts on a course of action which leads to two deaths and to the loss of his wife to Víctor. Jealousy also destroys the friendship between the Mother Superior and Sister Rat in *Dark Habits*. The institutionalized relationships of the convent place the Mother

Superior above Rat in the hierarchy, but Rat is more successful in making friends with the young girls in the convent, provoking resentment on the Mother Superior's part. The grim social and economic situation in *What Have I Done* is shown not to be conducive to friendship, though Cristal is an exception, helping Gloria whenever she can. In other films friendship is all but absent. The stylized fiction of *Matador* pares the film down to relationships as a function of the plot, and similarly in *Law of Desire* and *High Heels* the heightened charge of desire relegates friendship. In such films, the relationships that count are sexual ones. These gender and sexual relationships are the subjects of the next chapters.

4

Gender

When analysing the representation of gender in Almodóvar's films, the first thing one notices is the predominance of female characters. Only in *Matador, Law of Desire, Tie Me Up!* and *Live Flesh* do male characters really compete for the attention of the audience. Four films come close to dispensing with male characters altogether.[1] Almodóvar has said that females make better characters: 'women are more spectacular as dramatic subjects, they have a greater range of registers, etc.' (Cobos and Marías 1995: 100). But while it is true that women characters do dominate Almodóvar's narratives, as Smith (1994: 2) points out, he has still found himself 'accused of misogyny, of humiliating and fetishizing those same women'. This equivocal stance is largely due to the patriarchal legacy of cinema itself. Much auteur film bypasses this legacy by downgrading or disregarding gender as an issue. Not so the films of Almodóvar. Closer to classic genre movies, they frequently both represent and contest cinematic gender constructions. Where much of the pioneering work carried out by feminist film theorists reveals the hidden structures in classic Hollywood cinema, in Almodóvar these structures are foregrounded, turned into explicit themes.

Within the voluminous body of feminist film theory, three aspects can be singled out: the premise that in patriarchy the cinema's gaze is male, voyeuristic and sadistic; that classical film genres have constructed women as passive and often masochistic objects; and that the constructed nature of cinema representations can be contested through revealing its mechanisms (Mulvey 1989: 14–26). Almodóvar, an unlikely feminist, takes up the challenge inherent in the last of these premises, and proudly exposes such mechanisms, at the same time exposing the anxious hegemony of patriarchy itself. His films are self-consciously *about* voyeurism, *about* sadism, and *about* masochism in a way that mainstream Hollywood movies are not. Though written and directed by a man, they problematize questions of masculinity and often subvert gender through ambiguity and sexual role-playing. That this film phenomenon should arise in a country not especially regarded as a cinema-producing nation and, moreover, a country with a long tradition of machismo and repression of women, is surprising indeed.

Mother or Whore: The Hispanic Tradition

The tendency in Western culture to regard the female sex as either maternal or debased, angelic or demonic, stems from nineteenth-century philosophy and sexology (Bristow 1997: 42). In common with many other patriarchal attitudes, this one persisted longer in Spain. Contemporary novelist and journalist Rosa Montero describes the historical legacy for women in Spain thus:

> The influence of Catholicism, for which sexual difference is divinely ordained, plus the legacy of eight centuries of Arab occupation laid the foundations for a sexism that the Franco period would only aggravate. Forty years of dictatorship did more than halt the process of women's emancipation; the imposition of traditionalist National-Catholicism and ultra-reactionary social norms set the clock back dramatically for Spanish women. (Montero 1995: 381)

That Spain's treatment of women historically has left them virtually a stark choice between the roles of mother or prostitute is a paradox which Almodóvar's films both recognize (retrospectively for an older generation) and also confute (for Spain's new women).

Two of the films articulate this dichotomy directly in their characters. In *What Have I Done*, Gloria is the mother and housewife, oppressed by her existence and profoundly frustrated and unfulfilled. Cristal is the whore with a heart of gold, free from domestic constraints to live a fantasy of escape to Las Vegas. Gloria's desperate situation, which owes as much to her gender as to her social class, is contrasted with the attitude of her uncaring husband Antonio, whose job takes him out of the house for most of the time. His attitude towards Gloria is that of the typical *machista*: 'Who on earth can keep women at home [...] I give the orders in this house.' The futility of Gloria's life is illustrated as, one by one, her responsibilities disappear and she appears to be heading for a life on her own. Her trajectory is the opposite of traditional cinema narratives which show women on a journey to self-fulfilment through marriage and motherhood. Left with nothing, she contemplates suicide but the return of her son Miguel gives back a purpose to her life. Despite the clarity of the mother–whore dichotomy, this film offers no conventional truth about the merits of either choice. The prostitute Cristal, though sexually liberated and good-natured, is shown to be naive. Gloria is no ideal mother: she gives one son away, and escapes her husband only when she accidentally kills him. When little Vanesa asks Gloria to adopt her, she tells the girl, 'I'm not really a good mother either, you know.' But Vanesa's mother Juani is the antithesis of a good mother, repaying the bitterness she harbours for her estranged husband in cruelty towards their daughter. Moreover, Juani is clearly envious of prostitute Cristal when she criticizes her: 'Sometimes I think you only have feeling in your pussy.' Similarly, in *All About My Mother*, Manuela and Agrado represent the whore–mother dichotomy but they are not so different. Manuela is happy to pretend she is a prostitute to accompany Agrado to the sex-workers' shelter and help centre. Later she confesses to Sister Rosa, 'I'm not a whore despite how I've been treated sometimes', significantly equating 'whore' (*puta*) with what is *done to* someone rather than what they do. On the other hand, Agrado's role in life is 'to make other people's lives happier', not that different from the role of mother.

Masochism, Passivity and the Male Gaze

Moving away from purely sociological evaluations of gender roles, feminist criticism – armed with psychoanalytical models which can reveal human relationships in both capitalism and patriarchy – concentrates on how meaning is produced in films and not on their content. The construction of specific genres (especially melodrama) 'exposes the constraints and limitations that the capitalist nuclear family imposes on women' and serves 'to "educate" women to accept those constraints as "natural", inevitable – as "given"' (Kaplan 1983: 25). Psychoanalysis can offer reasons why women may tend to position themselves in passive roles.[2] Melodrama – a genre intrinsic to the so-called 'women's films'

(films for women but virtually always made by men) – constructs a female spectator 'who is made to participate in what is essentially a masochistic fantasy'.[3] To the extent that Almodóvar shows his female characters within a patriarchal society, these same structures are seen operating both in his melodramas and other genre films, as will be shown. The unmasking of such mediated patriarchal strategies may be largely unproblematic when analysing Hollywood's version of genre films for and about women; but in Almodóvar these ostensibly hidden (and therefore dangerous) strategies are turned into themes, and are self-consciously deployed, resulting in a parodic and often comic stance with regard to both female passivity and masochism.

This double-take on female masochism – both reflecting and subverting the mechanisms which hold women in subordinate positions in respect of men – is evident from Almodóvar's first film, *Pepi, Luci, Bom*. Luci's social relationships revolve around her sadomasochism. She tells Pepi, 'I need a firm hand', and admits that she married the policeman only in the hope of being mistreated by him: 'I thought that if I married him he'd treat me like his bitch.' It is no coincidence that Luci is a housewife: her masochistic tendencies are a grotesque inflation of her social position as the submissive wife of an unreconstructed and bigoted patriarch. Her husband makes every effort to affirm his *machista* credentials. He silences his wife, 'Shut up, you. This isn't women's business', and questions her 'Have you been in a bar? [...] In any case, you know quite well that I won't have any of that business of liberated women and the like.' At the same time, he is quite happy to enjoy forcibly the pleasures of the young Pepi or to indulge in pornographic magazines, or to attempt to seduce his wife's best friend Charito while upbraiding his wife for her degenerate actions as a groupie. When the policeman rings a colleague to see if there is some legal means of forcing his wife back home, he is echoing an earlier legal position of women in Franco's Spain. His friend tells him, 'Anyway, if it came to court we'd have every feminist in the country on our backs', an allusion to the new (if very modest) wave of feminist militancy in Spain. Luci, in turn, holds extremely conservative ideas: she knows a woman who could do a 'stitch-up' for Pepi, that is, sew up her lost virginity. Ultimately, Luci returns to her sadistic husband in keeping with her submissive role. For Yarza (1999: 120), the hospital bed scene represents her return to the law of Francoism (her fascist husband), sanctioned by the law of the Church (the crucifix over her bed).

Nevertheless, the film does represent a subversion of cinematic and social inflections of patriarchy. *Pepi, Luci, Bom* undermines traditional female roles in two ways. First, there are no mothers in the film, even if Luci is partially constructed as the passive housewife (though child-less). Second, the lesbian relationship between Luci and Bom removes the male power to construct women as either mother or whore. Although Luci returns to her husband, it is not because of patriarchal authority, but because of her perverse delight in masochism, and she tells Bom she did not treat her badly enough. More than this, though, both Luci's masochistic desire and the response of her partners (policeman husband and lesbian lover) amount to a caricature of masochism. Where classic melodrama sublimates female masochism in emotional violence, this film parodies dominant–subordinate relationships through the grotesque inflation of abusers and victims.

Caricature masochism is also a feature of the nuns in *Dark Habits*. They have an excess of humility that can be equated with masochism, and in the case of Sister Manure this is reflected in physical self-harm. Once again, the masochism is parodied: Manure's modes of self-flagellation have a hyperbolic medieval brutality about them. Sister Rat not only loves the sensationalist literature associated with female victims in novels such as *Largo de aquí, canalla* (*Out of Here, Scoundrel!*) but she actually writes such novels. And in *Flower*, another of Almodóvar's female victims just happens to be a writer of pulp romantic novels. Leo is perfectly in touch with her own emotional state and is able to isolate and articulate her own masochistic tendency. She cites a favourite writer, Djuna Barnes: 'You have before you a woman created for anxiety.' Leo's mother maintains traditional ideas about women, who, once they are without their men are 'like cows without a cowbell'. Even though she is a relatively modern and independent woman, Leo is oppressed by her inability to perform domestic tasks. (Paco complains about the paella being cold though Leo has other worries.)

Perhaps even more trapped in a passive gender role is Leo's sister Rosa, the downtrodden housewife, obsessed with being a good hostess. Here, social class plays a part in the construction of woman as victim. The same is true of *What Have I Done*, where consumer society con-stantly frustrates women without means. Gloria lists all the essentials she cannot afford and then Antonio smokes a cigar and watches an advert for coffee depicted in ridiculously romantic terms. Later, as Juani and Gloria discuss curling tongs, they look into shop windows; in a curious tracking shot, the camera placed inside the shops suggests they are excluded from this consumerism.[4] Even middle-class intellectual Patricia is consumer-obsessed, in her case about plastic surgery, objectifying herself as a gendered commodity. Gloria is a passive sex object, though not representing a specularized femininity – she is never a source of visual pleasure to be 'looked at' (Varderi 1996: 200) as she is insufficiently glamorized. On the two occasions she has sex, both at the instigation of men, she is not satisfied by either. She has sex on the demand of husband Antonio, but derives no pleasure from it, hence the ironic soundtrack of 'La bien pagá' (Well Paid). Almodóvar has commented that sexual satisfaction (of which Gloria is deprived) could have compensated for a harsh life: 'When in a family of this type the couple have good sex, everything is much more bearable' (Vidal 1988: 146). In *Women on the Verge*, female passivity is couched in comic terms. Candela's naiveté is absurd; she explains her victimization by 'the Arab world', 'many men have taken advantage of me; I have always realized it, but only later', and she asks Carlos: 'Why are you men the way you are?' When Pepa asks Carlos to stay in the apartment because there are 'too many women for such a large penthouse', it is not without irony; Carlos (Antonio Banderas) is more passively inept than any of them. The hysterical character of Lucía is also a caricature (as is her costume). Asked by the policeman if she has been talking about men, she responds, 'Is there anything more important?' In almost all the films, comedy takes the edge off the critique of gender stereotyping but it does not obliterate it. But in Almodóvar's most confused and flawed film, *Kika*, the comic reflection of female naiveté flounders with the attempted comic depiction of rape.

Even though Almodóvar has stated that his intention in the rape scene in *Kika* was to show the strength of female characters in difficult situations (Strauss 1996: 134), the scene may well have proved decisive in persuading some neutral observers of the director's alleged misogyny. The scene does not work, though not because rape is off-bounds to humour. In other films (*Pepi, Luci, Bom* and *Matador*) Almodóvar successfully portrays a humorous edge to rape (see Chapters 3 and 4). This episode is far too long (eight and a half minutes), and Kika's resilience does not triumph over her attacker. In fact, it's the two stupid policemen who finally remove the rapist from his victim. Smith (1996: 47) offers two suggestions as to Almodóvar's intentions here. He writes that 'Paul's parodic violence is offered as a paradigm of the supposed breakdown in social order'. Clearly, the crime-ridden and crime-obsessed city is a constant in this film. But Smith also suggests that one of Almodóvar's aims is 'to contest the operation of the state in the policing of "perversion"'. While this may be true of many of the films, the untrammelled freedoms of the newly deregulated media in 1990s Spain, whose bounds are not exaggerated by this cruel film, are hardly an endorsement for an unregulated (unpoliced) society. (See also Chapter 7 on the satire of the television transmission of the rape.) Whatever Almodóvar's intentions, playing a rape scene for laughs proved too much for US censors, who refused to give the film a rating (effectively making it commercially unviable in the USA).

Equally controversial but far more interesting in its construction of gender relationships, *Tie Me Up!* is Almodóvar's most sophisticated exploration of masochism. Its opening scene sets up a familiar melodramatic story of an older woman in love with a younger man, though this is a false start. Protagonist Ricky sets out in pursuit of his ideal woman, actress Marina, but his method is to abduct her and wait for her to fall in love with him. In an uncomfortably violent scene, he breaks into her house and silences her with a vicious headbutt. As Marina recovers consciousness, Ricky tells her, 'I have 50,000 pesetas and I'm alone in the world. I will try to be a good husband for you and a good father for your children.' Ricky's extremely conventional aspirations are pursued through a violence which differs only in measure from the conventionalized predatory instinct in all males. His naiveté – his lack of a social protocol – lays bare and seemingly magnifies this instinct. When he sees Marina looking around for some means of escape, he says, 'What are you looking for? I'm right here', assuming he is all she needs. Eventually – and here lies the controversy – she does fall in love with him. The film's title line 'Tie me up!' is unexpectedly uttered by Marina, not as a role-playing game (as hinted by the film's suggestive title) but as a genuine request. She doesn't know if she will try to escape or not, and now that she has come to realize her feelings for him, prefers not to be given the chance. Thus, the apparent premise of the film is that enslavement can lead to pure love. But this film, which is not intended to be either credible or politically correct, problematizes both the question of masochism and its representation in the film medium. The film's bondage is, in the words of Martha Nandorfy (1993: 60), in her incisive article on the film, 'a physical metaphor for the tyranny of marriage portrayed as a sado-masochistic arrangement'. For Nandorfy, the violence in the film is 'hyperbolically explicit', a 'parodic representation of the violence inherent in sexual relationships within a patriarchal society' (p. 55). Nandorfy argues that the actions of the violent male, Ricky (in a long wig which make him look like a Neanderthal), are 'an ironical conflation of psychotic symptoms and what Freud takes to be normal male behaviour' (p. 57). Ricky's pursuit of normality ('to work and form a family, like a normal person', as he puts it) is a parody, a grotesque exaggeration of accepted social norms. Almodóvar's comments suggest Ricky is not to be taken for real: 'Ricky's intellect is literal, animal. The only thing he ends up attaining is the comic, emotional side of an imitation of reality' (Strauss 1996: 99).

As well as a critique of patriarchy's instinctive violence, the film represents a satirical twist on politically incorrect sub-genres based on voyeuristic and sadistic titillation for men. The sexualized and objectified role of Marina is foregrounded in the narrative film-within-film, which draws attention to the rather suspect wish-fulfilment drive of director Máximo Espejo[5] (the desire in all directors and in all men to turn women into pure objects of their pleasure). A candid journalist tells Máximo (Francisco Rabal), 'You have the reputation of being a director of actresses.' Familiar with Marina's past as a porn actress, he wants to make Marina a sex object in the personal project of his last film (which he calls 'a horror B movie'). The director's sexual motivation is made explicit in a sequence where we see him watching a porn film staring Marina which Almodóvar obviously filmed especially for the video, clearly delighted at the opportunity to parody the genre (albeit with restraint). And Máximo's motives are confirmed by production manager Lola: she is angry with Marina for removing her pants 'because he looks at you and gets inspired; then he wants to save you and he changes everything'. Thus, Máximo even allows erotic desire to dictate the end of the film, not wanting his heroine to die. The shooting of the film, *El fantasma de la medianoche* (*Midnight Phantom*) looks very authentic, with all the machinery in full view, the cinematic illusion truly shattered. (In fact, the set was made up of a real film set, that of Almodóvar's previous film, *Women on the Verge*). The scene is high kitsch, parodying second-rate horror movies. And, once again, there are parallels between film set and life. In the film, Marina is being stalked by a monster, but there is a hint of a deeper relationship between the two. Off screen, Marina will also be stalked by Ricky, equally monstrous in his stolen wig, but eventually to become her lover. The shooting of the scene from *El*

10. *Tie Me Up! Tie Me Down!* Marina (Victoria Abril) on the set of
Midnight Phantom.

fantasma de la medianoche plays with the cinema–reality divide, moving
from the clearly film-within-film sequence where the whole crew, camera
and boom microphones are visible, to the discrete scene itself [fig. 10].
The length of the sequence is sufficient to absorb the viewer subtly in
the fictional metafilm, in which Almodóvar's own voice is used for the
monster. At the end of the shoot, there is a fadeout from the final
scene with Marina hanging from a rope over a balcony, to the same
image but with all the mechanics of filming (wind machines, set lighting,
etc.) clearly visible, as we hear Máximo say, 'Cut. We have finished.' The
film-within-film is yet another device which allows Almodóvar to explore
(and explode) within his films how men and women are reflected on
screen.

Feminist film criticism has attempted to demonstrate how classical
Hollywood cinema constructs males as subjects, as 'the bearer of the
look' and women as objects, denoting 'to-be-looked-at-ness'. Scopophilia
(sexual pleasure in looking) which in the darkened space of the cinema
allows the audience to look in on an ostensibly private world, combines
with the desire for self-recognition and identification with the (male)
characters on screen.[6] The female object image – constructed by and for

men – assumes an association between the male gaze of the camera (and the man behind the camera) and the male audience. However, there is a problem, explained by feminist critics in psychoanalytical terms: the female's lack of a penis implies the threat of castration. Faced with this, the male unconscious can either observe her obsessively in order to demystify her and simultaneously punish her, or, alternatively, disavow castration by 'the substitution of a fetish object or turning the represented figure itself into a fetish so that it becomes reassuring rather than dangerous' (Mulvey 1989: 26). The first avenue leads to voyeurism and sadism, while the second leads to fetishism. In Almodóvar, the assumption of an all-encompassing male gaze is problematic for a number of reasons. Where male characters assume voyeuristic or sadistic roles, this is critically questioned, and identification tends to lie with the female characters. This is the case in *Pepi, Luci, Bom* where the male sexuality of the policeman is shown as voyeuristic (pornographic magazines) and sadistic (his treatment of Luci), and in *Live Flesh* where the relationship between Clara and Sancho (the most dysfunctional relationship in all Almodóvar) is clearly the fault of Sancho's masculine insecurity.

In most of the films, the voyeuristic and sadistic tendencies inherent in cinema are openly and self-consciously questioned, a deployment of meta-cinematic distanciation which serves to 'destroy the invisible guest' to use Mulvey's (1989: 26) term. In fact, the films turn these hitherto unspoken, unconscious mechanisms of cinema into explicit themes: sadism in *Matador*, masochism in *Tie Me Up!*, voyeurism in *Kika*. Not content with playing out some of the cinema's strategies, Almodóvar actually satirizes the very tenets of film analysis. In this, the films raise something like the question asked by Ellis Hanson (1999: 11): 'Can psychoanalysis be a critical apparatus for interpreting films when it is already a self-conscious narrative gimmick for making them?' In *Kika*, Ramón's profession as a photographer is linked to his sexual obsession: he can only make love with a camera present. But the inauthenticity of the photographic set-up is made clear when we see that the bed is vertical not horizontal and Ramón is not on top of his model. In *Women on the Verge*, even from the titles women are coded as fetishized objects: lipstick, earrings, nail varnish, etc. These women and their accessories are 'fragments of women's costumes and bodies cut up and distorted', as Smith (1994: 96) puts it. The final title shows three women posing for cameras. And to portray the traditional male deceiver, Almodóvar chooses a stylized dream sequence: Iván (Fernando Guillén) moves along a parade of women suggesting he has had all of them, making con-descending remarks. Only the last woman has an answer for him; when he tells her, 'I accept you just as you are, darling', she replies, 'Big deal!' In her (unique) refusal to play Iván's game of 'boy wins girl', this dreamed character is flagging a challenge to masculine swank which is characteristic of Almodóvar's films as a whole.

Women on Top – Masculinity in Crisis

Quite apart from devices that raise consciousness about the workings of the cinema that serve patriarchy, many of Almodóvar's films prob-lematize gender binaries. This may involve simply portraying strong, positive, female characters, often in more professional social roles than men (García de León 1989: 81), while their male counterparts are shown as insecure or worse.[7] Even more significantly, Almodóvar inverts what Lehman (1993: 5) refers to as 'the dominant cultural paradigm wherein women's bodies are displayed and men's bodies are hidden and protected'. Almodóvar's male characters are frequently exposed physically and symbolically. This, of course, represents a gift for film criticism which is in the process of questioning 'unperturbed monolithic masculinity' and replacing it with images of the male which are complex, historicized and multiple (Cohan and Hark 1993: 3).

In *Matador*, the very first images are a montage of scenes of violence against women and Diego's sadistic fantasy could not be more explicit: he is masturbating, his legs straddling the television set. But the second sequence juxtaposes images of Diego explaining how to kill a bull with images of the predatory María who, in a reversal of roles, literally mounts her man before killing him with a phallic hairpin. Nor does the *corrida* provide a neat division of gender roles (see Chapter 2). *Matador* prob-lematizes the exclusively male preserve of both initiator of the action and bearer of the gaze. María Cardenal is as much a matador as Diego.

MARÍA: Men think that killing is a crime. Women don't look at it that way. That's why there is something feminine in all criminals.

DIEGO: And in all murderers there is something masculine.

MARIA: I looked for you in all the men I have loved. And I tried to imitate you when I killed them.

Although this suggests that María is simply following the master, Diego, it is she who finally kills him. Moreover, in *Matador*, and contrary to cinematic tradition, males become the object of both male and female gaze. María literally fetishizes Diego, hoarding all manner of objects which represent him for her. And the homoerotic look of the police inspector turns the other males (Ángel in particular) into sexualized objects.[8]

The character of Ángel perfectly illustrates a masculinity in crisis. Where male subjects in cinema are usually identified with activity, voyeurism, sadism, fetishism and narrative progression, Ángel is associated with passivity, exhibitionism, masochism and spectacle (Cohan and Hark 1993: 2). Voyeurism is integrated technologically into the film: Ángel watches Eva through binoculars and the camera takes his point of view with a blanked-off circular screen. Diego's malign influence ('You have to treat women like bulls: face up to them and hem them in') is naively put into practice by Ángel in his failed attempt to possess what his master possesses. But Ángel's attempt to rape Eva constructs *him* and not *her* as the victim. Ángel has problems getting the knife out (first he pulls out a corkscrew) and then, unable to penetrate her, ejaculates between her legs. Afterwards, he apologizes, Eva (Eva Cobos) calls him a 'son-of-a-bitch' and then slaps him twice. When she cuts herself he faints at the sight of her blood and falls on the wet ground. Then we see him in a bathroom after a shower looking at his face in the mirror, in an inversion of the usual bathing and cleansing of the rape victim. A naked shot of Ángel in the bathroom (one of many of nude men in Almodóvar) confirms him as the object of his own failure. His guilt complex is an inflation of masochism and, despite his attempt to assert an active voyeurism, he is frequently turned into the object of others' looks.

The opening scene of *What Have I Done* has proved a fruitful case study for critics of masculinities such as Peter Lehman (1993). Gloria, excited by the masculine spectacle of the men playing at Kendo, comes face to face with one of the men in the showers of the gym. The man beckons her to join him in the shower. She looks him up and down, visibly taking in his genitals. Vernon (1995: 62) has commented on how this scene inverts the traditional cinematic gaze, referring to 'Maura's character's unabashed gaze at the spectacle of the male body'. While the man is completely naked, Gloria remains fully clothed during the attempted sex act, which fails because the man, a policeman, is impotent. But this sequence departs even further from the conventional 'impres-

11. *Labyrinth of Passions*. Nymphomaniac Sexi
(Cecilia Roth).

sively dramatic' male sexual representation, in that the policeman – the
archetypal male, symbol of power, and in this case of the law – has a
small and flaccid penis (Lehman 1993: 9–10). After this disappointment,
Gloria picks up the phallic weapon of Kendo, equated by Lehman (p. 9)
with her taking up masculine positions. (The same position and a similar
weapon is later used by her to kill Antonio.) The opening scenes of
Labyrinth of Passions also establish males as the objects of both the male
and female gaze: both Sexi and Riza are looking at male crotches and
bottoms and Madrid's famous market the Rastro has now become a
marketplace for men. Nymphomaniac Sexi [fig. 11] is very much in
control; she has two men at once and invites no other women to her

parties. Sexi and her friends are typically liberated sexually, as their collection of dildos suggests. The principal males in this film, on the other hand, are less secure in their sexuality. Riza begins as a gay man and is apparently converted to heterosexuality through the love of Sexi. Queti's father is impotent and responds to the loss of his wife by taking aphrodisiacs and raping his daughter. Sexi's father, Doctor de la Peña, is also a male in crisis: he finds sex repugnant.

The women in *Pepi, Luci, Bom* are self-sufficient, not dependent on men for happiness.[9] The resolution of the film presents friendship as a greater priority than sexual love. Luci and Bom's lesbian relationship bypasses men, while Pepi, determined not to be made into a victim by men, takes revenge on the policeman who rapes her. Pepi's obvious sadistic pleasure ('give him a good beating') as she watches her friends beat up Juan (the policeman's brother) inverts traditional cinematic voyeurism and sadism. And while Bom has pictures of nude women by her punchbag, and Luci delights in lesbian sadomasochism comics, the painters (Las Costus) who share their house have interests which are more traditionally feminine (celebrity magazines, folkloric figures and images of royal families). The party competition '*erecciones generales*' also inverts the traditional female role as specularized, passive sex object. It represents a parody of a beauty parade, putting the male organ itself under the spotlight. Perhaps the ultimate gender swap is Pepi's friend (played by Assumpta Serna) who has a mute but, crucially, 'very good-looking' boyfriend. Two avenues are offered to waning masculinity: to accept the new freedoms and exploit them – Moncho and Toni are not worried about selling sex to men – or to lament the loss of a more primitive period in male–female relations – the policeman resorts to the law to control his wife.

In *Women on the Verge*, the portrayal of a range of women of different social types does not disavow the role of men in their lives; rather it chooses to focus on their interrelationships and on how they each resolve their problems, largely independently from the men who have oppressed them. The men in the film are all weak: Iván is placatory with women and clearly unable to make relationships work. His son is naive, though good-natured. As he watches his fiancée Marisa absorbed in her erotic dream, he innocently remarks, 'I have never seen her looking like this' [fig. 12]. Clearly, he does not yet possess the technique that Marisa is looking for in a lover. In fact, the couple have not had sex. Marisa confesses to Pepa that after her dream she no longer feels like a virgin.

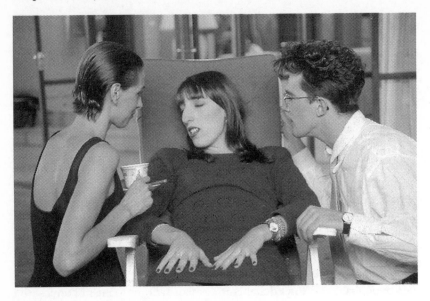

12. *Women on the Verge*. Marisa (Rossy de Palma) enjoys her dream as Candela (María Barranco) and Carlos (Antonio Banderas) look on.

Pepa tells her that she will be better for it, 'virgins are very unpleasant'. The conclusion of this film appears to be that happiness for women is not dependent on men. In fact, Pepa expresses male psychology as an enigma: 'It's much easier to understand mechanics than male psychology. You can get to know a motorbike really well but you can never get to know a man so well.' The eternal unfathomable is now the male.

All About My Mother largely dispenses with a male perspective altogether. The only conventional male is the satirized character Mario, the curious child whose only wish is to experiment with the kinky novelty of the transsexual Agrado. Mario represents the typical *machista* in both his on-stage role as Tennessee Williams's brutish Kowalski and off-screen as the vain male lead. The casting of peak-viewing television presenter Carlos Lozano not only increased media interest in the role, but also exploited the high-profile, high-masculine image of the actor. When Mario comes to ask Agrado for a blow-job, he has none of the subtleties of operation that characterize the women in the film, appearing shallow, vain and transparent. The female characters all demonstrate as much depth in their capacity to suffer as in their capacity to support one another. Manuela tries to take control of her destiny against the

13. *All About My Mother.* Manuela (Cecilia Roth) with Rosa
(Penélope Cruz).

odds and she does not look to be fulfilled through relationships with
men. She has the empathy of those who work with her when Esteban
dies; she has the support of her Madrid friend Mamen; her relationships
with both Agrado and Huma are ones of mutual support; even Rosa,
who on the surface depends so much on Manuela [see fig. 13], gives her
something in return (a reason for living, an opportunity to project
affection and, eventually, a substitute child). The moment when Agrado,
Huma and Rosa coincide in Manuela's flat is a good example of female
comradeship in an exclusively female space, which brings the best out
of Almodóvar in one of the few light and amusing moments in the film
[fig. 14].

Solidarity is unfairly assumed as a masculine virtue in dominant film
genres such as the western or gangster film. In Almodóvar, solidarity is
principally a feminine virtue. Pepi and Bom's relationship is an example
of such a female support structure; in *High Heels* there exists a solidarity
among the women in the prison who care for Rebeca when she faints;
in *Live Flesh*, Doña Centro demonstrates similarly generous support for
Isabel as she gives birth to her baby; and, in *Kika*, feminine friendship
has a particular value for Kika who says being unfaithful to Ramón is

14. *All About My Mother*. Manuela (Cecilia Roth) with Rosa
(Penélope Cruz).

not the same as Amparo lying to her, because Ramón is a man and
female friends demand a special confidence and loyalty. This is confirmed
in *Flower* where Betty, who is having an affair with Paco, puts her
friendship with Leo first, and goes to comfort her after Paco has left.
Even a film which most unambiguously portrays its female protagonist
as the victim of male abandonment, none the less devotes a great deal
of attention to relations between women (Leo–Betty, Leo–Mother,
Mother–Rosa, Leo–Blanca, Leo–Amanda Gris).

Live Flesh is perhaps Almodóvar's most sophisticated representation
of traditional gender roles and their more modern counterparts. The
competition between the male egos of David and Víctor – described by
Almodóvar in the script as 'pure genital masculinity' to indicate the
origins of their posturing – is swept aside by the effects of male bonding
over television football. A goal scored by the adored Caminero suspends
their animosity before David remembers his mission and aggressive
masculine control returns. The young men in *Live Flesh*, however, are
reconstructed, 'new men'. We see David perform cunnilingus on Elena
– a selfless and sophisticated technique in contrast to the thrusting
selfishness of men in earlier films. Victor admits to having little sexual

experience. When receiving sexual instruction from Clara he asks her what she likes, even what she thinks about when masturbating. His desire to be 'the best love-maker in the world' is reflected in his willingness to learn. But we also see how, at the end of the film, he is supporting his partner when she is about to give birth. Crucially, however, it is the men who suffer in this film, inverting female masochism. Both David and Victor are seen to cry in the course of the film. By contrast, Sancho – the representation of an older, more aggressive masculinity in the film – explicitly tells David he does not want to cry. Sancho's jealousy of his wife Clara, and, in particular, his murderous response to such suspicions and the violence which he metes out to her, all reflect a basic insecurity which is equated with his antiquated version of masculinity. Both this and the corresponding female masochism of Clara are shown in the film to be anachronistic and they die with these arch-protagonists of old-style gender relationships at the end of the film.

Parody and Satire: Gender Problematized

In many of Almodóvar's films, the mechanisms which construct gender roles are exposed, destroying the pleasure of the 'invisible guest' which is, for Mulvey (1989: 26), one way 'to strike a blow against the monolithic accumulation of patriarchal film conventions'. This may be through strong female characters, weak males or female-centred drama. Another way is to satirize gender stereotyping or, more radically, to parody gender, something which, according to Yarza (1999: 73), Almodóvar accomplishes through camp theatricality. The films typify the assertion – made by Judith Butler (1990: 25) in *Gender Trouble* – that all gender is 'performatively constituted'. In Almodóvar, gender role play is often 'camply' self-conscious, but this does not exclude a more social, anti-hegemonic representation. When Bom first meets Luci in *Pepi, Luci, Bom* her response is, 'Forty-something and soft just as I like them', prefiguring a lesbian sadomasochistic relationship which parodies patriarchal gender stereotypes. Similarly, Bom and her group Bomitoni's performance is punk but with its typical male aggression replaced by female desire. Luci even parodies her husband's right-wing discourse on sexual mores, admitting she is 'a victim of the wave of eroticism which is invading society', a line which sounds as if it comes from a reactionary tract. Her relationship with the policeman is no model for society, but the other heterosexual relationship (a neighbour of Toni's uncle and his wife) is also dysfunctional. The latter is a ridiculous parody of femininity with an absurdly high-pitched voice and a beard, he is a repressed homosexual. Pepi's advert is also a send-up of traditional gender roles (girls are not expected to fart on dates, wet their pants, or be seen to require the services of a dildo, according to the gendered stereotypes of publicity). Pepi's next product is a doll which sweats and menstruates. In *Labyrinth of Passions*, psychiatrist Susana's Lacanian diagnosis of Sexi's Oedipal crisis is crass, a parody of psychoanalysis, as is the facile backstory of Sexi and Riza's childhood trauma on the beach which is supposed to explain both their sexual problems.

By far the most common way Almodóvar parodies gender is through transvestite and transsexual characters, themselves often a parody of gender. The drag queens which populate the early films are both a reflection of the licentious and carnivalesque *movida*, and a theatrical element of comedy. Drag queen Roxy in *Pepi, Luci, Bom* exudes a scandalous and entertaining sexuality. Fabio McNamara repeats the role in *Labyrinth of Passions*, here Fabio is ambiguous and effeminate: 'I'm hysterical,' he says, using the feminine adjective. In *High Heels*, the transvestite who comes into the changing-room (one of the drag group Diabéticas aceleradas) is more stereotyped, clearly a man in drag. The same is true for the two drag queens who appear in *Flower*. In typically bitchy style we hear one say to the other, 'I'm not surprised with *your* weight'. The only truly developed transvestite in Almodóvar's films – Letal in *High Heels* – is heterosexual, making the point that transvestism is not directly connected to homosexuality. Indeed, Letal's heterosexuality is strongly affirmed in the scene where he has sex with Rebeca. As is usual in Almodóvar, the scene is filmed with an intimacy which is slightly uncomfortable, with shots filmed from behind and underneath as Rebeca hangs from a bar. The reasons for Judge Domínguez's transvestism are neither sexual nor gender-driven. But the character nevertheless problematizes gender, accentuates feminine features and gestures. Rebeca's reactionary husband Manuel, for one, is disturbed by the gender parody. He asks, 'Is Letal masculine or feminine?' and he is clearly uncomfortable with what he calls '*travestones*'. For Smith (1994: 125), the transvestite Letal represents 'the primacy of voluntarism, the freedom of the subject to place him/herself on either side of the sexual divide'. Yarza (1999: 89) sees the transvestite as a metaphor for the radical 'restructuring of traditional binary gender oppositions' that characterizes all Almodóvar's films. But in *High Heels*, femininity is represented as performance by women as well as by cross-dressing men. Shaw makes the point that 'Rebeca, Becky and Letal are all seen carefully applying their lipstick as performances of their femininity'.[10]

Transsexuals appear in two films: *Law of Desire* and *All About My Mother*. In the first the transsexual character is the vehicle for melodrama, in the second, she represents comic relief. But in neither is the transsexual character mocked. In both cases they are played by female actresses. *Law of Desire*'s Tina as a transsexual exaggerates her feminine features with spectacular dress and constant worries about her physical appearance, but Almodóvar says of her, 'The most feminine thing about Tina is her paranoia.'[11] Tina is also exceptionally good at mothering. Her female ex-lover is played by Bibi Anderson, real-life transsexual, a fact that Spanish audiences were acutely aware of, and one which Almodóvar exploits perhaps to indicate that gender divisions are not so rigid. In *All About My Mother*, Agrado's speech about authenticity confirms gender as a mobile construct: 'The more you become like what you have dreamed for yourself, the more authentic you are.'[12] Agrado's maxim is close to Baudrillard's example of 'the play of femininity' which he sees in transvestism:

> What transvestites love is this game of signs, what excites them is to seduce the signs themselves. With them everything is makeup, theater, and seduction. They appear obsessed with games of sex, but they are obsessed, first of all, with play itself; and if their lives appear more sexually endowed than our own, it is because they make sex into a total, gestural, sensual and ritual game, an exalted but ironic invocation. (Baudrillard 1990: 13)

The wit of Almodóvar's transvestite and transsexual characters is part of the 'game' of playing the woman, and humour is often a protective mechanism against potentially hostile reactions. But of course, Joan Riviere's (1986: 35) early psychoanalytic study of 'womanliness as masquerade' equates playing the role of the feminine with the need 'to avert anxiety and the retribution feared from men' by women who aspire to masculinity. Many of Almodóvar's successful female characters (Pepa in *Women on the Verge*, or Leo in *Flower*) are constructed as fragile or even hysterical in their relations with men, and most know how to 'play' womanliness to achieve their aims.

Doubtless Almodóvar's construction of gender in his films will continue to receive a significant degree of critical scrutiny: by feminists who are troubled by what they see as an irresponsible frivolity; and by film theorists who continue to deconstruct the portrayal of gender as if Almodóvar were innocent of such discourses at work (and at play) in his films. The director's knowing problematization of the ongoing debates around gender and its cinematic representation, by relentlessly exposing its own mechanisms, leaves the theorists themselves curiously exposed.

5

Sexuality

The Sex Drive

In 1974 Almodóvar made his first short film, *Two Whores or Love Story Ending in a Wedding* (*Dos putas o historia de amor que termina en boda*), which was closely followed by *The Fall of Sodom* (*La caída de Sodoma*), *Sex Goes, Sex Comes* (*Sexo va, sexo viene*) and finally the feature-length Super-8 *Fuck, Fuck, Fuck Me, Tim* (*Folle ... folle ... fólleme, Tim*). All these early, non-commercial films have overtly sexual narratives, a trend which was to continue in the early commercial features. While this owes something to the relaxation of censorship in the final years of the dictatorship and to the liberalization after Franco's death – when film-makers exploited the novelty selling power of female nudity in the so-called *destape* films – the films go beyond the established boundaries of acceptable titillation for male audiences, introducing hitherto taboo sexual practices. Much of Almodóvar's sexually explicit content is designed with shock tactics in mind. One of the legacies of this strategy of acclimatization is the opening up of sexuality as a site of debate in Spain. Another is the international reputation Spanish film has gained for scenes of explicit sex (Jordan and Morgan-Tamosunas 1998: 112). For this, Almodóvar shares responsibility with other directors (such as Juan José Bigas Luna) and with the explosion of a range of sex industries, made possible by a new, politically validated sexual licence, which, arguably, turned Spain almost overnight into the most liberal nation on earth.

Almodóvar's early full-length films certainly reflect this licentiousness, but they also contributed to it. *Pepi, Luci, Bom* is a virtual catalogue of taboos, a carnivalesque sexual and scatological challenge to accepted public taste. The impulse to shock gives way to a more contextualized (though no more credible) sexual maze in *Labyrinth of Passions*. The labyrinth of sexual desire is established by the opening which alternates between shots of Sexi and Riza wandering around the Rastro (Madrid's fleamarket). Their initial connection is a common desire for men. They are both successful: Riza picks up Fabio, both happily admitting they are cruising; and Sexi is organizing an orgy in which she is the only woman. Later, in a session with her analyst, Sexi relates that she took eight or ten men home and slept with them, and calmly admits to being a nymphomaniac. Her Lacanian psychoanalyst, the voluminous Argentinian Susana, is also sex-obsessed, and assumes Sexi's father – a gynaecologist working on artificial insemination – must be also. She gleefully announces to Sexi her intention of sleeping with him. In fact, the doctor's research stems from a deep-seated repugnance towards sex. This attitude contrasts sharply with that of Queti's father who is also obsessed with sex. Since his wife has run away, he has substituted his daughter Queti as an alternative sex object, tying her up and forcing her to have sex with him, deluding himself that she is a schizophrenic – becoming, according to him, both his wife and his daughter – while commenting, 'You're a kinky little thing.'

All the characters in *Labyrinth of Passions* are driven by sex. Sadec (Antonio Banderas) is a Tiranian terrorist whose political ambitions are compromised by an addiction to homosexual sex and whose acute sense of smell becomes impregnated with the smell of Riza after only one encounter. Riza moves quickly from sex with Fabio to a one-hour stand with Sadec. But meeting Sexi changes him. As he receives a blow-job from band member Santi he loses his erection, so powerful is his love at first sight for Sexi. In perfect reciprocity, Sexi, too, can think of nothing but Riza. Though she has two young male bedfellows, her mind is elsewhere. She hums the song she had heard Riza sing in El Carolina nightclub. A fluidity of sexual orientation – one possible explanation for Riza's sudden departure from sex exclusively with men – is subtly suggested by the look exchanged by the two men abandoned by Sexi who is unable to concentrate on the job in hand. As Sexi extricates herself from in between her two men they are left facing each other naked and aroused; a rapid cut-away to the next scene leaves open the question as to whether their discomfort triumphs over their immediate

15. *Kika.* Juana (Rossy de Palma) tied up by her
brother.

sexual needs. In fact, the explanation for both Riza and Sexi's sexual
compulsions are revealed in flashback, induced by Susana in a parody
of psychoanalysis. Sexi and Riza had met as children and liked each
other. But Riza's stepmother, the jealous Toraya (Helga Liné), had come
between them, sending Sexi to nymphomania and Riza to homosexuality.
Thus their reunion and sexual union as adults will 'cure' them both,
providing their escape from the labyrinth which began in the Rastro. In
a symmetry worthy of Shakespearean comedy, Queti also discovers true
sexual union with the hitherto frigid gynaecologist. Queti tells the
redundant psychologist Susana, 'no more problems with sex in this
family'.

A more abstract desire replaces genital sexuality in *Matador* and *Law of Desire*.[1] In the latter, desire is personified in transsexual Tina, and memorably in the scene in which she is hosed down in the hot Madrid street. Sex is a powerful force in Almodóvar's narratives (with the possible exception of *Flower*). In *Tie Me Up!*, a long sex scene (which led to the film being granted an X certificate in the USA) is shown from various angles and reflected in multiple mirror-images of the roof light. But the scene is not gratuitously graphic. In typical dramatic conceit, it is their lengthy copulation which allows Marina to recall their first meeting which altered the course of Ricky's life and subsequently hers. In *Kika*, sex maniac and rapist Paul Bazzo (literally 'Big Fuck') associates everything with sex. When his sister Juana tells him to tie her up so that he can steal things from the flat, he asks her 'are you into S & M?' [fig. 15]. And in *Live Flesh* the naive Víctor confesses to Elena that he was motivated by the desire to prove to her he was 'the best fuck in the world'.

Sex as Commodity *Business*

According to Lawrence Birken (1988: 49), the idea of sex as consumption emerged with the bourgeois concept of the individual with personal tastes in a kind of open market. Writing about contemporary society, Baudrillard describes our culture as one of 'premature ejaculation' and continues,

> all seduction, all manner of enticement – which is always a highly ritualized process – is effaced behind a naturalized sexual imperative, behind the immediate and imperative realization of desire. Our centre of gravity has been displaced towards a libidinal economy concerned with only the naturalization of desire, a desire dedicated to drives, or to a machine-like functioning. (Baudrillard 1990: 38)

The early work of Almodóvar, in particular, with its plethora of wandering desiring characters, seems to encapsulate Baudrillard's concept of sex-as-capital.

Pepi, Luci, Bom begins with the rape of the young Pepi by the reactionary and *machista* policeman. The rest of the film charts Pepi's attempted revenge, not for the violation of her body but for the thwarting of her plan to sell her virginity for 60,000 pesetas. Sex is a business for Pepi. When housewife Luci helpfully recommends a woman who can 'sew it back up', restoring a saleable virginity, Pepi coolly replies, 'No thanks. For the moment I want to keep on using it.' Pepi is not alone in selling sexual favours. Toni and Moncho sell sex to older men and willingly put the exterior signs of their virility on show at the bidding of a wealthy, closeted neighbour. In *Labyrinth of Passions*, Riza reads the lurid sexual stories of Patty Diphusa, self-titled 'famous porn star' whose memoirs, written by Almodóvar himself, featured in the magazine *La Luna de Madrid* (see Chapter 1). And Riza's first sex partner, Fabio, turns out to be the star of a sado-masochist *fotonovela*, in a scene where Almodóvar plays the director.

The sex trade depicted in *Dark Habits* is much more subtle. The lesbian Mother Superior rescues fallen girls from the danger of the streets in return for their sexual favours and under the guise of a project in social redemption (see below). In a sophisticated reading of the film, Ryan Prout (1999: 61) suggests this commerce in sexual attraction may be a symptom of the lack of alternative models for relationships outside exploitative or matrimonial relationships. The idea of matrimony as the result of romantic love dates from the eighteenth century, before which it was indeed considered primarily an economic liaison (Bristow 1997: 172). This follows Foucault's (1978: 103) point that sexuality is socially inscribed and historically contingent. Blatantly less socially acceptable and institutionalized is Gloria's sale of her younger son Miguel in *What Have I Done* for the price of a pair of curling tongs. After selling him to a lascivious paedophile dentist, the next shot shows her buying the tongs. While the context for this maternal dereliction is Gloria's desperate poverty, her neighbour, the prostitute Cristal, is both the happiest and most likeable character in the film. Indeed, those who choose prostitution as a career are usually likeable characters in Almodóvar, among them Agrado, the hilarious transsexual prostitute in *All About My Mother*.

In *Law of Desire*, the opening meta-film suggests the relationship between film-maker and actor is one of prostitution; in the same film, a young would-be actor accompanies Pablo home and is willing to sleep with him to obtain a part in a film. In *High Heels*, the signer for the news broadcast clearly exploits her sex for personal gain, sleeping with the director of the television station and assuring a judge that he can 'bother her whenever he likes' as she suggestively straightens her implausibly short skirt. The selling power of the miniskirt also moves ageing film director Máximo Espejo in *Tie Me Up!* His actress Marina kneels on the stage after filming in a wet short dress with no knickers on. (This sexy image from the film-within-the-film was also used on publicity photos for Almodóvar's film: in conjunction with the sado-masochistic allusion of the title, the plot of the film thus foregrounds the selling power of the pornographic allusion.) And, as is usual in Almodóvar, erotic scenes are approached from an unusually intimate angle: an aerial shot reveals Marina in the bath playing with a wind-up toy diver between her legs, her breasts in the foreground, an allusion to her past in porn films. But far from a celebration of the violent, abusive behaviour of exploitative males which radical feminists see in all pornography (McNair 1996: 13), Marina is seen here alone and enjoying herself. The little porno film-within-the-film featuring Marina, which Máximo watches, casts him as the sad voyeur more than it degrades Marina. Pornography – the ultimate in mediated sex – is never far from Almodóvar's depiction of sexual activity. The films show signs of the 'radical individualism' that Weeks (1995: 115) identifies as the downside of promoting specialized markets, that is, sex as commodity. This liberalization of economic markets which turns everything into com-modity is particularly free in contemporary Spain, where sexuality – so long repressed – was in one constitutional act liberated from political and social control. Almodóvar's films, all products of democratic, liberal Spain, benefit from that liberation, but they have also played their part in (re)presenting it, in promoting it.

The Closet

In his *History of Sexuality*, Foucault (1978: 140) examines power structures which affect the discourses surrounding sexuality, concentrating at one point on 'the subjugation of bodies and the control of populations'. Two of the nineteenth-century phenomena which he includes have a direct bearing on both the repression and the representation of homo-sexuality: what he calls the 'socialization of procreative behaviour' (p. 154), which equates heterosexuality with moral responsibility, and the 'psychiatrization of perversions' (p. 153), which separates healthy and pathological manifestations of sexuality. Together, they clearly impact on the reception of homosexuality in society, inscribing it as unproductive and unhealthy. More originally, Foucault claims that the nineteenth-century discourse designed to subjugate homosexuals (as perverts) provided them with their own discourse of resistance, which he calls 'reverse discourse' (p. 101). The suppression of sexuality has long been a staple of narratives. In particular, the political question of liberation among repressed minority sexualities – coming out of the closet – has characterized Anglo-Saxon stories about gays and lesbians. Indeed, it has often represented the *only* thematic treatment of gay storylines. The case of Almodóvar's depiction of homosexuality is somewhat problematic, for such Anglo-Saxon 'coming out' narratives cannot apply in an ideal world of absolute sexual licence, which is how Almodóvar's sexual universe is often perceived.

Within the generalized sexual freedoms of post-Franco Spain, none of the old taboos exists. In fact, the repression of sexuality (straight or gay, though the terms are largely absent in Almodóvar) is a greater taboo: Almodóvar takes acceptance of gay and lesbian characters for granted.[2] The closet is always inscribed as an individual rather than a social predicament. Almodóvar's characters have nothing to come out of but themselves. The closeted homosexual in *Pepi, Luci, Bom* is hopelessly married to the squealing, bearded Cristina Pascual, who thinks he is upset only because his best friend has come out as gay. Her husband's self-repression reduces him to buying sex and to the voyeuristic pleasure of exiled witness to the members on parade in the 'general erections' contest. In *Matador*, Diego wonders if Ángel is gay because he has never been with a girl. Ángel, whose sexual repression is clearly attributed to his strict religious education, sees this as an insult. To prove he is not *maricón*, he attempts to rape Diego's girlfriend Eva. Later, when Ángel goes to the police station to confess the rape, he also confesses to the murder of a young man who, he says, was about to penetrate him, a suggestion that the murder was the result of what some people controversially call 'homosexual panic'. Ironically, the police inspector to whom Ángel offers this confession is overtly gay and apparently closeted. He subjects the young Ángel to an objectifying sexual gaze (the inspector's image is cleverly reflected in the police station window juxtaposed with Ángel's face). Ángel reports the rape and the inspector assumes he is the victim not the perpetrator. With a smile of anticipation, the inspector tells him, 'Come in and tell me how you did it.' Confirmation of the inspector's sexual orientation comes when we see his lingering point of view on the crotches and buttocks of the male bullfighting students. Later, he asks Diego if he thinks Ángel is homosexual, and tells his 'girlfriend' they won't be sleeping together tonight, even though she assures him 'I don't mind if you don't fuck me.'

The character of Antonio in *Law of Desire*, as played by Antonio Banderas, is a continuation of the actor's role as Ángel in *Matador*. At the start of the film, after watching the erotic final scene from director Pablo Quintero's *The Paradigm of the Mussel*, Antonio goes into the bathroom and repeats the word 'fuck me' (as spoken in the film) while he masturbates. After stalking Pablo for a while, he finally picks him up and goes home with him. Antonio is uncomfortable about his sexuality. He is clumsy and asks Pablo to teach him how to kiss. Pablo tells him not to kiss 'as if he were unblocking a sink'. Antonio interrupts the sex three times to ask about sexually transmitted diseases, and about penetration. Camera angles and *mise-en-scène* also emphasize Antonio's sexual repression; a high-angle shot of Pablo penetrating Antonio, the latter's feet in the foreground, makes their sex act look awkward and uncomfortable. The sex itself is depicted realistically: Antonio's face expresses the difficulty of penetration and Pablo subsequently reaches for the lubricant. Almodóvar has stated that sex scenes have little interest in themselves, and more for what they tell us about characters (Vidal 1988: 205). Here, Antonio's inexperience becomes the main focus, despite the clearly ground-breaking depiction of explicit gay sex in the scene as a whole. Commenting on the potentially alternating dominance in gay relationships, Smith (1992: 192) suggests that the camerawork – an unusual use of crossing the line – is mobilized as a metaphor for 'the instability and reciprocity of homosexual relations'. Later, Antonio in anger writes Pablo a note saying if he were sixteen and not twenty he would report him as a child molester, revealing his deeper reactionary streak. He exaggerates masculine features (overcompensating for his sense of a deficit in his masculinity): he shouts *'Buenos días'* like a brutish workman, and possessively tells Pablo, 'I don't want to find out that you've been with other men' (a possessive *machista* attitude unusual in gay relationships). He is also predatory, as in his attempt to possess Juan at the lighthouse. Antonio can be seen as the embodiment of self-repressed sexuality. As José Arroyo (1992: 42) puts it, 'the same characteristics that oppress Antonio as a gay man are here attributed to him personally: competitiveness, power, domination, violence, the need to control, and the need to possess'.

In *Dark Habits* the convent functions like a metaphor for desire suppressed. The repressed sexuality of the five nuns emerges in the scene in the chapel where Sister Rat, in hypersensualized tones, reads a passage from a book called *The Christian Damsel*, warning young girls of the levels of danger in different types of kisses. The nuns' reactions are revealed in a slow frontal tracking shot. Though the sexual promiscuity which characterizes Almodóvar's first two films is curtailed by the walls of the convent, the nuns are clearly not insulated from worldly desires. Despite their seclusion, they 'already embody the sensual obsessions of contemporary Spain' (Smith 1994: 38). The Mother Superior keeps secret both her sexual attraction for girls and her heroin habit. Drugs represent a bridge to the world outside, but also, as Yolanda does not reciprocate the Mother Superior's sexual love, taking heroin together is a substitute for sexual relations between the two women. At the end of the film, Yolanda sings 'I left because I left' at the Mother Superior's party, a song which speaks of forbidden love, and at one point includes the phrase, 'Don't tell me anything, mother', verbalizing a love that should not speak its name. The Mother Superior is not alone in her secret desires. Sister Rat sublimates her desires in a love of sensationalist literature and turns out to be a writer of romantic novels. Sister Damned lovingly (and obsessively) attends to the domestic welfare of the convent. And the romantic–platonic relationship between the chaplain and Sister Snake is wilfully confused with religious admiration by the nun. She sings 'Lord of my life, life of my love' as a hymn not to God but to his more worldly messenger. At the end of the film the couple leave the convent to 'form a family'.

Lesbians and Gay Men

Those seeking progressive images of happy homosexuals in Almodóvar's films are most frequently disappointed, for Almodóvar is always interested in crisis and imbalance. Gays and lesbians are just as likely to be unhappy as heterosexuals. Almodóvar does not perceive any duty to compensate for decades of repression and invisibility by substituting politically correct 'positive images' of gays and lesbians. They are present in his world but their political or social context does not interest Almodóvar. Smith takes up Richard Dyer's point, that if homosexuality is treated as incidental, it runs the risk of becoming marginal (Dyer 1990: 166). In Almodóvar this makes it difficult to see the films as progressive in terms of sexuality (Smith 1992: 168–9).

Almodóvar's first feature has a lesbian relationship which does little for the positive political affirmation of lesbians. Paradoxically, *Pepi, Luci, Bom*, on the one hand, takes lesbian love entirely for granted, and, on the other hand, goes out of its way to make its scenario as sensational as possible. For the first sexual relationship in Almodóvar's work is between a housewife and a sixteen-year-old punk singer whose first encounter is among the film's most famous scenes. Luci has agreed to give Pepi knitting lessons. Pepi quickly perceives Luci's sexual fix and the housewife soon confesses, 'I need a firm hand'. Pepi assures her that as long as they have their knitting classes, she will get her share of physical punishment, and Luci replies that she is wet just thinking about it. Her use of the word 'wet' gives Pepi an idea. Their class is interrupted by the young punkette Bom (signalled by Holy Week music) who squeezes Luci, remarking 'forty something and soft just as I like them'. She heads for the toilet but Pepi stops her and suggests, 'Make the most of it, and piss over her. She's hot and it will cool her down.' The first sexual congress of the film is thus a sensational perversion, emptied of all politically transgressive content by its decontextualization: a knitting class rather than a porn studio, and females with no male audience. A parody of sadomasochism, this scene is followed later by one in which Bom obliges Luci to eat her snot, and then another where Bom has Luci on a dog-lead. Despite her visible transformation (and Bom admits that she's 'incredible in bed'), housewife Luci finally returns to her husband who proves himself capable of giving her true punishment. Female friendship (not necessarily sexual friendship) proves the lasting virtue of this film, wonderfully portrayed in the scene where Pepi prepares for her friend Bom her favourite dish *bacalao al pil-pil*, a scene of natural affection between women though subtly charged with a sexual frisson.

Lesbian desire is again decontextualized in the unlikely setting of the convent in *Dark Habits*. But despite the incongruity, the all-female desire is taken seriously. When cabaret singer Yolanda arrives at the convent, fleeing the scene of her boyfriend's death, she interrupts a service in the chapel. The nuns sing 'Divine heart, sweet as honey' and, as the doors open, Yolanda appears, a divine presence bathed in heavenly light (note the light is from the street, the outside world). The Mother Superior walks towards Yolanda as a bride to a groom. The chapel becomes the locus of a secular love.[3] When they reach the 'suite de honor' where Yolanda is to stay, the young woman takes off her coat, revealing a red lurex dress. The Mother Superior is lost for words. A little later, when Yolanda is frightened by the tiger, the Mother Superior puts her hand on Yolanda's bare arm, and the gesture's erotic charge is heightened by the social barriers between them.

Significantly (in this film and in others), the tentative rapprochement between the two women is facilitated by the first of many romantic songs, *boleros*. In one of the most sublimely romantic moments in all Almodóvar's cinema, the Mother Superior sings along to 'Encadenados' ('Chained Together'). With a rapturous expression, she sings to the young woman, 'Perhaps it would be better if you didn't return. Perhaps it would be better if you forgot me.' Yolanda can do no less then return the gaze, despite being as yet unaware of the full truth of the Mother Superior's look. She returns the line, 'Affection like ours is a punishment, carried in our souls until death.' Their singing over the deep masculine voice of Lucho Gatica, though played without irony, nevertheless subverts heterosexual romance. As Smith (1992: 184) puts it, 'in this highly stylized and emotionally charged sequence the audience is addressed directly as a participant in lesbian seduction'. Later, they comment on this type of sentimental music and the Mother Superior takes advantage of their mimed intimacy, telling her she looks lovely today. The Mother Superior reminds Yolanda of her feelings on various occasions, and eventually admits her only sin is loving her. After her party Yolanda undresses and the Mother Superior hesitates long enough to see her naked breasts. It is the last she sees of her unrequited love. Her scream at the end when she discovers Yolanda's vacant room signals the desolation of lost love. While the Mother Superior's relationship with Yolanda is unconsummated, there is a strong indication of a sexual relationship between her and Merche. The former protégée pleads with her protector, amorously kissing her hands, 'Don't you like me even a little any more?' But the Mother Superior reminds her, 'You were quite clear before. You don't have to explain anything now.' Confirming the possessive nature of the Mother Superior's relationship with the girls under her care, Sister Rat correctly accuses her of being jealous of Rat's relationship with the girls.

Lesbians in later Almodóvar films are minor characters. An out lesbian couple among reporters in *Law of Desire* defuse an argument between transsexual Tina and the sensationalist press. The aggressive reporter asks Tina if it's true she's become a lesbian. Pablo rescues her: 'If all men were like you, even I would become a lesbian.' At this point the female couple chime in that they are already lesbians. The idea of lesbian desire as a choice, rather than an involuntary orientation, is exemplified in the character of Nina in *All About My Mother*, who leaves a lesbian relationship with Huma to get married and have children at the end of the film. Even her lover Huma, who claims she is 'hooked on Nina like Nina is hooked on drugs', later admits to having had sex with a man ('It's a long time since I dined on dick,' she laughs). Less compromising, though still humorous, is Rossy de Palma's Juana in *Kika*, a somewhat stereotypical lesbian complete with a moustache, pronouncing 'the moustache is not unique to men. In fact, men with moustaches are either queer or fascist or both.' She tells Kika she'd like to be a prison governess, surrounded by women all day long. The close encounter with her mistress Kika is too much for her: 'You've got me excited. I need a bit of cold water to cool my erection.'[4] Juana's lesbianism is linked, by Kika at least, to incest with her brother:

> KIKA: That's why you're so traumatized.
> JUANA: Traumatized? Give me a good pussy and that's all I need.

When Kika makes her up in a more feminine way, she blames 'the mistress who got it into her head today to dress me up in women's clothes'. Juana thinks her brother Pablo should have stayed in prison; he objects, 'in jail there are no women'. She replies that there are queers, assuming they are interchangeable.

Unlike Juana's moustached lesbian, Almodóvar's early gay men are not stereotyped. These early scenes of gay sex are in no way sensationalized but neither is there any attempt to sanitize the gay milieu, as demonstrated by the scene in *Labyrinth of Passions* where Toraya goes to a gay cruising area.[5] In *Labyrinth of Passions*, the first sex act is between Riza and Sadec, a gay encounter which is not shown, though we do see Riza washing his penis (just out of frame) afterwards. Later, there is a full shot of Santi performing oral sex on Riza. Similarly, in *Flower*, Alicia, Leo's publisher, describes the scenario of one of her 'new' darker novels which includes, much to the scandal of her publisher, 'a queer son who happens to like black men'. In *What Have I Done*, the portrayal of homosexuality is more ambivalent. On the one hand, the paedophile dentist is a caricature of the predatory effeminate homosexual. Gloria's attitude to her younger son's precocious gay sex life is typical of her inability to do more than merely enumerate the unpleasant details of their lives: she tells Miguel she knows he's been in bed with his friend's father just like every day. And her son replies that he's the master of his own body. However, Gloria's relationship with Miguel is all that remains for her at the end of the film. Marvin D'Lugo (1991: 55) draws a positive conclusion from this ending: 'The film's final reconciliation between Gloria and her gay son underscores the persistent bonding of female and gay characters throughout Almodóvar's cinema as they each recognize the city as the place of their liberation from the tyrannical sexual and social codes of the patriarchy.'

Law of Desire, Almodóvar's story of a gay love triangle, is a perfect illustration of his equivocal attitude to homosexual relationships. He has claimed that the same-sex relationship is not a determinant, but entirely 'anecdotal' (Cobos and Marías 1995: 140). Interestingly, this is exactly what Fassbinder said of his gay storyline in _Fox and His Friends_ (1974).[6] It is true that both directors have found themselves appropriated by assimilationist gay and lesbian critics and audiences, despite a reluctance to be thus categorized. Pablo Quintero, the principal character of _Law of Desire_, is a writer and director who has much in common with Almodóvar. The film opens with a scene which, rather than naturalizing gay sexuality, is a 'scandalous provocation' (Smith 1992: 189). José Arroyo (1992: 38) comments that this initial challenge to audience sensibilities determines whether the spectator will stay or leave; after this scene 'nothing in the rest of the film will be as problematic'.[7]

Aside from its shock value, this opening scene is among the most complex in Almodóvar's cinema. An attractive young male enters a room and is instructed by an off-screen male voice to undress, and, after a number of commanded indulgent gestures of solitary foreplay, to masturbate. The youth attempts to look at his interlocutor and is reminded, 'Don't look at me. I'm not here.' Dyer (1992: 104) suggests the male model, as object of the gaze, has the option to look elsewhere, ignoring the viewer, or to look up (suggesting a mind on higher things) or even to look _through_ the viewer in an attempt to reassert male power. Here, the actor is deprived of the chance to return the gaze of the viewer: he is ordered to turn around, facing away from the camera, emphasizing passivity – here explicitly offering himself for anal penetration. And when he shows reluctance to ask the other man to fuck him, he is informed 'it's only a word'. A reverse-angle shot (the first indication that there is a real interlocutor present) reveals the director and dubber to be an older man who continues to issue orders. The young man is dubbed by a second (also older) man, who takes a handkerchief to his sweating bald head as the simulated excitement builds. When the young man reaches orgasm, he is told 'you did very well' and paid. A shot of the cash on the bedside table is frozen and is then cut to an identical shot in black and white. To signal the editing process, we hear director Pablo instruct 'freeze and End', before this same frame cuts to the black and white freeze frame with the word 'FIN', visible on a cinema screen, just as Pablo's sister Tina comes into the frame, leaving the première. The film is called *The Paradigm of the Mussel*. The soft porn sequence is actually a film within this film. As always the meta-cinematic effect is not gratuitous, but provides a context for the introduction of all three main characters, Pablo, Tina and Antonio. The film medium is also connected with homosexual desire in the figure of Antonio, who goes straight into the toilet to masturbate, imagining himself in the film and mimicking it, 'fuck me'. This meta-film sequence makes explicit the equation of film-directing with a kind of de-moralized prostitution, reinforced by the older man's payment to the younger. Almodóvar uses the word prostitution to describe the transaction in which 'the director pays someone to do and say whatever he is asked' (Vidal 1988: 210). This represents a new take on the male gaze: in a challenge to the great male directors who directed female stars for the pleasure of male viewers, here a male directs another male for voyeuristic pleasure.

Subsequent to this strange, distanced gay commerce, the relationship between Pablo and Juan is depicted with complete naturalness. We see Pablo in Juan's arms in a tender parting scene in which their sexuality is immaterial. Pablo puts on the record which becomes the soundtrack for their separation, 'Ne me quittes pas'. The intimacy and domestic normality of their relationship contrasts with the hitherto brief physical gay liaisons in Almodóvar's films. Juan asks Pablo if he minds not having sex tonight. And the final shot of the lovers entwined at dawn is Almodóvar at his most sensuously romantic. When Juan leaves for a summer job in the south, their correspondence is like any other love affair across the distance with the exception that Pablo writes all the letters; their sexuality is not an issue. Not so for Antonio, whose personality knows only absolutes: an absolute horror of homosexuality, and a homophobia typically masking desire; once in love, Antonio equally gives himself entirely to his love object. He sets about the conquest of Pablo with a systematic list of objectives: to impress him, support him, complement him, protect him as well as to possess him. At their final meeting, after he has kidnapped Tina in order to get to Pablo, he puts his own soundtrack on the turntable of Tina's record-player and sings along with Los Panchos' 'Lo dudo' ('I doubt if there is a love more pure than the one you have in me'). This heartfelt sentiment coming

16. *Law of Desire.* Pablo (Eusebio Poncela) with Antonio
(Antonio Banderas).

from Antonio is ironic because Antonio's love, though pure, is tainted
by his irrational and murderous commitment to it. He admits 'loving
you this much is a crime and I'm ready to pay the price' [fig. 16]. The
essential paradox of Antonio's character, as identified by Almodóvar in
an interview, is that his enslavement to desire makes him the only free
character in *Law of Desire*, because he is ready to pay the price for what
he wants (Cobos and Marías 1995: 138).

The use of the actor Antonio Banderas in three successive gay-
coded roles (*Labyrinth of Passions, Matador* and *Law of Desire*) has had a
curious effect on film audience reception of homosexual characters.
Marsha Kinder (1997: 6) suggests that Antonio Banderas has gained a
'liminal antihomophobia [...] in the performative space of Almodóvar's
sexually mobile melodramas'. If straight Banderas (or Tom Hanks in
Philadelphia) can play gay men without compromising a commercially
viable heterosexuality, perhaps straight men in general need not fear
homosexuality. This is an example of how, at least in terms of simple
visibility, Almodóvar has contributed to the normalization of gay characters in world cinema.

How, then, can we evaluate Almodóvar's construction of lesbians and gays? If we look for identitarian sexual affirmation we may well be disappointed. Almodóvar does not, apparently, like labels. The films represent sexuality in terms of what Kosofsky (1990: 90) calls 'universalizing' desire as a continuum of choice, rather than as the 'minoritizing' desire of inborn essential identity. In this sense, queer theory and politics may be useful means of accessing the almodovarian world which includes many choices or 'different ways of being' (Weeks 1995: 115). In the 1990s, queer theory replaced essentialism (being born with a homosexual, gay or lesbian identity) with constructionism (a socially inscribed range of identities) (Penn 1995: 25–6).[8] The fluidity of sexual choices in Almodóvar seems to uphold the idea that there are homosexual acts but no homosexual people.[9] Indeed, for those looking in on Almodóvar's world from outside the context of contemporary Spain itself (and its idiosyncratic, hedonistic libertarianism), the most interesting aspect of Almodóvar's work as a 'gay'-coded director is 'his rejection of fixed positioning and earnest politicking in favour of a celebration of the "unnaturalness" and fluidity of all sexuality' (Burston 1995: 142). In this sense, 'queer' Almodóvar runs parallel to queer theory in both its benefits and its dangers: it shares the aim to 'destabilize the boundaries that divide the normal from the deviant and to organize against heteronormativity' (Penn 1995: 31); but it also runs the risk of dismissing outright the categories of lesbian and gay and the search for positive representations to compensate for decades of invisibility (Penn 1995: 33). On balance, that search in Almodóvar's films bears considerable and, at times, delicious fruit.

Part Three
Construction

6

Madrid: Cinematic and Socio-cultural Space

Like my characters, Madrid has a history: but the past is not enough because the future still excites it.[1]

Although Spain has its symbols, at least as potent as those of other nations, Madrid is not among them. There is no capital landmark which tells the international cinematic traveller 'this is Spain' in the same way that Big Ben is cinematic shorthand for 'action moves to London, England' or the Eiffel Tower indicates France. If Spain really is *diferente* (as affirmed in Spain's famous 1960s advertising campaign), so too is its capital, as unassuming as London is brash, or as Paris is chic. Madrid's modesty in auto-definition (where other cities such as Seville or Barcelona tend to overdetermine their identity) can be deceptive. The fact that the characters, situations and action of all but one of Almodóvar's films are almost entirely located in Madrid can go unnoticed by the viewer. Though many films have been set in Madrid since it gained advantage over Barcelona in film production after 1939, few directors have paid homage to the city quite as directly and consistently as Almodóvar.

In the script of the opening sequences of Almodóvar's twelfth film, *Live Flesh*, the Spanish capital is mentioned no fewer than seventeen times. A novel originally set in specific areas of London is adapted as a film in which Almodóvar gives Madrid a prominence bordering on adoration. These preliminary sequences narrate the birth of Víctor who, next seen twenty years later, will be the protagonist of the film. Víctor is absolutely a child of Madrid, born on a city bus and offered lifelong free transport as a result. His birth in 1970, on the night information minister Manuel Fraga declares on national radio a 'state of exception', is mirrored at the end of the film by the birth of his own son, also en route to hospital in the streets of the Spanish capital. And Víctor draws the parallel in one of Almodóvar's most emotionally and patriotically (yes, patriotically!) charged lines of dialogue. He speaks to his about-to-be-born child, telling him the bustling city was not always like that. Madrid is the mirror of a transformed Spain as well as its capital. After the desolate atmosphere of the 1970 city scenes, described by Almodóvar (1997: 23) in the script as the 'total absence of the typical Madrid merry-making', now in 1990, we see a resplendent Puerta de Alcalá, former city gate and perhaps the symbol *madrileños* would choose for themselves. Behind this landmark, Víctor, now a young man, is revealed on a motorbike. Twenty years on, Madrid still belongs to Víctor and Víctor still belongs to Madrid. To mark the comparison with the start of the film in the deserted streets of the capital, the end, also at Christmas, is the Madrid we experience today, even more spirited and teeming than usual. In the published script, Almodóvar describes the lively avenue as 'a prostitute turned into a street'.

The Spanish capital is a city which signifies differently according to historical, social and geographical situation. For the provincial conservative Doña Perfecta in Galdós' nineteenth-century novel, it represented iniquity, an evaluation which would be re-adopted by an anti-urban Francoist state. Paradoxically, Francoism's assumed anti-urban idealism (the restating of 'healthy' rural values to counter the perceived chaos of an overpoliticized and corrupt urban class) was accompanied by an unparalleled concentration of power in the fascist-urban ministry buildings of the Spanish capital. For this, some Basques and Catalans see Madrid as the embodiment of the repression of their national identity. Nevertheless, for many throughout its history it has been a city of possibilities, open to immigrants. Madrid saw the highest growth in population over the course of the twentieth century of all Spain's regions. The largest wave of migration to the city came in the 1960s. By the end of the century the city accounted for 10 per cent of the national population and was home to more than three million (excluding the metropolitan area).[2] The rural–urban divide is pronounced in Spain, and, heightened perhaps by Madrid's location in the exact centre of the

17. *What Have I Done?* Grandmother (Chus Lampreave) with
her lizard Dinero.

peninsula, the struggle between centripetal and centrifugal forces had
become a trope by the sixteenth century. The debate survives today,
manifest in Almodóvar's Madrid. The grandmother in *What Have I Done*
hates the city and longs to go back to her village. At one point she is seen
on wasteland (the nearest thing to the countryside) in a long shot
silhouetted against the darkening sky. She finds a lizard, which she seizes
upon as a link to nature [fig. 17]. But the subsequent reverse-angle two-
shot reveals in the background another unnatural, unsightly and decidedly
urban block of flats. She is also obsessed with cold: 'In Madrid it's so
cold even lizards can't stand it.' She articulates the desire to escape from
urban enclosure and isolation: 'Here in Madrid we can't go on. We're
drowning.' At the end of the film her wish is granted. Her return with
grandson Toni to the *pueblo* recalls the similar journey taken by the family
at the end of the Spanish neo-realist classic *Surcos* (José Antonio Nieves
Conde, 1951).[3] Leo's mother in *Flower* is also obsessed with the return to
where she was born, worried about skinheads and cars. 'I don't want
Madrid,' she protests. When she does return, along with her convalescing
daughter, leaving the city represents an escape for both women. But
leaving the city also represents a futile attempt to regain an idealized rural

past. When Ricky in *Tie Me Up!* returns to his native village, Granadilla in Cáceres, he finds it completely in ruins, an idyll long disappeared.

This town versus country trope is not, however, the norm in Almodóvar, where non-urban locations are rare. Marvin D'Lugo (1991: 47) sees the omnipresence of Madrid as 'imitating the American cinema's unself-conscious universalization of particular milieus as the natural mise-en-scène of action'. But the limited presence of rural locations in Almodóvar often points to an alternative to urban life. Moreover, his use of Madrid is celebratory, even self-conscious at times rather than self-effacing and normalizing. In many of his films, Madrid is quite simply the entire world. This is especially true in the early films, the action of which never strays beyond the city limits. Almodóvar's first two full-length features, *Pepi, Luci, Bom* and *Labyrinth of Passions*, are products of the post-Franco cultural renaissance known as the *movida madrileña* as much as they are representations of it (see also Chapter 1). These two films stand as almost documentary evidence of an époque firmly rooted in Madrid, providing a view of the city that is partial (in both senses): restricted to the antics of a youth culture yet to challenge the hegemony of the city's cultural elite; and, unlike in Warhol's films, selecting what is interesting in the subculture, rather than filming everything. The marijuana plants Pepi keeps on her balcony demonstrate the licentiousness of the period. The images of the city may show its shabbiness, but these are followed immediately by the rehearsal of the local rock band which indicates that this is a happening place. The ludic quality of the film testifies to the fact that parties were the true spirit of Madrid. And the spectacle of Roxy (president of the Bomitoni fan club), played by Almodóvar's friend and night-life sidekick Fabio McNamara, represents a genuine record of the times of the *movida madrileña*, part of its cultural geography. Even the mode of conversation is finely tuned to a time and a place: while Pepi mimics the razzmatazz American English as compère for 'erecciones generales', Toni talks with a mixture of his native Andalusian accent and acquired speech which is distinctly *pasota madrileño*, adding both to the authenticity of the dialogue and to its humour.

By the time of *Labyrinth of Passions*, Madrid is described, even by an outsider (Toraya's spy in the island of Contadora), as 'the most fun city on earth'. Almodóvar himself speaks of a certain 'glorification of Madrid' in *Labyrinth of Passions* (Vidal 1988: 41). But Madrid's *movida* is happening not in high society or the elite arts, but in places like the Rastro which is the setting for the opening of Almodóvar's second feature. The Rastro, famous madrilenian flea market, is a place where one discovers trash items and cobbles them together to make something interesting, a suitable definition, perhaps, for both the *movida* and for many other postmodern art forms. *Labyrinth of Passions* brings together the elements which were central to the period in Madrid: pop groups (an embryonic Radio Futura, Alaska, Los Pegamoides, etc.), artists (las Costus and Ouka Lele) and performers like Fabio McNamara and Almodóvar himself. It is fitting that *Labyrinth of Passions*, once released as a film, should become the product *par excellence* of the *movida*, screened every weekend in the midnight film screenings at the Alphaville cinema all through (as well as long after) the phenomenon it portrayed.

The Alphaville is one of many existing and functioning urban spaces which are utilized by Almodóvar throughout his films to give them authenticity, and perhaps to counterbalance the tendency towards a certain postmodern artificiality and excess style characteristic of studio-filmed sequences. Such real spaces range from the newest, like the Torres Kio which feature prominently in *Live Flesh*, to the most *castizo* elements in the city. *Labyrinth of Passions* opens with the sequence in the Rastro, and the market appears also in *Dark Habits*, where even cloistered nuns cannot keep away from this ubiquitous Madrid ritual. Such landmarks as the Puerta de Alcalá, the Plaza Mayor, the Almudena cemetery, the María Guerrero theatre, and the Café Bellas Artes appear, all filmed on location. The martial arts centre featured in *What Have I Done* still exists today (in the Plaza del Conde de Barajas where the action of the film opens), as does the recording studio EXA where Pepa and Iván work in *Women on the Verge*. In fact, the same recording studio is used in reality by Almodóvar himself. All this is punctuated by the array of street scenes with yellow post-boxes, lifts, stairwells, telephone boxes, refuse collectors, and the typical Madrid bar with the perpetual sound of slot-machine jingles and television in the background. The range of urban locations used by Almodóvar is limitlessly extended, the offices of *El País* newspaper making an appearance in *Flower*. The constant use of such real places conveys a sense of an entire city where studio-filmed scenes are mixed seamlessly with on-location scenes. At times, the coherence of Madrid's existence is subtly overdetermined, perhaps an affirmation of the smallness of the city, microcosm rather than metro-polis. In *Women on the Verge,* for example, the Torre España (home of Spanish television) first appears as a symbol on the Telediario (Spanish television news); Pepa subsequently walks past it as dawn breaks.

On occasions Almodóvar enlists the direct intervention of his adopted city. In *Flower*, the view from Ángel's apartment is of the Plaza Callao and the FNAC store building, upon which a giant hoarding advertising the novelist Amanda Gris is displayed (see Chapter 1). This novelist, a fictitious creation of the director, was promoted as a real writer, prior to the release of *Flower*, the city's commercial interests actually collaborating with Almodóvar. Many of the institutions and organizations which feature in the film credits are Madrid-based. More than most directors, Almodóvar knows how to make the most of his city. Moreover, Almodóvar admits that searching for locations in the city has brought him into contact with a range of beautiful buildings and locations he did not know existed (Albaladejo et al. 1988: 46).

The script of *Live Flesh* specifies the name of each street in which the action is to take place, Almodóvar directing even from the printed page. The very first scene is set in the Calle de la Bolsa, a stone's throw from the Puerta del Sol in the heart of the city, and home to one of its most *castizo* locales, El oso y el madroño (The Bear and Strawberry Tree), named after the city's emblem. The organ-grinder who often plays there performs in *Matador*, in the pensioners' club in Arganzuela, where pensioners dance Madrid's local dance, the *chotis*. There are many more examples of authentic *castizo* which give verisimilitude to Madrid as a city with a popular cultural heritage: the Villa Rosa night-spot with its Goya-like frescoes in the background, appears in *High Heels*; the Viuda de Vacas restaurant; the Catedral de San Isidro and Plaza de la Cebada in *Flower*. But elements of 'el Madrid *castizo*' are used both for added authenticity and for more dialectical, often satirical or even parodic commentary. The *chotis* danced by the pensioners is juxtaposed with the extravagantly psychotic behaviour of Diego and María. In *Pepi, Luci, Bom*, the night street scene offers a parody of traditional Madrid folkloric stereotypes: *chulos* and *chulaponas*. This parodic discourse (rock musicians dress in *chulo* costume as a cover for their violence) is not without homage to the paradigmatic Madrid performance of *zarzuela* and to its localized ambience and costume. And towards the end of *Women on the Verge*, the traditional chase scene of action films is parodically transposed to Madrid, the mambo taxi, the pink dress of Lucía, the *pasota* tone of Ana, and the construction sites of the A-100 road to the airport providing a mixture of standard genre and localized elements.

Another particularly prominent urban feature of Almodóvar's cinema is transport. As well as offering greater verisimilitude to the films, transport's crucial role in the lives of city-dwellers (both in a practical sense and in terms of social status) is fully integrated into their narratives. Almodóvar lists taxis among his favourite things (Vidal 1988: 138). Taxis play a crucial role in Madrid, being more economically accessible than in many cities of the world. All taxis in Madrid have the city's emblem on their doors – the Oso y madroño (see paragraph above) – making their connection symbolic as well as real. In *Labyrinth of Passions*, all characters come and go by taxi, a sign of the relative affluence of the sons and daughters of the middle classes, with hyperactive social lives and no time to waste on foot. Taxis appear in twelve of Almodóvar's thirteen films. In *What Have I Done*, Antonio is a taxi driver, a fact which accounts for his lack of money, his above average general knowledge given his education, and for his chance meeting with the desperate writer Lucas. This kind of chance meeting – reflecting the notion that Madrid remains a *pueblo* despite its millions of inhabitants – is famously taken to an extreme in *Women on the Verge*, where protagonist Pepa forms a friendship with a taxi driver after three encounters. Where characters travel by bus (Yolanda in *Dark Habits*, Ricky in *Tie Me Up!*, Víctor in *Live Flesh*) it is because of their low socio-economic status, and only in *What Have I Done* are characters reduced to travelling on foot. In almost all cases real buses are filmed on location, as in *Live Flesh* where those familiar with the city will recognize the Circular line bus, connecting it with their own sense of the geography of the real, lived city. The simple and single-minded Ricky in *Tie Me Up!* appropriates the efficiency of schematic urban transport maps to simulate his life-line as a metro line with his love object-victim Marina as the final stop.[4]

In the later films dealing with more affluent classes, characters have their own cars and, in the case of *High Heels*, a chauffeur-driven limousine. In *Kika*, the first view of Madrid is on the arrival of the high-speed AVE train at Atocha, and Manuela travels three times on the Madrid–Barcelona train. Once again transport says a great deal about the city and the country, displaying a modern, sophisticated urban society. Airports, like cities themselves, act as meeting places, and they also figure prominently in Almodóvar's films. Madrid's Barajas makes its first appearance in *Labyrinth of Passions* where it is used as the setting for the coincidence of all interested parties in pursuit of the Emperor of Tiran's son. The symbolism of an airport finale is obvious: the open ending offers a journey, for protagonists Sexi and Riza it is a sexual journey, their first union noisily taking place on board the departing plane. In *Women on the*

Verge, the airport is once again the scene for the final episode in the film, and also ends in a journey – the departure of the cause of all Pepa's problems. More significantly, perhaps, is *High Heels*, which begins at the airport. Here, the journey commences at the outset and the film concludes not with an open ending but with the closure of Becky's death.

While all on location shooting serves to enrich the tapestry of Madrid's existence, there are a number of constants in Almodóvar's portrayal of the social geography of the city: shots which socially contextualize characters; shots which draw attention to change, either in fortunes or over time; and shots of views from windows or balconies. Even more eloquently than dress, behaviour and speech (often the most potent social signifiers), Almodóvar's camera discovers the social milieu of his characters: the rich and famous in *Women on the Verge*, *Tie Me Up!* and *High Heels*, the intellectual bourgeoisie in *Flower*, or the desperately poor working class in *What Have I Done*.[5] It is in the latter film – Almodóvar's veritable neorealist masterpiece – where the director's social realism is most dependent on urban geography. The Madrid it depicts, though a reality for many, is far from the bright lights and strong colours often associated with Almodóvar. An establishing shot of the M-30 motorway puts housing blocks into context beside the major artery. The urban landscape portrayed is forbidding: children play football alongside the busy motorway, and more high-rise low-quality accommodation in the background seems to close in on the diminutive characters in its shadow. In *What Have I Done*, modernity is an ambiguous commodity; while the proximity of the motorway impoverishes quality of life for the inhabitants, Antonio thinks Ingrid Muller will enjoy a tour of the Madrid orbital motorway in his taxi. But modernity has not fully installed itself in these areas, hence the striking image of the conglomeration of modern blocks with a gypsy's horse and cart collecting scrap; the old meets the new, but life in the slums changes little. Rain intensifies the drabness of the scene and, unique in Almodóvar's films, characters complain of the cold. Winter makes the city much less habitable. In a city which suffers from extremes of temperature, the rich need not worry about the cold.

The social geography of Madrid in Almodóvar even extends to death, the Almudena cemetery also contextualizing social status. In *Live Flesh*, Víctor's prostitute mother is buried in a *nicho* (a hole in the wall) metres away from the elaborate grave of Elena's ambassador father. The script describes the social division: 'Only a tarmac path separates the line of miserable, hole-in-the-wall graves from the elegant zone of the cemetery'

(Almodóvar 1997: 112). It also makes reference to the similarity of the *nichos* of the cemetery with the blocks of flats beside the M-30, those dwellings seen in *What Have I Done*. In shots of interiors, too, social commentary can be found, often in more local urban spaces. The bar is an essential part of Madrid life. The Alhambra bar which Toni and his grandmother visit in *What Have I Done* is a faithful depiction of such an urban locale, dreary and derivative (just how many of Madrid's bars attempt to re-create the native region of their owners?). The irony of the grandmother's remark, 'If you haven't seen Graná [Granada] you haven't seen anything', draws attention to the longing for escape shared by many immigrants in the Spanish capital.

Almodóvar has a particular urban fascination with the views from windows and balconies, important urban features in a city which is built vertically towards a famously bright sky. The view from a character's flat indicates social status. Pepi sees only the windows of other flats, including the infamous policeman's window. The policeman spies on her from his flat, discovering the marijuana plants and providing the catalyst for the main storyline of the film. (*Pepi, Luci, Bom*, like Hitchcock's *Rear Window*, could only take place in the confines of an urban environment where the lives of others are on display for those who want to watch.) The voyeur motif of *Kika* depends on the view from Ramón and Kika's balcony which includes the Torre Picasso (a modern, expensive location). Gloria, from her balcony in *What Have I Done*, sees nothing but grey concrete jungle. But by the late 1980s (the time of *Women on the Verge*), *terrazas* are fashionable status symbols, and Pepa surveys a splendid panorama of the city from her terrace, including the Telefónica building. This particular view, however, is studio-built, a 'fantasized skyline' according to D'Lugo (1991: 62) to match the desires of Pepa herself.

Just as social status is potentially mobile, so, too, the social geography of the city allows for changes in the fortunes of characters. In *Pepi, Luci, Bom*, once Pepi moves up into the world of advertising, we see her no longer in the 1940s and 1950s working-class districts of Madrid but in the ultra-modern area around Azca including the Torre Picasso skyscraper. This parallel economic–geographical movement is shorthand for progress for those who know Madrid, and is used in other films and in the differentiation of one film from another. Films like *Women on the Verge* or *Tie Me Up!* portray characters of an altogether higher standing economically, and this is reflected in the areas of Madrid in which they move. Urban social change is also reflected in the films. Earlier films portray a somewhat drab city while the later ones feature designer lofts and sleek high-speed trains. In *Live Flesh*, the clash of the old and the new Madrid is seen at La Ventilla, the dilapidated quarter which is home to Víctor, but now finds itself in the shadow of the futuristic Torres Kío. In the script, Almodóvar likens the area to a war zone, progress clearly identified as the enemy. And in *High Heels*, the ultra-modern buildings of the city demonstrate the passing of time for Becky; she prefers the old quarter, the Plaza del Alamillo, where she was born.

On many occasions the city is used as a metaphor, or in some cases an urban pathetic fallacy; the city seems to conspire with art to the benefit of the film. In *What Have I Done*, time-lapse shooting is used to demonstrate the passing from night to day, the changing light falling on the inhospitable block of flats. The architecture of the city also provides for metaphorical use of *mise-en-scène*. In *Pepi, Luci, Bom*, Bom's change of artistic direction at the end of the film takes place as she crosses a footbridge from one side of the orbital motorway to another. And in *What Have I Done*, Gloria's parting with her son and mother-in-law takes place at a bus depot on the very edges of the city, a tracking shot following her as she turns her back on them, framed by the vast expanse of desolate land behind. When she returns to her empty flat, the desolation is no less intense. She surveys the emptiness of the rooms in a long panning shot from her point of view. The panorama from her window and the point of view down to the ground is like a vacuum threatening to suck her in. But the return of her other son Miguel gives her a new role and saves her. The subsequent final shots focus on the balcony of their flat, then dissolve into a medium shot of a section of the building, then the whole block, then a cluster of blocks with the motorway in the foreground, the re-establishing shot both the geographical and social context for Gloria and the return of her domestic and needed role within it. In *Live Flesh*, *mise-en-scène*, camerawork and editing are all used to integrate the inclining Torres Kío (fast becoming a new symbol for Madrid) into the narrative and symbolic structure of the film. As Clara writes to Víctor, 'leave Madrid', we see the towers, and they are then used repeatedly to mark the convergence physically and metaphorically of the main characters for the climax of the drama.

At times the interaction between city and characters is more direct, even personalized. Madrid is a labyrinth and full of prying eyes; when characters have something to hide they choose to go outside the city. Nick (Peter Coyote) buries the body of Susana in his chalet outside

Madrid in *Kika*; in *Matador*, bodies are also buried outside the limits of city; and in *Women on the Verge*, Candela (María Barranco) takes the belongings of the Shiite terrorists to a site far from the centre, an evocative use of on-location shooting as she scrambles over the rubbish dump overlooking the city, the sun setting in the background. There are moments when the city accompanies the characters, as in *Law of Desire* where the warm tones of the rising sun reveal the golden bodies of the lovers entwined in bed, or at the end of *Women on the Verge* where the city shares the intimacy of Pepa and Marisa. Pepa recognizes the value of her apartment and its marvellous view of Madrid: 'I think I won't rent it after all. I love the views.' Perhaps the most famous example – and the most emblematic of all Almodóvar's cinema – comes in *Law of Desire*. Unable to stand the heat of the city any longer (the heat is metaphorically as much as physically linked to the provocation of extremes of desire), Tina asks a street cleaner to point his powerjet hose at her to cool her down. The city's nightly cleaning and cooling is thus applied to Tina. In *Tie Me Up!*, the same street cleaners who relieved Tina also revive Ricky as he lays on the ground bleeding.

The personalization of the relationship between city and character is strongest, however, in *Live Flesh*, the starting point for this chapter. When the protagonist Víctor is born, the landlady Doña Centro tells him, 'What a hurry you were in to get to Madrid!', and then, holding him up, proclaims, 'Look, Víctor! Madrid!' This is followed by a shot of the golden-lit Puerta de Alcalá, the city introducing itself. At times, the city is referred to in almost mythical terms. In *Women on the Verge*, Pepa discovers an old postcard of the Cibeles fountain (Madrid's equivalent to the fountains in Trafalgar Square) on which she and Iván had written to each other as if they were on holiday. In *Matador*, Diego and María come together on the viaduct in the Calle de Segovia, the traditional place for suicides in the city, a part of its popular mythology perfectly suited to the death-obsessed lovers. And in *Flower*, in a touching scene after the flamenco performance, walking with Ángel in a deserted Plaza Mayor, Leo recalls a trip to Athens, and points out: 'Over there it's not like Madrid; there are virtually no bars.' Earlier, when she rings Paco in Brussels, he tells her it's late. She replies that in Madrid midnight is not late. His response is loaded, and perhaps a fitting epigram for Almodóvar's adopted city: 'In Madrid it's never late.'

7

Genre

Genre and Auteurism

There are three good reasons not to include genre as a subject for a chapter in this book. The more film theorists have engaged with genre, the more sophisticated and problematic its workings have proved, and any attempts to define genres in an accepted taxonomy have been quickly contested. Second, genre is a term often used in opposition to the auteurist approach (see below) to film study and Almodóvar is clearly regarded in this book as an auteur, as is apparent from its title. Third, Almodóvar's work defies clear generic definition, the term 'un film de Almodóvar' denoting almost a genre in itself (much as one might refer to 'a Woody Allen film'). But, far from being inapplicable to Almodóvar's films, genre greatly informs them. Paradoxically, resistance to generic definition in Almodóvar is born out of an acute awareness of genre, how different genres can be mixed into a hybrid product, and, most importantly, how it can be enlisted as a vehicle for the distinctive expression of an accepted 'auteur'.

The history of auteurism or authorship in cinema – in its critical, theoretical sense – is relatively short, deriving from the 'Politique des Auteurs' expounded in *Cahiers du cinéma* during the late 1940s and the 1950s, although the common-sense notion of a controlling authorial voice in all art dates back to Romanticism and arguably to the Renaissance. Alexandre Astruc's concept of 'le caméra stylo' equated the director's art with that of the poet, while François Truffaut differentiated between auteurs and *metteurs-en-scène*.[1] Rather than merely recording what was in front of the camera, true auteurs were able to stamp their films with a signature of their style, their personal vision, or even their general world view. Looking at the whole of a director's *oeuvre* would provide an insight into authorial style, and often the positive associations of a director's name were able to attract an audience (sometimes a faithful minority, sometimes a mass audience sold on the name of the director as a mark of quality). The 'best' auteurs controlled their work (often despite the pressures of industrial production) to the point where their presence as an organizing force turns them into 'a kind of protagonist in the drama'.[2] This is particularly true of Almodóvar, whose directorial style and persona make him more famous than his actors or any of his films.

Auteurism soon came under fire, for its subjectivist and canonizing tendencies, for its 'ahistorical idealism',[3] and for its failure to recognize the relationship between the text and its socio-historical context (Cook 1985: 189). Clearly, Almodóvar's film output both resists a canonizing rigidity (if anything, it is iconoclastic), and is firmly wedded to its historical, cultural context. Following the tremors of 1968, the idea arose that an author was progressive because he attempted to destroy the illusion of reality – illusionism being a central tenet of mainstream bourgeois cinema. Here Almodóvar proves a fine case study, his films full of anti-illusionistic gestures, self-reference and parody, all of which undermine the 'naturalizing' logic of cinema. Meta-cinematic devices abound in Almodóvar. The effects of post-structuralism, and in particular of Derridian deconstruction, had an impact in author criticism from the 1960s onwards. In particular the interaction of his films with other texts is one of their most engaging 'deconstructive' features. Almodóvar's film world is full of references to the media, film, television, popular culture and music. Almodóvar's corpus dates entirely from an age we can classify as postmodern and post-structuralist. It should come as no surprise, then, that his films clearly demonstrate the notion that the discourse or voice of the author is just one of many codes operating in cinema.[4] Almodóvar-author can be thought of as a mobilizer of the diverse codes which make up his films. These include codes typically associated with auteurs (vision, poetry, distinctive style, etc.) but also – and more significantly – other codes which originate in non-auteurist film criticism. Of these, perhaps his use of genre (the often wholesale borrowing of generic codes from Hollywood) is what sets Almodóvar apart from many of his European 'art-house' peers. Indeed, the *Cahiers du Cinéma*'s critical re-evaluation of certain Hollywood directors of genre films as auteurs seems entirely appropriate for Almodóvar's idiosyncratic utilization of genres.[5]

Of the many approaches to film, genre is perhaps the most complex because it comprises, as Pam Cook (1985: 58) suggests, a 'repertoire of conventions running across visual imagery, plot, character, setting, modes of narrative development, music and stars'. But genre is also a useful theoretical tool in the analysis of films as commodities: it reflects audience expectations, and relates to the marketing and consumption of films. For Stephen Neale (1980: 19), genres are to be seen as 'systems of orientations, expectations and conventions that circulate between industry, text and subject'. Given his attention to publicity and to the reception of his films, it is hardly surprising that Almodóvar makes much more use of genre conventions than has often been the case with Spanish cinema. Genre functions as a marketing tool to persuade audiences to watch the product. Films perceived as thrillers, melodramas or comedies will attract certain audiences; critically, audiences who may be reluctant to see films perceived as 'difficult' such as auteur cinema or 'art films'. Here, Almodóvar's appeal clearly outweighs that of most of his fellow Spanish directors (for example Carlos Saura or Víctor Erice whose films are much more introspective). Based largely on what John Ellis (1981: 30) has called a film's 'narrative image' – in Ellis's words, 'what is the film like?' – audience expectation plays a role in the reception of films. As more Almodóvar films appear, expectations change, and the narrative image of each film (based on the title, publicity stills, posters and on genre expectations) is a fundamental part of Almodóvar's use of genres, as will be shown.

Two of the constituents which determine the genre of a film are narrative and iconography. The principal commodity of mainstream cinema is narrative, as Neale (1980: 20) points out. Many classic Hollywood films employ established, even formalized narrative structures which enable audiences to make sense of the films.[6] The kinds of narrative structures operating vary from genre to genre, and, in the case of Almodóvar, combinations of genres produce variations on these narrative models. Thus, crime narratives tend to use restricted narration, whereby the viewer does not have all the information and has to solve the enigma (e.g. who was the murderer?). The action of such films is based on a rational and appreciable causality, where each event is a consequence of another. Melodrama, on the other hand, uses omniscient narration, where the viewer sees everything, and therefore is in a position of superior knowledge over some or all of the characters, able to anticipate character responses. Narration in comedy often depends on chance encounters, misunderstandings or scheming characters, and invariably leads to a happy ending.[7] The incorporation of such narrative structures and their modification by Almodóvar forms a substantial part of the following analysis. Almost as important as narrative is iconography, defined by Edward Buscombe (1977: 37) as a 'cluster of images and conventions'. Genre iconography (cars and guns in crime films, telephones and letters in melodrama) always plays a part in Almodóvar's films.

The theorized study of film genre began in the 1960s, mainly as a response to auteur theory, positing an approach to film study which looked at the similarities between films in a particular category, rather than the difference between one director and another (Cook 1985: 58). But rather than rejecting the notion of the auteur altogether, the introduction of genre into film studies allows the investigation of both 'standardization and differentiation' across groups of films (Cook 1985: 58). As Frank McConnel (1977: 10) puts it, 'the artist's individuality [...] manifests itself only *in tension with* the genre within which he works'. This is particularly relevant where a film-maker with an individual authorial style is none the less working within a genre context, as is the case with Almodóvar. Many of the elements in his films which exploit genre conventions also subtly undermine them, or combine usually separate conventions. Taken one step further, this 'dialogue' with genre becomes parody. Jean-Loup Bourget (1977: 62) has observed that 'whenever an art form is highly conventional, the opportunity for subtle irony or distanciation presents itself all the more readily'. This is often exactly the strategy adopted by Almodóvar as will be seen. His films are in a constant dialectic with genres – comedy, melodrama, crime – often combining elements of different genres and making explicit references to other genre film texts.

Comedy

Comedy necessarily trades upon the surprising, the improper, the unlikely and the transgressive in order to make us laugh; it plays on deviations, both from sociocultural norms, and from the rules that govern other genres and aesthetic regimes. (Neal and Krutnik 1990: 3)

Neale and Krutnik's definition is a good starting point for understanding the comedy in Almodóvar's films. His work amply demonstrates the kinds of comedy included in this definition. The distinction between those elements which play on deviations from socio-cultural norms (satire), and deviations from aesthetic norms (parody), is particularly relevant in Almodóvar, because his films coincide with a new freedom in Spain, both to express socio-cultural deviation, and to use new and more transgressive modes of presentation. This accounts for the prevalence of irreverent humour or black humour, both of which treat subjects traditionally off-limits to comedy.[8] It also accounts for the frequent comparisons made between Almodóvar's cinema and that of John Waters whose gross comedies set out to break taboos and violate the sensibilities of conventional US audiences.

As with all genres, comedy plays upon the expectations of audiences, and humour is looked for where audiences expect to find it. This has sometimes had a deleterious effect on the reception of Almodóvar's films. London audiences laughed even at the sex scene in *Live Flesh*, indicating that an expectation of comedy ('Almodóvar is a comic director, isn't he?') predisposes audiences towards laughter, even where the director's intentions lie elsewhere. Jerry Palmer (1987: 21) makes the point that humour can be either immanent or negotiated. The generic contextualization of comic elements can enhance (as well as detract from) their impact as comedy. Thus, while murdering one's husband is not usually the stuff of comedy, the context of satire and the absurd in *What Have I Done* allows such an action to become comic. To return to Neale and Krutnik's (1990: 10) discussion of comedy, a point they make about the genre is its 'formal diversity'. The film comedies which are discussed in the following pages testify to that variety: satire, irony, the sardonic, parody, the absurd, even slapstick are all represented in Almodóvar's gallery of comedy.

Of all Almodóvar's films, his first feature, *Pepi, Luci, Bom*, fits most squarely into the genre of comedy. Its narrative image (the long title of the film, its amateurish, pop advertising and the local notoriety of Almodóvar himself at the time of its release) provides a context for a comedy which the build-up of comic elements in the first scene confirms. The relatively simple narrative chain of events begins with Pepi offering sexual favours in return for a policeman's silence about her marijuana plants, her subsequent rape by him and her desire for revenge, which leads to a more or less continuous struggle between the two.

Chance typically plays a large part in the plot. Pepi's friends beat up the policeman's twin brother by mistake. Twins and mistaken identity are age-old tropes of comedy. Pepi discovers the policeman is not injured and wants to hurt him in some other way, thus landing on idea of reaching him through his wife, who, in turn, happens to be a masochist, perfect for 'perverse-looking' Bom.[9] The happy ending, essential for comedy, comes when Bom goes to live with her true friend Pepi and starts a new life. The comedy in the film is fleshed out by much satire, social commentary, moments of absurd or grotesque humour and parody.

The characters are all stereotypes, offering Almodóvar the chance gently to criticize contemporary Spanish society. Pepi is 'a rich heiress', economically supported by her father and thus free to live life to the hedonistic full. The policeman is an extreme right-winger (exaggerated but not entirely implausible), who rapes Pepi and treats his wife with clichéd machismo. Luci and her child-like friend Charo are passive housewives (especially in comparison with the assertive Pepi), whose conversation about the price of potatoes, shouted over a barking dog and car horns, is made even more ridiculous by what is soon to be discovered about Luci's real nature as a masochist. Charito is duped into a sexual encounter with the rampant policeman (thinking he is the gentler twin brother) and innocently exclaims, 'How silly I am.' (The script is less generous, calling her 'peasant-cum-retard'.) Then there is the hot-tempered Andalusian flamenco-rock singer, played by Kiti Man-ver, who is seen arguing with her agent who apparently wants to get her work as a prostitute. Finally, minor characters add colour and humour to the picture: a pair of Argentinian girls (with no connection to the plot) who take money from a boy in the street, and Fabio as the drag queen drug dealer who arrives with a fruit cocktail face mask (a tin of fruit).

Transgression of both social and aesthetic norms plays a prominent part in *Pepi, Luci, Bom*, which is not surprising given its emergence in the taboo-smashing environment of post-Franco Spain. Nothing is sacred and Almodóvar sets about demolishing national myths about the police, politics, family, even virginity. Pepi challenges the policeman's authority, mockingly grabbing his badge and examining it closely, claiming to be short-sighted. The indecency of Pepi's proposal to the policeman – to trade sex for silence – is matched by his willingness to accept. The script tells us 'she lifts up her skirt like a stage curtain'.[10]

Faced with more than she bargained for, Pepi tells the policeman, 'I'm a virgin and I don't want to lose my honour yet', thereby consigning to comedy the highly serious tradition of the Spanish honour code, frequently the staple of seventeenth-century plays.[11] Next for demolition is marriage, in the shape of the housewife Luci, married to a policeman in the hope of some reactionary domestic violence which she indeed finally secures. Bom's uninhibited reaction to Luci leads to an early scene which is emblematic of the film's radical transgression: Bom, bursting for the toilet, is urged to relieve herself over masochist Luci (this 'golden shower' scene is one of many aesthetically shocking moments in the film and the first instance of regular scatological humour in Almodóvar). Pepi's final line, 'That's it. It's all gone', echoes a mother's words to her child as milk or food is finished. The food metaphor for sexual acts is later used again when Bom instructs Luci to perform fellatio on the party's best-endowed male: Bom tells Luci, 'Come on, eat up before it gets cold.' As Luci becomes absorbed into the groupie world of drugs, sleazy sex and masochism, even her language changes. Her husband challenges her to remain in her rightful domestic place: 'I have told you to stop those knitting classes. Or do I have to tie you up?' But Luci is having none of it and says so: 'That wouldn't be a bad idea at all, but the fact is I don't give a flying fuck what you say anymore.'[12] The scatological lyrics of Bom's song to her lover Luci ('Murciana marrana', see Chapter 9) mark her descent into the comically sordid Madrid subculture and we soon see her kept on a dog's lead by Bom.

Apart from the generalized exaggeration of the crazy world of Pepi and her friends, the film contains absurd episodes such as the appearance of Cristina Pascual as a sexually frustrated wife who has an incredibly high-pitched voice and stubble, as well as a repressed homosexual husband. Absurd parody also plays an important part in Pepi's new profession as advertising agent. Her idea for next Christmas is for dolls who menstruate and sweat, and her idea for multi-use panties provides perhaps the most hilarious sequences in the film. The sample adverts designed by Pepi (and to feature in many of Almodóvar's earlier films) are ridiculously exaggerated parodies of the advertising medium, but they also transgress social decorum in their subject matter (see Chapter 3).

Transgression is also central to Almodóvar's second feature. The publicity poster for *Labyrinth of Passions* displays an enormous, pink pair of female buttocks forming the shape of a heart which has a pink arrow through it. This narrative image, along with the title, accurately reflects the film's generic position as a crazy comedy about human and especially sexual relationships. The narrative, which is far more complex than in Almodóvar's previous film, follows the romantic fortunes of Sexi and her eventual lover Riza, as well as the various secondary relationships among the characters. A great deal is owed to chance: it is a coincidence that Riza is in Madrid at the same time as his stepmother, that she is being treated by Doctor de la Peña, and that Riza meets and falls in love with the doctor's daughter, Sexi. Among the other implausible situations typical of farce are Sadec's extraordinary olfactory talents, dry-cleaner Queti's successful transformation into a Sexi lookalike, and, indeed, the psychoanalytical solution to the mystery of Sexi's phobia of direct light. The narrative follows the typical pattern of exposition, complications and happy resolution.

Among the comic ingredients are examples of stereotypes and satire, as well as the usual transgression of social and aesthetic sensibilities. Notable stereotypes include the rude and unhelpful airport assistant (played by comic actress Eva Siva), the over-attentive Cuban maid, and the Argentinian Lacanian psychoanalyst (a species prevalent in Madrid in the 1980s). Often, character traits are exaggerated to the point of black humour or the grotesque: the impotent dry-cleaner, Queti's father, takes aphrodisiacs and then rapes his daughter (though his daughter gives him an antidote). Blacker still, as he ties up his naked daughter, there is a crucifix on the wall behind the bed. Deviation from socially acceptable behaviour is everywhere, especially in the realm of sexual practices. Sexi calmly tells her analyst that she has just slept with eight or ten men at once, and other characters are seen having sex with one or more partners. Scatology is another source of grotesque humour: Angustias and Ángel talk about flatulence in the lift, while the rehearsal studio's constipated caretaker tries repeatedly to get to the toilet after taking a laxative, before finally succumbing and allowing it to run down her leg. And the shooting of a pornographic *fotonovela*, starring Fabio as a masochist who is being ravished by a sadist with an electric drill, provides the occasion for further aesthetic deviation. Almodóvar plays the director, both characters keep their real names, and Almodóvar cannot help but laugh at the exaggerated effect produced by his friend.[13] (Later, both will appear on stage performing 'Suck It to Me'.)[14] Such grotesque and scatological moments disappear altogether by the time of Almodóvar's most conventional (and most successful) comedy.

Almodóvar described *Women on the Verge* as 'a realistic comedy, in the

American style, that is, very false'.[15] Once again the narrative image of the film signals comedy. Its poster reveals four female characters seated on a sofa, all in poses which exaggerate their predicaments: nervousness for Candela, haughtiness for Marisa, a crazed expression for Lucía and anxiety for Pepa who also holds a telephone. The film's long and yet catchy title, along with Almodóvar's reputation as a comic director, reinforce the expectation of comedy. Certainly, the film can be classified as a comedy though elements of melodrama are also present, as will be shown. Despite some genre mixing and the complex plot, the elements of the film coalesce into a more concentrated genre experience. As Evans (1996: 53) puts it, 'this was the film in which Almodóvar moved from gratuitousness towards coherence in patterns involving minor as well as major characters'. More than in any other film by Almodóvar, the narrative of *Women on the Verge* conditions the genre following the typical pattern of exposition, multiple complications, climax and resolution.

In the first five minutes of the film we learn about Pepa's broken relationship with Iván, her job and her pregnancy. The story consists of her pursuit of Iván to tell him she is pregnant, but this is complicated by the characters around her with their own problems, and the comic conceit is furthered by many coincidences. Pepa is standing in a phone booth outside Lucía's flat when Lucía throws Carlos's suitcase out of the window; it falls on top of Pepa and she discovers a photo of Iván with his son Carlos (Pepa thus discovering he has a son). Even more coincidental is that Carlos and girlfriend Marisa are flat-hunting and they arrive at Pepa's flat, thus discovering who Pepa is. Thus one of the character components is in place on the stage of Pepa's apartment (though this particular woman, Marisa, is far from nervous breakdown at this stage). The next woman on the verge is the naive Candela ('Don't call me a pain. I'm feeling very sensitive'), who provides much of the hilarity in the film. Further narrative complication is provided by her relationship to the Shiite terrorists. In a moment of pure farce, the desperate Candela tries to jump off the roof, fails and is left hanging ridiculously. This, in turn, affects the coldly self-assured Marisa, who is deeply shaken by Candela's attempt at suicide; she goes to the kitchen and drinks Pepa's spiked gazpacho, falls asleep and misses the rest of the drama which transpires around her for hours. In a conjunction of improbabilities, just when Pepa goes out to get rid of Iván's suitcase, he tries to phone her while his lover Paulina is waiting in the car just outside Pepa's apartment. Pepa walks right past her and does not see her. Meanwhile, Iván's ex-wife Lucía is approaching. When Pepa throws an LP out of the window it hits Paulina on the head, and this missile is closely followed by the answering-machine which Pepa throws out in an angrily symbolic gesture renouncing her goal of communicating with Iván. Then comes the comic climax: the police arrive to track down the Shiite terrorists, along with Lucía in pursuit of Iván; once Pepa works out Iván's plan she has to escape the police interrogation. The gazpacho provides the solution, putting the two policemen to sleep. The accumulation of coincidences is actually questioned by the policeman who remarks incredulously, 'I get the feeling you are making fun of me.'

To a certain extent, this film is also a comedy of manners, the characters themselves stereotypes (subtle or otherwise) providing opportunities for satirical comment. A good example is Paulina Morales, a hard and uncaring feminist, capable of stealing Iván away from two of her political 'sisters'. The studio receptionist, wonderfully played by comic actress and television personality Loles León, is the opposite of Paulina: witty, sarcastic, with a heart of gold, but also a stereotype – the receptionist who knows everyone's business. She chides Pepa with the loudspeaker of the public address system still switched on, a metonym for her indiscretion. Comic contrast is set up in the father–son pairing of Iván and Carlos. Where Iván is cool and arrogant, his son, the stammering Carlos, is absolutely dominated by his girlfriend Marisa. But he takes after his father in his voracious appetite for women: making the most of Marisa's gazpacho-induced indisposition, he kisses the nearest female at every opportunity. His psychotic mother Lucía, whose fashion sense alone is cause for comedy, provides the ultimate in female hysteria, her incongruous hijacking of a motorcycle to track down and kill her ex-husband Iván, the last resort in her mad scheme of jealousy and revenge. The image of her, a psychopath in baby-girl pink with two pistols, is one of the most memorable in the film. Finally, there are two cameo roles which are comic gems. The doorwoman of Pepa's flat (played by veteran Spanish comic actress Chus Lampreave) is an exaggerated stereotype, a notorious busybody (as usual) but also, in a delightful comic twist, a Jehovah's Witness, a sect which proscribes lying and therefore obliges her to tell the whole truth no matter how much trouble it causes. Then there is the taxi driver (played by Willy Montesinos) who repeatedly picks Pepa up, eventually becoming a friend, who is an implausible (but not impossible) Madrid stereotype (i.e. over-friendly). His mambo taxi contains a little shop with products to buy or rent and a sticker which reads 'thanks for smoking' as well as an eclectic selection of music. His pursuit of Lucía's taxi is the first of several chase sequences. At their next meeting Pepa is upset and the amicably servile taxi driver cries too. In the final chase sequence he at last loses his composure, protesting that he is a taxi driver not a bounty hunter.

There are also moments of undiluted comic business in the film. When Pepa throws sleeping pills in the gazpacho she says, 'I'm sick and tired of being good', and then proceeds to throw matches on the bed, setting fire to it. And when Candela explains how she is in hiding from the police on account of the Shiite terrorists, there is a classic comic gag:

CANDELA: They will be looking for me as a collaborator and you too for not revealing them.
PEPA: Don't worry about me. I collaborate with whoever I like in my own home.

Similarly, Candela cannot resist an ironic stab at the poor stammering Carlos, who needs to make the quickest phonecall of his life:

CARLOS: They won't trace the call. I'll give the information very quickly.
CANDELA: Yes, as you're so good with words...

And later, drawing attention to the extreme farcical situation, when she is kissed by Carlos in the kitchen, she chides him, 'Carlos, for goodness' sake. With this scene, the police, your girlfriend, your mother. Aren't you scared they'll see us?'

Parody also serves the comedy in both subtle and exaggerated forms. The final car chase is a tribute to decades of comedy. Then there is the typical parody of the television advert, in this case 'the mother of the famous Cuatro caminos murderer' (see Chapter 3). *Women on the Verge* also contains melodramatic elements. The iconography in the title sequence (lipstick, roses, etc.) suggests a female world devoid of social problems. With the exception of Carlos, whose partial feminization is a virtue in a machismo-tainted society, the main characters are women who are victims of men. Indeed, the most important man, Iván (likened by Pepa to a terrorist) is characterized more by his absence than anything else (Cobos and Marías 1995: 141). The omniscient narration, which is Almodóvar's usual form, is particularly suited to a melodramatic story. For example, Pepa's secret (her pregnancy) is known to the viewers but to no one else, her opening monologue voice-over an invitation to hear her story, and the action which follows rather like a flashback. But much of the melodramatic genre is really put to work in the service of comedy and much of the comedy here is only melodrama pushed to an incongruous limit. For example, the chance encounters of melodrama become comic coincidence, the objects or paraphernalia of a bourgeois lifestyle – for example, Lucía's outlandish and out-moded costumes – become stylized high kitsch.

By the time of *Kika*, Almodóvar's comic vein is far more critical. The UK video cover for *Kika* describes the film as 'Brash, kinky, fun'. Critics and the public saw it as comedy, though in many ways this is Almodóvar's least generically stable comedy. Uneasily combining moments of melo-drama, crime thriller and even documentary (though this is grotesquely caricatured), the effect is to produce a disturbing comedy. The narrative is perhaps the least problematic element. The characters (lovers and ex-lovers, the bitter and scheming along with the happily naive) struggle against their passions and against one another until the contrived happy ending which sees bad guys (Andrea and Nick) both dead at each other's hands, and protagonist Kika left with either the dubious prize of Ramón to go back to, or the distraction of the delicious Manuel Bandera.

Much of the humour is decidedly black, such as the scene where Kika goes to Nick's house thinking she is going to have sex, but ends up making up the seemingly dead Ramón. And in the central (and most controversial) rape scene, ex-boxer, ex-legionnaire and porn star prison escapee, Paul Bazzo (his star name, when uttered quickly in Spanish, sounds like 'Big Fuck'), goes straight to his sister Juana's house and rapes her employer Kika. The sequence, played for laughs, is one of the least successful in Almodóvar's work. The reason for the relative failure of this sequence may be the difficulty for the viewer in locating a target for the satirical humour.[16] Far from making light of rape, the film attempts to de-traumatize the rape itself, and relocate the trauma else-where. The whole sequence is set up as farce. Pablo arrives dressed in a plastic Groucho Marx wig and false nose. All his actions are those of a naive but predatory male animal. His brutishness is matched by his sister Juana whose plan for his escape involves him knocking her unconscious. He goes into Kika's room and is aroused by the sight of her on the bed. He removes his shirt to show off his muscles, but she sleeps on. Only when he cannot wake his sister for sex does he return to Kika's room. He manages to penetrate her without waking her. When

18. *Kika*. Andrea (Victoria Abril) waits for the scoop of her career.

she does wake her squeals are comic. She asks him, 'You are Paul Bazzo, aren't you?', and, ridiculously, they introduce themselves. A conversation ensues with Kika asking him about his problems and complaining about his drooling. She protests, 'One thing is a rape, another is keeping me here all day.' She even tries to help him towards climax with orgasmic-like squeals. After slapping him on the buttocks, the policemen finally prise Paul off Kika. In a final twist, Paul Bazzo's orgasm is reached as he masturbates over Kika's balcony, ejaculating on to the face of Andrea who is waiting for the scoop of her career, camera ready, at ground level [fig. 18]. Almodóvar has stressed Kika's refusal to be the victim as the reason for the understating of her trauma during and immediately after the rape scene: 'indifference, which in Andrea's case is a symptom of her cruelty, becomes with Kika an indication of her optimism, her sunny disposition' (Strauss 1996: 133). But that Kika finally breaks down when she sees the rape transmitted on television suggests the real target of Almodóvar's satire: the media coverage of sensational(ized) events. Kika is more traumatized by the sight of her ordeal on television than by the rape itself. What feminists have described as the 'metaphorical second rape' of the courtroom here becomes the 'post-violation violation' of media intrusion (Martín Márquez 1999: 36). The principal source of humour in *Kika* is satire of the excesses of the media, though much of it is so caustic (and so close to the truth, notwithstanding caricature) that it produces a wry smile rather than a giggle. The television show *The Worst of the Day* is among Almodóvar's most grotesque creations (see Chapter 3).

It is difficult to tell whether comedy is always a conscious strategy of Almodóvar's film-making or sometimes an instinctive humanizing reflex. Funny things do happen in life, of course, though verisimilitude would hardly be used by Almodóvar as justification for much of his work. None of the films is devoid of comedy altogether. And even where the exigencies of the plot do not demand it (or indeed may be more directly served without it), a space is found for comedy. Neale and Krutnik (1990: 18) point out that 'local forms responsible for the deliberate generation of laughter can be inserted at some point into most other generic contexts without disturbing their conventions'. In the later films (melodramas and thrillers), comedy is introduced by means of exclusively comic characters, who, while not essential to the plot, are perfectly integrated into it. But the comedy inserted into these later films acts like a balm, soothing the emotional tension in the principal characters. (Those who suffer are principal in Almodóvar.)

In *All About My Mother* the character of Agrado is an oasis of comedy in this most traumatic of films. Agrado is a half-operated transsexual and an old friend of protagonist Manuela. At one level she is a stereotypical transsexual: heavy make-up disguising a less than attractive appearance; an affected Andalusian accent frequently used in outrageous and mildly bitchy comments. When actor Mario asks her to give him a blow-job (ostensibly to relax him), she realizes it is the typical male curiosity about transsexuals and asks him if *he* is always being asked to give blow-jobs just because *he* has a penis [fig. 19]. But, far more than comic relief, Agrado is the exclusive custodian of both comedy and optimism in the film. When we first see her, despite her appearance (recently attacked by a client), she quickly recovers the wit that characterizes her throughout. When Huma and Nina are indisposed, Agrado takes to the stage to explain why the play has been cancelled. In a sublime episode, she offers those in the audience not in a position to exchange their tickets, the story of her life. But what follows is the story of her body and its relationship to plastic surgery and silicone. Part by part, she explains how much it has cost her, much to the

19. *All About My Mother*. Agrado (Antonia San Juan) with Mario (Carlos Lozano).

amusement of the theatre audience. But this theatrical price list culminates in a small piece of Agrado's own philosophy: 'The more you become like what you have dreamed for yourself, the more authentic you are.' This observation marks Agrado's essential function in the film: she provides a constancy of optimism towards which other characters, notably Manuela, have to work.

In *Flower*, the scenes involving Leo's mother and sister provide a diversion from the main storyline and the only true comedy in the film. Both characters are social stereotypes: Rosa is the long-suffering housewife with the added burden of an hysterical yet strong-willed mother. They are constantly arguing: about skinheads and yuppies (mother can't tell the difference); about fashions ('Your sister likes these chairs; as they are gold-coloured ... you'd think she was a gypsy').[17] The sequence also provides the opportunity for a typically scatological observation: mother is constipated and insists on using suppositories every day. Rosa comments, 'She wants to be shitting all the time.' The mother is stereotypically set in her ways, insisting that she will not be wearing her new dressing gown, as it is 'for a museum'. Once she begins her attack there is no stopping her: 'I can't do anything to please your sister; after lunch

20. *The Flower of My Secret*. Rosa (Rossy de Palma) argues with her mother
(Chus Lampreave).

when I doze off, there she is waking me – "get up, get up" – Christ,
what does she want me to do, aerobics?' Finally, the mother decides to
go back to her village, telling her elder daughter, of her younger one,
'she treats me like a dog' [fig. 20].

There are isolated comic incidents in many films, a reminder of the
transgressive elements which formed the bulk of the humour in the
earlier films. Often the comic impact of these brief comic asides is
greater because of the non-comedy generic context. Mick Eaton (1981:
25) affirms that the comic involves both a 'transgression of the familiar'
and a 'familiarization of the transgression'. Outside the comedy genre,
these comic elements are not familiarized, not expected, hence they are
potentially more poignant. Examples of such isolated transgressive
comedy include mildly shocking or outrageous touches such as the
candour with which Tina tells her young charge Ada in *Law of Desire*,
'How many wanks I have had within these walls!', referring to the chapel
in her former school; or the image of Lola sitting on a toilet in *Tie Me
Up!* accompanied by dramatic music.[18] When, in *Matador*, Ángel accuses
himself of raping a girl, the female police officer tells him 'some girls
have all the luck'. A similar moment of light relief is provided in *High*

Heels when, at the Villa Rosa, Letal asks for one of Becky's earrings as a souvenir. Manuel suggests Becky ask for a false breast in return. She holds up the item, exclaiming, 'Thanks for the tit, now I have three of them'. The opportunity for a gag or a joke paradoxically reinforces Almodóvar's particular brand of melodrama, providing a counterpoint to it or a means of release, as the following discussion will show.

Melodrama

> In its dictionary sense, melodrama is a dramatic narrative in which musical accompaniment marks the emotional effects. This is still perhaps the most useful definition, because it allows melodramatic elements to be seen as constituents of a system of punctuation, giving expressive color and chromatic contrast to the story line, by orchestrating the emotional ups and downs of the intrigue. (Elsaesser 1987: 50)

This definition of melodrama, from Thomas Elsaesser's seminal piece on the genre, could readily be applied to the cinema of Almodóvar as a whole, determining thus as melodrama his whole corpus. Certainly, Elsaesser's essential starting points, music and colour, are central to all Almodóvar's films. When some of the detail is added to the generic make-up of melodrama, this too confirms a strong presence in the Spanish director's work. Buckland (1998: 81) lists the following as 'primary attributes' of melodrama: women-dominated narratives, the perspective of the victim, moral conflicts, omniscient narration, twists and reversals, chance events and encounters, secrets and dramatic knots which complicate the plot. To these can be added the prevalence of flashbacks, which, according to Pam Cook (1985: 80), result from the need for dramatic action while remaining in the same place – hence the circularity of melodrama. All these narrative features of the genre are clearly present in much of Almodóvar's work.

Beyond this, less immediately apparent but just as decisive in melodrama, *mise-en-scène* plays its part. In classic Hollywood melodrama (Douglas Sirk being the most celebrated example), the *mise-en-scène* was made to work to compensate both for the limited length of the films (in contrast to melodramatic novels) and for all those topics which could not be directly expressed in them. The importance of *mise-en-scène* over dialogue means that sophisticated melodrama was, as Elsaesser

(1987: 52) puts it, 'the most highly elaborated, complex mode of cinematic signification that the American cinema has ever produced, because of the restricted scope for external action determined by the subject, and because everything, as Sirk said, happens "inside"'. One of the consequences of this is that objects take on meaning as visual metaphors. Elsaesser (1987: 62) takes the example of Claudette Colbert looking at and touching objects she had just used with her now departed husband in John Cromwell's *Since You Went Away* (1944). In Almodóvar, an equivalent is the new meaning the objects in her flat take on for Gloria at the end of *What Have I Done* now that she no longer shares these with her family. The importance of objects in the *mise-en-scène* in Almodóvar is discussed in Chapter 8.

Almodóvar has stated that if anything requires artifice and elaboration, it is melodrama (Cobos and Marías 1995: 139). Geoffrey Nowell-Smith (1977: 117) refers to melodramatic *mise-en-scène* as 'excess': a surplus of music, colour and movement, which compensates for what cannot be accepted in plot or dialogue. In Almodóvar's cinema, almost entirely freed from such socially inscribed or industrial constraints, the excess in *mise-en-scène* combines with a more general overdetermination which borders on self-consciousness and parody. Mulvey (1989: 46) writes about Sirk and Fassbinder, 'both brought to the cinema a sense of theatrical distanciation (drama as spectacle) that works against the tendency of the film to absorb the spectator into itself', an affirmation equally applicable to Almodóvar, as the following analysis shows. However, while Fassbinder insisted that his highly stylized melodrama did not amount to parody (Waugh 2000: 55), Almodóvar frequently permits and even encourages a parodic reading.

Regarded by many as Almodóvar's best film, *All About My Mother* taps into melodrama's richest vein. The content is certainly that of a melodrama: a mother loses her son and goes in search of the long-lost father to inform him; the father is a transsexual, a drug addict and HIV-positive; in her search she encounters old and new friends who quickly grow to need her. The characters are almost all female, victims of circumstance, of the men in their lives, their dramas involve the moral conflicts typical of the genre: for Manuela, to follow her dead son's donated organs in a desperate attempt to be close to him, then to determine to let the father know, despite the certain pain of a reunion; for Agrado, to give up prostitution; for Nina, to give up drugs; for Huma, to give up Nina; for Rosa, to give birth to a baby who will be

HIV-positive like her; and for Rosa's mother, to accept or reject the baby. The secrets these women keep testify to their strength; once again Almodóvar is demonstrating his admiration for women.

The story unfolds using simple linear time (one event after another in chronological order) and omniscient narration. There are only two flashbacks, justified diegetically: Manuela, on returning to the performance of Tennessee Williams's *A Streetcar Named Desire* which she had seen with her son the night he was killed, has a visual memory of him as he was waiting for her on the night of the play; and when she tells actress Huma about her son, Huma also recalls the night, and remembers seeing the boy's face through the taxi window asking her for an autograph. The story is dependent on coincidences and sudden twists or reversals, as is the case in classic melodrama. It is chance that brings Rosa into contact with Esteban-Lola, so that she ends up having his second child (his first being Manuela's dead son). Coincidence also brings Manuela into contact with Huma and Nina, a meeting which changes all their lives. In another stroke of melodramatic fate, Rosa dies in childbirth, leaving Manuela to bring up the second child of her husband, now dead. The circularity of the story (Manuela loses one Esteban and gains another) is not gratuitous. For this is a subtly but none the less consistently crafted film, artistically wrought, and self-conscious in the established almodovarian manner. The *mise-en-scène* and visual style of the film have all the qualities which enabled Sirk to say so much more than the plotlines of his films could say: in particular, they demonstrate the expressive power of what Elsaesser (1987: 53) refers to as 'the contrasting emotional qualities of textures and materials'. (See also Chapter 8 on visual style.) But where Sirk's *mise-en-scène* and visuals are essential compensatory functions of his art (making up for what could not be said directly), in Almodóvar this richness in texture combines with a freedom to be sensational (especially in language). The result is close to rhetorical self-consciousness, but not quite as close as in films like *Law of Desire* or *High Heels*. Even the location of much of the action in the domain of the theatre (so common in melodrama) never allows slippage into theatrical distanciation or parody. This is probably in part due to the earnestness of the drama: the loss of a child is part of society's mythology of traumas and thus comprehensible to all. But the masterful insertion of a comic catharsis in the figure of Agrado (see above) also plays a part.

In *Flower* also, the melodrama is complemented by discrete comic episodes involving secondary characters which are not unlike the traditional comic roles often assigned to the servants in bourgeois Hollywood melodrama. And, a constant in Almodóvar, the measured excess which characterizes classic melodrama is taken just beyond its limit of generic verisimilitude to become, at times, somewhat self-conscious, too melodramatic.[19] This is true of the film's narrative image: the title reads like a pulp romantic novel; the poster, with its heart of roses and typewriter, alludes to the themes of the film and to its style. Almodóvar has suggested that *Flower* even has the structure of a novel, and that originally the 'chapters' had individual titles (Strauss 1996: 162). All the classic elements of melodrama are here: the omniscient narration follows Leo's emotional trajectory from hope to despair and then, finally, the beginnings of recovery; the musical accompaniment is very pronounced in this film (see Chapter 9); the action concentrates on emotionally motivated actions and reactions. From the start Leo is portrayed as a victim. She has no one to help her take off her boots, and Betty tells her 'you can't go on being so fragile'. The emotional force of Leo's abandonment is expertly depicted in key moments of painful recognition. When Leo calls Paco in Brussels to tell him about her invitation to write for *El País*, her excitement is interpreted by Paco as alcohol-induced – this lack of understanding on Paco's part is deflating and cruel; and when Leo talks to Paco about her feeling of abandonment he leaves the room and she goes on talking unaware. Leo responds with a gesture of anger, projecting her momentary hate on to a portrait of her husband which she throws on the floor, the marbles in its frame scattering. The use of slow motion for this action draws attention to the pent-up anger released like the marbles in a perfect example of the visual metaphors which populate classic melodrama. There are two further examples of this: Leo's boots, given to her by Paco, which she is unable to take off, she herself interprets as a metaphor for her obstinate love for her husband; and when Paco returns for his two-hour home visit, Leo follows him into the bathroom and watches him through the shower curtain, until he realizes and turns away (anticipating his abandonment of her).

Leo has a degree of self-awareness: she is, after all, a writer of melodrama. She tells Ángel (who has asked her to write a piece attacking sentimental novelist Amanda Gris), 'I don't want to write against anything. There are enough negative things in my life.' Of course, the viewers know 'the flower of her secret', that *she* is Amanda Gris. Leo also knows she has a problem with alcohol, remarking, 'If I keep drinking I will end up in alcoholics anonymous [...] except drinking how difficult everything is.' Leo drinks when things don't go her way, for example, when she cannot remove her resistant boots, or before her interview with Ángel. When Leo plagiarizes Djuna Barnes's phrase, 'you have before you a woman created for anxiety', she is, of course, writing about herself as much as her character. And it is one of Almodóvar's authorial quirks that a melodramatic story-teller should be framed in a melodrama of her own life. As if to reconfirm the 'melodrama within melodrama', Almodóvar chooses to begin the film with what first appears to be a mini soap opera – the contemporary small-screen incarnation of melodrama. Doctors inform a mother that her son has died. The themes (family situation, moral conflict, female victim, chance event) all indicate soap opera and it is filmed on video. The mother's performance is also like soap and her family background too: her husband is dead and her mother-in-law is a problem for her. Even here, Almodóvar cannot resist the temptation to destabilize genre expectations. This sequence is not a soap opera, but an educational simulation to train doctors in the art of breaking bad news to relatives before asking for organ donations. The acting is made explicit. There is a list of common feelings: sadness, anger, pain, impotence, relief, solitude, a list which reads like the emotions of a melodramatic plot. Nurse-cum-actress Manuela even asks the psychologist Betty if her acting was 'over-sentimental'. This little melodramatic simulation later became the departure point for arguably Almodóvar's finest melodrama, *All About My Mother* (see above).

A more hybrid genre product, *High Heels* (more accurately translated as 'Distant Heels') has much melodrama about it, though its composite narrative image (the poster image of a high-heeled shoe which is also a gun) testifies to the combination of two genres, melodrama and crime thriller.[20] The themes are typical of melodrama: family relations dominate the storyline as do relationships between men and women. The narrative charts the reuniting of a long-absent mother with her daughter and their competition over men (one man in particular) and over professional success. All the characters have secrets that the viewers know. The omniscient narration, typical of melodrama, allows suspense only in terms of how other characters react to revelations the viewer anticipates. Thus, Becky conceals her heart condition from her daughter, Rebeca conceals the truth about murdering her husband, and the Judge conceals his triple identity as Femme Letal, Hugo and the investigator. Where necessary, the narrative resorts to flashbacks to fill in essential details. When Becky and Manuel see each other again after many years, there is a brief flashback of their time as lovers in Mexico. At the very start of the film, a flashback shows Rebeca's relationship to her mother and stepfather, her resentment of the stepfather, her desire to see her mother happy and how she killed her stepfather to liberate her mother from his tyranny. This same scene is replayed as Rebeca narrates the truth about this murder to Becky at one of the film's dramatic climaxes. This scene of confrontation is perfect melodrama, the iconography of the court-room for the exposing of the truth, and the reference to *Autumn Sonata*, combining to produce one of Almodóvar's most powerful melodramatic scenes. The ending – Becky's sacrifice for her daughter's liberty – is also melodramatic in the extreme.[21] Also typical of melodrama, objects embody particular memories, such as the earrings which Rebeca puts on as she awaits her mother's return, earrings given to her by Becky some twenty years earlier. When they are reunited, Becky does not make the same connection, forgetting the origin of the earrings or, as Smith (1994: 124) expresses it, more melodramatically, she 'fails to validate her daughter's memory'.

On occasions, the narrative departs from melodrama. The unhappy ending is explained by the auteur's will for a satisfyingly credible ending (as opposed to the model of Hollywood melodrama where the studio might well have demanded a happy resolution). Thirty-five minutes into the film there is a murder, which destabilizes the genre: but the murder investigation does not turn the film into an investigative narrative for several reasons. First, there is no real restricted narration, despite the fact that we do not see the crime committed; instead, the omniscient narration of melodrama is retained, and the narrative follows Rebeca and Becky not the crime investigator, Domínguez. We know that Letal is the Judge and that Rebeca probably killed her husband. But, moreover, the crime genre is undermined by subtle parody and comic deflation. Immediately after the murder of Manuel, the investigators at the scene of the crime argue about the minutiae of every forensic detail. The investigative role of Judge Domínguez is further undermined by the fact that his motivation is love for the murderess Rebeca rather than solving the crime. Rebeca's television confession is beyond the limits of either external or generic verisimilitude. And at what could be the most poignant of moments, as an ambulance takes the dying Becky home, she hears that her daughter did kill Manuel and coolly tells her, 'You have to learn to solve your problems with men in some other way.' At times, Becky's melodramatic performance mode is so evident that her daughter Rebeca draws attention to it – 'stop putting on an act' – foregrounding and thereby deflating melodrama.

Hybridity and Intertextuality

Almodóvar's preferred generic location is somewhere on the scale between comedy and melodrama, most of his films having elements of both. The transitional films *Dark Habits* and *What Have I Done* are the most finely balanced between comedy and melodrama. *Dark Habits*, Almodóvar's third film, is the first to combine a strong element of comedy with burgeoning melodrama, indicating a way forward for the director's work after the first two pop comedies. The film's narrative image suggests generic hybridity: the title is decidedly dark but the poster (a tiger dressed as a nun, a cabaret singer and a heart pierced by syringes) suggests comedy. Typically, for comedy, the narrative is pushed forward by both coincidence and the scheming of the characters. But, critically, there is no happy ending. All the nuns but one leave and the Mother Superior is abandoned by Yolanda just like all the other 're-deemed' girls. In fact, the ending is Almodóvar's bleakest. The director relates how the original ending had Yolanda with Tarzan (the Marquesa's grandson) in a swimming pool, but that Julieta Serrano's final scream impressed him so much he decided to end it there (Vidal 1988: 93). Nevertheless, there is ample comedy in the form of character quirks, caricature, and gags. (On the film's satirization of institutionalized religion, see Chapter 2.) While the convent location and the individual eccentricities of the nuns constantly edge the film towards absurd comedy, if these elements were removed, the remaining drama of relationships has much melodramatic potential. Yolanda is a victim (though perhaps a willing one), and her flight from the guilty secret of boyfriend Jorge's death precipitates the action. As is common with melodrama, females dominate the film (here, unusually, at the expense of male characters altogether). Tensions in the convent are like those in a family, and the mission of the convent can be seen as a projection of the needs of the family unit into a space which normally excludes families, Almodóvar reinscribing the conventions of family melodrama in a somewhat incongruous context. There even exists a moral conflict, frequent in classic melodrama but usually absent in Almodóvar: a conflict based on the interpretation of religion as discipline and hierarchy, or the personal (and highly suspect in the case of the Mother Superior) interpretation as the charitable provision of shelter for 'immoral' women.[22]

Other melodramatic features include the ubiquitous mobile camera which follows Yolanda from the start, and its concomitant omniscient narration, and the flashbacks such as the one narrating Yolanda's meeting with the Mother Superior in the nightclub. The title music is perhaps the most melodramatic of any of the films. The opening instrumental bars of 'Encadenados' which is used for a panning shot that shows the viewer the room previously occupied by Virginia (which looks like the bourgeois interior of classical melodrama), also fits the melodramatic tone, though the rendition of the song itself, sung by Yolanda and the Mother Superior, is perhaps not subtle enough for melodrama, being too self-consciously contrived. This is in keeping with Almodóvar's prevalent mode of near-parody, revealed in too-melodramatic lines like the Mother Superior's 'my only sin is loving you too much', or the incredible story of Virginia (a novice who entered the convent after her boyfriend killed himself, and then left the convent for Africa where she was eaten by cannibals). The austerity of the convent – not immediately obvious as the locus for melodrama – is compensated for by a home-made urban jungle. Nuria Triana illustrates the symbolic function of this savage garden:

> Here typical melodramatic excess is represented by a wild garden, a point of religious symbolism at the centre of this non-religious order. This paradise/jungle re-created by Almodóvar is not based on realistic memories but rather on the exaggerated exuberance of Hollywood's constructed settings. [...] Its function is purely melodramatic and symbolic, heightening the emotions and reinforcing the idea of the characters' 'untamed' natures, the aura of the nuns themselves. (Triana Toribio 1996: 182)

What Have I Done, Almodóvar's fourth feature film, is an unusual (and successful) amalgamation of diverse and normally incompatible genres: it layers both absurd comedy and melodrama on to what can justifiably be described as neorealism. Indeed, Almodóvar himself describes the film as 'my Italian film, par excellence' (Cobos and Marías 1995: 134), though elsewhere he adds that it is neorealist in intention not in execution, 80 per cent of it filmed in studios rather than out on the streets as the Italians did it (Vidal 1988: 118). The narrative image suggests comedy; the title the sardonic; the poster (a small Gloria superimposed on to a background of the blocks of flats, and with the lizard, Dinero, superimposed over her figure) alludes to the comic and the absurd. The narrative is structured around the journey of housewife Gloria from desperately overstretched wife and mother, who gives away one son, and accidentally kills her husband, to freedom and solitude (until her youngest son returns to look after her at the very end). Even the relatively happy ending is unable to compensate for the extreme material and emotional poverty which characterizes Gloria's life before. Moreover, unlike in mainstream comedy where the cause and effect chain begins with either human actions or pure coincidence, here narrative causality is dispensed with altogether: Gloria's life is ruled almost as if by an immovable fate. Causality is, of course, further subverted by the absurd, unexplained telekinesis of Vanesa. And a further contributor to this obscuring of causality is the narrative dispersion inherent in a sub-plot about forged Hitler diaries which even Almodóvar admits does not quite work.[23]

Unsurprisingly for Almodóvar's most socially conscious film, much of the humour derives from social observation, either by simple satire or by more typically almodovarian transgression. The film begins with an unexpected and uneventful sexual encounter, as Gloria is enticed into the shower by a policeman who is in fact impotent. This is the first of many frustrations for Gloria who seeks respite for her burdened existence everywhere and never finds it. To underscore her frustration, her neighbour, the prostitute Cristal, is totally uninhibited. Nowhere is this juxtaposition more evident than in the scene where Cristal asks Gloria to sit and watch an exhibitionist make love to her. Curling tongs in hand, and still wearing her coat, Gloria sits next to the exhibitionist as he tries in vain to impress Cristal. The whole scene is virtuoso satire and transgression at the same time. The exhibitionist, in an exaggerated and absurd display of insecurity, draws attention to his physical weaknesses, but suggests his penis compensates for the rest. He fails none the less to have much effect on prostitute Cristal. The element of transgression inherent in the breaking of taboos in his monologue can also be seen as satire on the newly sexually liberated Spain: 'Each time my glans enters a woman's vagina I destroy her. That's why I have to go with prostitutes who have bigger pussies because they use them more.' The same theme of excessive sexual licence is caricatured in the figure of the dentist who has an unhealthy interest in young boys and proposes to 'adopt' Gloria's son, Miguel. Cristal, too, is a stereotype: the kindly, naive prostitute with dreams of going to America to become famous. Much of the comedy in the film derives from the character of the grandmother, also a stereotype. We first see her offering to help her grandson Toni with his homework, in fact giving him all the wrong answers. He asks her whether a list of writers are romantic or realist:

GRANDMOTHER: How's the homework coming?

TONI: The worst...

GRANDMOTHER: Well, look – I'm going to help you.

TONI: OK, tell me which of these writers are romantic and which are realist...Ibsen.

GRANDMOTHER: Romantic.

TONI: Lord Byron.

GRANDMOTHER: Realist.

TONI: Goethe.

GRANDMOTHER: Also realist.

TONI: Balzac.

GRANDMOTHER: Romantic. Isn't it easy?

She also offers expert advice on the properties of the saints and comments that her son's feet smell as strongly as her husband's did. Then there are examples of absurd humour, such as Gloria killing her husband with a ham bone, the inspector referring to the lizard as the only witness to the crime and an appearance of Almodóvar himself in a television spoof of the Miguel de Molina song 'Bien pagá' (Well Paid).[24] The scene's first shot shows television cameras with no attempt to hide the machinery of production. There is a certain amount of self-conscious indulgence here (Almodóvar performs alongside his best friend and drinking partner, Fabio McNamara), but the scene is also integrated ironically into the story of the desperate housewife Gloria. She certainly is not '*la bien pagá*' (well paid) for her efforts to make ends meet. But the contextualization of the television performance raises other questions, as pointed out by Rosanna Maule:

In placing his parody of Spanish popular culture and reception from within a popular medium (television) and in popular re-interpretations of popular genres (the cabaret parody of a love song), Almodóvar demystifies not only the identification of authorship with high culture and tradition, but also its postmodern appropriation as an item of commercial consumption. (Maule 1998: 127)

Among the film's more melodramatic elements are the omniscient narration, female protagonist, the domestic sphere and moral conflicts (how to survive while retaining some decency and self-respect). For much of the time, Gloria is too concerned with survival to devote time to her emotional life (thus, the main 'hysterical' content of melodrama is impossible). The melodramatic discourse around maternal sacrifice is characteristically ambivalent: 'there is an ironic slippage between the altruistic act of maternal self-sacrifice in its most characteristic movie form and Gloria's more venal desire for a curling iron, but this subversion works against the sentimentalizing tendencies of the traditional maternal melodrama' (Vernon 1995: 67–8).

There are moments when melodrama takes over completely, such as that when Gloria is refused pills in the pharmacy: her outburst to the cold chemist's assistant is followed by a shot of her walking across an empty park in front of her flat, the opening of the sentimental German song 'Nur nicht aus Liebe Weinen' (Don't Cry Over Love) by Zarah Leander accompanying her desperation. The German ballad is reminiscent of Fassbinder and his sometimes eccentric, self-conscious use of music. Like Fassbinder, Almodóvar has taken melodrama 'outside the confines of the bourgeoisie', as Mulvey (1989: 45) puts it, but more than this, melodrama is completely infiltrated by a peculiar brand of (social) realism mixed with satirical (and at times surreal) comedy.[25] In the remainder of the films, *Law of Desire*, *Tie Me Up!*, *Live Flesh* and *Matador*, the genre base – which is then combined with other generic elements – is the crime film/thriller.

Theoretical discussion of the thriller, and associated crime film genres such as the detective film, focuses on the iconography of the genres, and, most importantly, on narrative structuring. The narrative patterns operating in these genres are limited in number: their purpose is to allow the viewer to figure out the *fabula* (story) by means of the *syuzhet* (narrative sequence in film), and therefore too many paradigmatic choices would hamper the recognition of familiar patterns. This rigidity – the institutionalization of generic conventions – is too limiting for Almodóvar. His instinct is not to respect conventions but to flout them. In this, he is in good company, for most renowned Hollywood directors worked in genre films, nevertheless leaving their personal imprint on the movies and often subtly changing the genres themselves. The most interesting aspect of Almodóvar's utilization of crime genre elements is their degree of departure from generic conventions. Where Almodóvar is comfortable with much of what classic melodrama has to offer, he is more radical in what he borrows and what he rejects from crime genres. He critically departs from the convention of crime genres in privileging the human motivation for crime over its investigation. Psychologist Julia (Carmen Maura) aptly expresses this in *Matador*: 'You're only interested in whether or not he killed. You don't care about his reasons.' There is, of course, a tradition in classic Hollywood which exploits the melodrama in crime. Michael Curtiz's *Mildred Pierce* (1945) is a good example of a crime framework largely serving melodrama. Curtiz's genre hybrid is also one of the movies to which Almodóvar makes visual reference, intertextuality becoming another means by which genres are cross-referenced and combined.

Almost an hour passes in *Law of Desire* before the crime – Juan's murder at the hands of Antonio – is committed. The first fifty minutes of the film amount to melodrama with much more emphasis on human motivation – in the case of Antonio, jealousy – provoking the murder than on the crime itself. Even after the crime is committed, the narration continues to be omniscient, which works against the enigma–resolution pattern typical of restricted narration crime fiction. The viewer sees the murder so the investigation does not provoke curiosity about the culprit. The film's thriller element derives from suspense about whether Antonio will be caught or whether the initial murder will unleash further violence. In an unexpected twist, it emerges that Antonio has picked up Tina, which causes suspense (Pablo guesses he is armed and knows already that he is desperate enough to kill) and this suspense continues until Antonio shoots himself at the end of the film. There is much appropriation of thriller themes and iconography. But the thematic material of crime is adapted to Almodóvar's hybrid of passionate romance, melodrama and suspense thriller. Pablo's amnesia is pure melodrama (almost soap opera). Antonio is obsessed with Pablo and when we first see him at the nightclub he is holding a shotgun, practising his shot in an arcade game. His last action in the film also involves a gun, turned on himself. The police figure heavily, but the investigation is like another element of iconography rather than a structuring device of the narrative. In the climactic scene, Antonio takes Tina and a policeman as hostages and demands an hour to negotiate with Pablo. In a classic crime thriller this time would be for making criminal demands (money, time to escape, etc.). Instead, the negotiation is Antonio's last desperate attempt to prove his love for Pablo. The crime-coded scenario (hostage-taking) is disturbed by the infiltration of melodrama, and the masculine-coded violence associated with crime is replaced by homosexual love. Kinder suggests that Pablo almost consciously wills a melodramatic ending to his story. In her words, 'he stops trying to manipulate the plot and concentrates instead on the mise-en-scène' (Kinder 1993: 249).

While murder and its consequences constitute the pivotal narrative moment of *Law of Desire*, melodrama is its mode of address. On three separate occasions in the film, transsexual protagonist Tina claims that three different things are all she has left: first, she claims, 'I have had to pay too high a price for those failures. They are all I have'; she later tells her brother, 'You are all I have'; and then again, 'Memories are all I have left.' Tina is melodrama personified. When Pablo questions her about what she plans to do, she responds, 'Cry until I am too tired to cry any more.' At her amnesiac brother Pablo's bedside, she endeavours to tell him their family backstory. The melodramatic mode of Tina's story is clearly shown to be the result of a melodramatic life, though its content is well beyond what would be acceptable in classic Hollywood melo-dramas. (It comprises Tina's incest and eventual elopement with her father, her sex change, abandonment, meeting with her long-lost brother at their mother's funeral and so on.) In her self-conscious femininity, Tina is also an exaggeration (almost a parody) of the female victim. Pablo, too, represents the victim, his predicament described during his last night with Juan: 'It's not your fault that you aren't in love with me and it's not my fault that I'm in love with you.' The relationship between Pablo and his sister Tina is at least as important as the sexual relationships in the film, thus preserving the centrality of the family (a melodramatic paradigm), despite the non-standard family unit represented by Tina, little Ada and Pablo. Other melodramatic features include chance en-counters such as Antonio meeting Tina, the letters and phonecalls which are the stuff of melodrama, and the secrets, like Pablo's invented character Laura P., and Antonio's hidden sexuality. The traditional excess in *mise-en-scène* (compensating for lack of physical movement) is amply illustrated by such sequences as the now classic scene where Tina asks a street cleaner to hose her down fully clothed. Almost equal in spectacle to this is the stage rendition of 'Ne me quittes pas' and the explicit meta-

drama of Cocteau's *La voix humaine*, staged by Pablo. The stage environment itself is also reminiscent of classic melodrama like Sirk's *All I Desire*
(1953) and *Imitation of Life* (1959). Also self-consciously cinematic is
Pablo's admitted fetish for Juan's motorbike, which he caresses, remarking, 'It belongs to a friend who is leaving tomorrow. I'd like to keep it
as a fetish.' And Pablo's script entitled 'Laura P.' is a parody of melodrama:
in the script, Laura has her leg cut off after breaking her ankle in an
attempt to make her lover feel guilty.

Almodóvar's most controversial film, *Tie Me Up!*, is another hybrid.
Its narrative image sits precariously between erotic comedy and pornography. One of the publicity stills shows Victoria Abril on her knees in
a provocatively short dress. The English title seems designed to lighten
the pornographic suggestion (a sensible strategy in view of the film's
eventual and much-criticized X rating in the USA). Rather than the
iconography of crime, the film plays with that of pornography (rope,
gags, etc.). Despite the equivocal narrative image, the film is actually
a suspense thriller with a highly provocative resolution. The narrative
suspense (aided by Morricone's thriller music) is created by Ricky stalking
Marina's flat and then gaining entry. The violence of this first encounter
sets up expectations about the kidnapping and whether Marina will be
able to escape. The tension builds to a climax which, though prepared
for, is none the less disturbing. Ricky's plan to kidnap Marina so that
she may get to know him and fall in love with him is fulfilled. This
tension is built up through a series of episodes where expectation is
introduced and then frustrated: when Marina and Ricky go to her doctor
and she nearly has the chance to escape; when Marina pretends to be
asleep and tries to grab Ricky's keys; when Lola calls but Marina is
unable to make herself heard and cry for help. Then on Lola's final visit
they are nearly discovered. Only when Lola forgets her radiocassette
does she return and find Marina tied up – the twist being that now she
is no longer sure she wants to be rescued. As they flee the suspense
derives from the fact that we know Ricky is about to return. In terms
of narrative perspective, once again, the viewer is in a privileged position
of omniscience, which means that suspense is not of the enigma and
resolution pattern, but the emphasis is again placed on the characters
and how they will react to their circumstances.

The same is true for *Live Flesh*, the narrative of which begins and
ends with the firing of guns, and this framing of the story in crime
marks an otherwise melodramatic tale of love, sex and betrayal. Much

of the rest of film is about the passionate relationships between the five main characters. The iconography of crime is introduced immediately through policemen David and Sancho and their paraphernalia (squad car, walkie-talkie, guns). The introduction of the television screening of Buñuel's *Ensayo de un crimen* (1955) provides an opportunity for crime genre self-reference. The accidental shot in Elena's flat is confused with the shot in the film, blurring the boundaries between crime fiction and real violence. Subsequently, the image of the two policeman with their guns silhouetted against the stair wall in a pose which is a parody of crime genres, further adds to the genre self-consciousness. In narrative terms, the equilibrium is upset by Elena pulling a gun on Víctor; her overreaction starts a chain of dramatic events (though chance plays a large part). Once again character provides the motivation for action, focusing on the causes not on the investigation of truth. Víctor and Sancho's struggle with the gun is an example of suspense: we know something dramatic is going to happen (David is shot and paralysed). Then the action jumps to four years later. The viewer's next task is to fill in the immediate past; we see David in a wheelchair and Víctor in prison. Half an hour into the film, the perpetrator of the crime is (apparently) known and no investigation is necessary. As the viewer apparently knows what happened and why, the suspense derives from expectations about what will happen next, and how the characters will react. Once again this is as much the stuff of melodrama as of crime thrillers. But then there is an unexpected disclosure: Víctor tells David that it was Sancho who shot him out of jealousy and not Víctor. By then, sexual passions and jealousy have given the action an unstoppable momentum. The suspense climax begins when David tells Sancho that Víctor is having sex with Clara, and Sancho goes off to kill him, and it lasts until Sancho and Clara shoot each other.

Live Flesh is an adaptation of the eponymous novel by popular British crime author Ruth Rendell. Some elements are almost perfectly transposed: the garage which contains the furniture that represents Víctor's past becomes the dilapidated prefabricated house in La Ventilla; both in the novel and the film, David clasps at the banister as he is shot down by Víctor's bullet. Beyond these parallels, the way in which Almodóvar adapts Rendell's novel says much about Almodóvar's attitude to genre and to his characters. Where the crime novelist subjugates her characters to the needs of the plot, Almodóvar gives full integrity to his characters at the expense of generic integrity. Even the title is given a markedly different interpretation. Rendell's live flesh – Chorea, a medical twitch, and a metaphor for Victor Jenner's psychosis – becomes a metaphor for weak and easily tempted flesh in Almodóvar. Rendell makes Victor virtually a psychopath; he deludes himself that he was provoked by David's insistence that the gun was a fake. Almodóvar makes Víctor truly a victim of circumstance; Sancho (a crucial third party) is the real culprit of the shooting, thus giving a much more rational revenge motive for the crime. Also, where David Fleetwood is entirely innocent, Almodóvar's David professes himself responsible not only for the later massacre in La Ventilla but also for the shooting at the start of the film. Equally significant is the ending, 'happy' in Almodóvar with Elena and Víctor together, and David afforded at least a kind of anagnorisis. This is due to the fact that where Rendell is an essentially one-genre author (crime), Almodóvar is as ever a creator of hybrid products, hence the greater focus on the sexual passion between Víctor and Elena. In the novel David and Clare's acceptance of Victor into their lives is never really credible, where Almodóvar makes it much more so, since Víctor and Elena have at least already had sex (in a toilet), and Víctor is portrayed far more favourably. Where Clare describes Victor as somehow 'lovable', Almodóvar actually depicts Víctor as such.

Almodóvar also worked with a novelist (co-scriptwriter, Jesús Ferrero) in *Matador*. This film is simultaneously an erotic thriller, a horror film, a love story and an art film. This last category, though not a narrative or theme-related genre, is a film category consciously adopted by Almodóvar: the film is much more theoretical than the rest of Almodóvar's work. It offers a highly stylized version of a singular national mythology, which, though never aiming directly at verisimilitude, provides a sophisticated commentary on national identity (see Chapter 2). In Spain (where both the public and the critical environment can reasonably be assumed to be sensitive to its subtleties), the film benefited from government money, such was the perception of its worth to the national culture. Abroad it was understandably more slippery for critics and audiences expecting only comedy from Almodóvar. The *BFI Companion to Crime* (1997: 224) refers to *Matador* as a 'corrosive comedy thriller'. Paradoxically, it may well be his most studied as well as his most misunderstood creation. Both narrative image and title suggest stereotypically Spanish drama. But the sequence accompanying the opening credits is from horror films. After this a murder is committed, by a woman, and explicitly linked to sexual activity. We see murder and know who the murderess is, but her appearance is very different from when we see her later as a lawyer, thus delaying awareness of the perpetrator for some (less perceptive) viewers. The omniscient narration leaves only questions about possible links between the murder and ex-bullfighter Diego who appears in the next sequence. A further complication arises with Ángel's confession, as the viewer has not connected him with the crime committed. But Ángel recognizes María Cardenal when she comes to the prison to represent him, and it gradually becomes apparent that Ángel has seen María commit murder. Ángel's description of them is due to his visionary abilities (he witnesses the murders of the two girls by Diego and of the men by María). The irrational explanation for Ángel's false testimony subverts the traditionally solid and reliable causality in crime narrative. Psychologist Julia comments, 'There are things which escape reason and this is one of them.' As is typical in crime thrillers, the film's climax is a chase, but with the novelty of Ángel's visions guiding them.

Elsewhere, the subversion of the crime/thriller genre is more pronounced. Ángel accuses himself of rape and then confesses to the murders as well; but in the end, the inspector finds himself trying to prove Ángel's innocence rather than corroborate his guilt, to which Ángel's judgemental mother responds, 'A strange way of investigating, inspector.' When María tells Ángel, 'for the moment don't confess to any more murders. Four is more than enough', more than subtle comedy, there is a powerful retrospective irony operating; Ángel adds confession upon confession but is not guilty of any of the crimes. The police inspector, too, is a subversion of traditional genre conventions, though he is not comically incompetent. He does manage to discover María and Diego's guilt. What sets him apart from the conventional police inspector is his sexuality: crime inspectors are not gay in Hollywood films, and this man's small personal drama (he is in a hopeless relationship with a female psychologist) subtly detracts from his role as inspector. For example, when he first meets Ángel who confesses to raping Eva, the inspector is so fascinated by the young man that he asks if *he* was the victim of the rape and then begins his interrogation, 'tell me how you did it', an unusual angle for a supposedly disinterested investigator. The subtle subversion of genre extends even to the iconography of crime. Guns, for example, combine with the paraphernalia of *tauromaquia* and are explicitly converted into a sexual fetish. In her office, María threatens to kill herself, pointing the gun first at Diego then at herself, but when she is really ready to die, at the end of the film and with her dying lover still able to bring her to orgasm, she puts the gun in her mouth in a gesture which is unequivocally sexual.

Matador combines genre hybridity – the freedom to tell a story, wherever it leads, be it crime thriller, horror story, love story, even comedy – with film reference or intertextuality. The first scene includes video clips of scenes from horror B-movies, low-budget, sub-products by Italian, French and Spanish directors.[26] This masturbatory montage has been put together by the death-obsessed Diego to satisfy an erotic appetite which feeds on a mixture of sex and violence. These images reveal Diego's dangerous sexuality and his murderous inclinations, and their details prefigure the crimes he later perpetrates. Thus, while the instinct to kill is innate, murderous technique is apparently acquired from films. Later in the same film, Diego and María watch the end of *Duel in the Sun* (King Vidor, 1946), a film where the protagonists, played by Gregory Peck and Jennifer Jones, die in each other's arms at the end, a cinematic death which prefigures their own. Other film texts form an unusually rich part of Almodóvar's genre iconography.

Despite being self-taught, Almodóvar is a highly cine-literate director, largely due to an early diet of mainly Hollywood genre movies. Their influence is ever-present. Cinematic references within his films are sometimes no more than a casual mention, as in *Dark Habits*, where an amorous priest asks a nun to see *My Fair Lady* (George Cukor, 1964) with him, or at the end of *Labyrinth of Passions*, where Sexi tells her lover, 'We'll do it right here, just like in *Emmanuelle 1*', a reference to the soft porn film (Just Jaeckin, 1974). They can influence the actions of characters as in *Matador*, or in *What Have I Done*, where a visit to the movies to see the melodrama *Splendour in the Grass* (Elia Kazan, 1961) inspires the dreams of Toni and the grandmother to return to the countryside. Or they can consciously refer to other film-makers, as is the case in *Dark Habits*, where the resentful Mother Superior takes back the gift of a cake from the Marquesa, in a gesture reminiscent of Florence in *Le Charme discret de la bourgeoisie* (Luis Buñuel, 1972). Almodóvar sometimes pays homage ('theft' is his word for it) to his favourite films and directors.[27] He refers to Hitchcock and Bertolucci in his use of the psychological flashback to explain traumas originating in childhood. Critics and audiences alike noticed the homage to *Rear Window* in *Women on the Verge*. Celestino Deleyto explains its re-signification in a different genre context:

21. *Kika.* The 'wounded innocence' of Kika
(Verónica Forqué).

The parodic reference includes a case of transcontextualization, from suspense thriller to comedy, and a narrative reversal: *Rear Window* is the story of a man who, like the ideal spectator of a film, is more interested in what happens to others than in his own life [...] *Women on the Verge...* on the other hand, features a heroine who at first is only concerned by her unreciprocated passionate love for Iván, but who gradually learns to look at the world from the outside. (Deleyto 1995: 53–4)

At times, intertextuality takes the form of a visual quotation, which may be noticed only by film specialists. Near the beginning of *Tie Me*

Up!, the sanatorium director (played by Lola Cardona) lets the blinds of her office drop down as she looks out of the window while saying goodbye to Ricky, in a shot which is strongly reminiscent of *Mildred Pierce* where Mildred played by Joan Crawford does the same thing. Even the narrative situation is the same: both women have reluctantly said goodbye to men they were attached to. And the phrase uttered by Monty Barragon, 'account paid in full', is literally applicable to the situation between the sanatorium director and Ricky in *Tie Me Up!*

Often, these references are integrated into the narrative, even playing a key role in the plot. A good example is the use of *The Prowler* (Joseph Losey, 1951) in *Kika*. In the clip from the Hollywood film, which Ramón watches on television, a security guard shoots himself to make murder look like self-defence. This reveals to Ramón the manner of his mother's death at the hands of his stepfather. To acknowledge the cinematic inspiration of this revelation, Ramón's vision of the truth is seen in black and white, as close as possible to the borrowed crime film, *The Prowler*. Narrative interdependence, strongest here and in *All About My Mother*, provides the clearest example of Almodóvar's reliance on Hollywood genres, a feature which differentiates him from many other European and especially Spanish directors. Hollywood – its movies, stars and icons – are his frame of reference, his way of talking about films. He speaks about the character of Kika, played by Verónica Forqué [fig. 21], in terms of the 'wounded innocence' of Marilyn Monroe (Strauss 1996: 10), and the same eternal star features in the film *Law of Desire* where protagonist Tina has set up an altar with figures of Marilyn and photos of Elizabeth Taylor alongside the Virgin and other religious paraphernalia. Cinema is comparable to a religion for Almodóvar.

8

Visual Style

Many film-goers will think of the glossy and colourful visuals of films such as *Women on the Verge* or *High Heels* when asked about the style of Almodóvar films. In fact, the films are more varied in visual style, and there is a clear process of development in technique, as well as certain recurrent motifs. (Among these are objects, designer décor, the colour red, framing and mirrors.) Film-making is, of course, a collective enterprise, and Almodóvar has plenty of expert support from directors of photography (Paco Femenia, Ángel Luis Fernández, José Luis Alcaine, Alfredo Mayo, Affonso Beato), from his editor Pepe Salcedo, and from a range of designers, sound engineers and many others. Nevertheless, Almodóvar's own attention to detail approaches control freakery. Publicity stills often show him behind the camera [fig. 22]; many of the objects featured in the films are bought by him on his travels, and his first script analysis with the chosen actors often features Almodóvar as the voice and actor of every character.[1] This artistic omniscience may well be a product of Almodóvar's apprentice-ship as a self-taught film-maker, keen to learn everything about the craft. The earlier films are a fascinating testimony to this learning process.

The Camera: Learning to Manipulate

The visual style of a film comprises more than merely aesthetic decisions. Many of the choices open to a director also affect characterization, narrative development, the degree of omniscience or subjective authorial

22. Almodóvar with the camera on location in
Barcelona.

comment of the narrator, and the film's tone. Thus, as Katz (1991: 106)
sets out, the visual or graphic decision as to where the camera is stationed
corresponds to the narrative question about whose point of view is
represented; the size of the shot equates to the viewer's distance (physical
and figurative) from the subject; and the angle of view determines our
relationship and attitude to the subject. Marshalling such technique in
the service of narrative and characterization was an intuitive priority for
Almodóvar. In the camera and in the editing suite, the decisions made
about cutting or moving the camera determine whether we are com-
paring points of view (cutting can show different angles, or points of
view on the same subject), and how we perceive time (cutting can

indicate time moving ahead or suggest simultaneity). In editing, the earlier films show a certain naiveté, when compared with Almodóvar's more assured mature work. The degree of subjectivity is also related to a film's visuals: an objective perspective is generally associated with longshots, deep focus and a static camera, while subjective shots are more likely to be close-ups in shallow focus and/or with a moving camera. A crane shot, apart from being expensive, is not analogous to normal experience, and is therefore self-consciously cinematic.

In Almodóvar's work, the balance of the composite visual elements differs from one film to the next. The earliest films experiment with the camera, with lighting, location shooting, *mise-en-scène* and editing in roughly equal measure, the novice director perfecting his craft. By *Dark Habits*, aesthetic considerations supplement the needs of the narrative and so camerawork and *mise-en-scène* are mobilized to a larger degree than in the two preceding films. In the highly stylized, almost pictorial *Matador*, *mise-en-scène* and, above all, colour dominate the visual style. From *Tie Me Up!* through to *Kika*, the use of the camera is much less experimental but the *mise-en-scène* engages conventional genre associations to a greater degree than in the other films. Visual masterpieces all three, *Flower*, *Live Flesh* and *All About My Mother* nevertheless differ in their balancing of visual elements: where the consistently melodramatic *Flower* favours *mise-en-scène* (in keeping with the genre's tradition), both *Live Flesh* and *All About My Mother* exploit the versatility of the camera (mobile and imaginatively varied) to seek out the intimate suffering and joys of their protagonists. While in many ways Almodóvar's imaginative conception of narrative and characterization have proved consistent (and even suffered something of a temporary lapse after *Women on the Verge*), his directing skills have improved consistently since his early apprenticeship.

The distinctive style of *Pepi, Luci, Bom* is bricolage: the 're-ordering and recontextualization of objects to communicate fresh meanings', an idea formulated first by Lévi-Strauss.[2] Almodóvar takes the visual context of his world in late 1970s Madrid, its people and places, references to the political world outside his circle, as well as to other art-forms (including film itself), puts them together in a slight but imaginative plot, and then films the result with the very limited technical means at his disposal. This is very much the film of an amateur, of a director learning his trade as he goes along. After the comic-book-inspired titles by the then virtually unknown illustrator Ceesepe, the first shot of the film is a one-minute-long, rather clumsy pan from an establishing shot of a dilapidated apartment block window, which then pulls back to a close-up of Pepi's marijuana plant collection, losing its sharp focus as it does so and encountering problems with the change of light from exterior to interior. This awkward shot ends in Pepi's room, where there is then a cut to a close-up of a photograph of Superman in a magazine, then back to Pepi lying on the floor and finally to the policeman ringing the doorbell. The absence of smooth cutting is made more apparent by the breaks in the soundtrack, where the Little Nell song seems to be cut and restarted on several occasions. Almodóvar is, however, already aware of the expressive possibilities of *mise-en-scène* and camera positioning: placing the camera above Pepi makes her appear smaller in contrast to the policeman who towers above her. The use of close-ups for this first encounter has two advantages: the proxemics (how near the characters are to each other) here suggest an inappropriate intimacy between the two characters, their actions, reactions and feelings revealed in their facial expressions; and tight shots are also easier to handle, requiring less space to position the camera, and less attention to *mise-en-scène*, as little is seen apart from the faces of the characters.

Many of the visual choices in this film are made on a practical basis rather than an artistic one. In the next sequence there is a full shot of Pepi pacing up and down her room, but the room is very small as Almodóvar had no money for studio shooting, and not all of the room is visible since the camera is inside the room and unable to pull back sufficiently. When she looks from her balcony to locate the window of the policeman, the camera zooms and pans at the same time and this double camera action is not even completed before the next cut. There are also technical lapses in the film which in normal filming circumstances would be re-shot: as Pepi waits opposite the apartment building for the policeman to appear, deep focus is used to reveal Pepi in the foreground and Luci's building in the background. But as two more characters are about to appear in the foreground there is a perceptible zoom out to accommodate them into the frame. Later, the camera cuts off the head of Almodóvar himself as he acts as compère for the general erections contest. At the end of one scene, Almodóvar's voice is heard saying 'that's it', obviously indicating a shot completed. This may have been a genuine slip, allowed to creep in due to the difficult and erratic nature of the film's shooting, but it is made into a virtue in this engagingly self-conscious film.

Another feature of Almodóvar's apprenticeship of his directing craft is the extensive use of panning to cover movement and incorporate characters into the frame, reflected in the tendency to follow actors around (e.g. Cristina Pascual in her bedroom). Makeshift lighting reveals shadows on walls behind the actress, where interior light sources would not normally create such shadows. Improvised lighting is also used for the interior of Pepi's flat at night, the attempt to justify this diegetically not quite successful because Pepi switches on one of the lamps a fraction of a second earlier than the extra lighting, a lapse betrayed by a shaky reflection on the white walls. The use of lighting in the spoof advert for Bragas Ponte, however, displays an awareness of its expressive properties. A translucent screen lit from behind provides a diegetically motivated backlight which gives actress Cecilia Roth a clarity of image (in combination with classic Hollywood key and fill lighting) and a glamour befitting the enhanced images of publicity. The focus is also slightly out, suggesting a softness also associated with adverts for sensual, pleasurable products.

In the absence of a film studio, Almodóvar has to make productive use of on location shooting. Given the freedom of space in the street, the variety of shots increases with close-ups, medium close-ups and an extreme long shot from Pepi's point of view on her friends' attack on the policeman's twin brother, as well as a dramatic point-of-view shot from the perspective of the victim, blows and kicks raining down on him. On location shooting also has the virtue of a certain scruffy realism, given the areas of Madrid chosen for filming. But locations necessitate open framing as the camera cannot take in all of the visible panorama. This open framing, associated with realism, contrasts with Almodóvar's later closed and stylized framing. Almodóvar's self-confessed predilection for street corners derives from their possibilities for characters entering often into the middle of the frame (Vidal 1988: 27). Also making the most of what was available at the time, costume reflects the reality of late-1970s Madrid, most of the characters far from glamorous. Almodóvar recounts how the film was taken by some as a social document and one which has lasted well (Vidal 1988: 15). Interiors, too, reflect a generally realistic shabbiness and the décor is often in poor taste (e.g. the wallpaper and tablecloth in Luci's flat). This 'visual poverty' – far from the style associated with Almodóvar – is aided by the subdued colour in this film, caused by the poor quality of the filmstock.

Unlike most of the characteristics mentioned so far, which set this film apart from the remainder of Almodóvar's work, certain features and visual motifs which characterize the rest of Almodóvar's work are present here. The extreme close-up – a constant feature in Almodóvar and an obsessive one in the later films – is debuted in a shot of Pepi's typewriter, revealing the phrase 'Pepi, Luci, Bom', the title of Pepi's filmscript (and of Almodóvar's film). And at the end of the most intimate scene in the film which depicts the strength of Pepi and Bom's friendship, there is an extreme close-up of Bom's favourite dish *bacalao al pil-pil* cooked for her by Pepi. *Mise-en-scène* also contributes to the sense of intimacy between the girls: Pepi and Bom are filmed through a window, in the first of countless instances of double framing (a frame within the frame) in Almodóvar.

Generally, *mise-en-scène* is used in a pragmatic but imaginative way in this film. The blocking of characters is straightforward. Luci and Charito face each other and are filmed in a two-shot as their conversation is insignificant and requires no close-ups or shot/reverse shot pattern. Later, during their knitting classes, Pepi and Luci are filmed in a medium close-up frontal shot, to allow more attention to their conversation. But when Bom enters, the proxemics are altered because of the sexual attraction between them: a close-up of Bom urinating over Luci suggests an invasion of personal space. However welcome for Luci, this is uncomfortably close and even quite shocking for the audience. Similarly, during the 'general erections' contest, a close-up of the competitors' bare bottoms, with Almodóvar as compère very close behind, filmed through their open legs, is effective precisely because it is unexpected. Other features which prove constant in Almodóvar are the conventional use of masking to form a circular iris indicating binoculars as the policeman spies on Pepi's flat, or the appearance of a mirror in which we see the policeman's attempt to seduce Charito. Editing effects (or opticals) are also introduced in this film, the examples being a rather well-executed split screen to show twin brothers, both played by Rotaeta and filmed separately, or the freeze frame used for the end of the Bragas Ponte advert with the slogan in letters over an image of Cecilia Roth's ecstatic expression. The overall visual effect of this piece is a roughness that – cinematography textbook technique aside – adds to the charm and freshness of the film, and is reminiscent of the early work of John Waters such as *Pink Flamingos* (1971). While there are nevertheless elements of a visual style yet to come into its own, this film is less stylized (and certainly less stylish) than many of the later ones. Almodóvar's second film, properly produced, marks the beginning of a trajectory towards an increasingly technical and artistic competence in visual style.

Shot directly on 35 mm film and with better colour quality, *Labyrinth of Passions* is from the outset technically superior to *Pepi, Luci, Bom*. This is particularly clear in the use of the camera. An establishing shot of the Rastro is followed by shots of Sexi and Riza, both separately hunting men in the streets of the market. Riza is first seen reflected in sunglasses hanging from a market stall (the nearest visual motif to a mirror in this film). Smith (1994: 24) remarks that this is 'a telling image in a film which will stress the multiplicity of identities and their tendency to uncontrollable reproduction'. The sequence ends with an aerial shot of the market, more ambitious and self-conscious than the do-it-yourself style of *Pepi, Luci, Bom*. In general, camera use and editing are much less intrusive, the *modus operandi* largely based on the classic continuity model. There is much less panning, much more use of cutting (especially the shot/reverse shot for conversations) as well as cutting from one side of a telephone conversation to another.

Almodóvar is more adventurous with camera angles here. For example, at the start of the incest scene, we see only a close-up of Queti's naked foot tied to a bedpost, then there is a high angle shot of her torso tied to the bed with a crucifix in view above her, and then a side angle shot of her horizontal on the bed, the dislocating of her various body parts suggesting fetishization. There are also shots on a moving train and a two-shot in a taxi (the first of many). Good use is made of a deep focus shot of Toraya in the phone-box and Sadec with Riza on the street behind. The variety even extends to an exterior tracking shot from Toraya's point of view on her visit to a cruising area in search of Riza. In editing, too, this film experiments with new techniques: fast motion photography (conventionally used to denote slapstick comedy) is used for a shot of Angustias hastily applying lip balm and doing exercises, and a split screen is used again for a single actress playing two roles (Sexi and Queti), the image reflected in two circular mirrors.

The title sequence of Almodóvar's third film, *Dark Habits*, heralds a change in tone from the upbeat comedies before it to a sombre melodrama with comic elements (see Chapter 7). Almodóvar uses time-lapse filming to convey the arrival of night. This clearly metaphorical use of the camera is echoed in an altogether more aesthetically motivated film, where *mise-en-scène*, camera angles, editing, lighting and colour all contribute to an impressively harmonious piece of film-making. *Dark Habits* is a dark film with relatively little colour. Only the psychedelic colours of Sister Manure's acid-induced hallucinations and the shimmering red dress worn by Yolanda break from the stark black and white of the convent. Almodóvar's visual signposts for his director of photography, Ángel Luis Fernández, were Douglas Sirk and seventeenth-century Spanish painter Francisco de Zurbarán, reflecting both cinematic and pictorial influences (Vidal 1988: 73). Where Sirk's *mise-en-scène* could provide a model for the interiors associated with melodrama, Zurbarán's dark religious paintings are a referent for the shadows cast by the light entering the bleak convent. The aesthetic handling of both the static and mobile camera utilizes a range of angles with differing effects, the overall variety of which mitigates the immobility of a narrative with less action.

The opening sequence, which narrates the death of Yolanda's heroin-addict boyfriend, is filmed in shadows with low contrast blue lighting. After a tracking shot following Yolanda along the street, into the building and up the stairs, there is a very low angle shot of Yolanda and her boyfriend Jorge. This is followed by a high angle shot of her in the bathroom and then another very low angle of Jorge dead on the floor, a metaphor, perhaps, for the highs and lows of drug addiction. In this case Jorge's low is death, dramatically but simply filmed by a ground-level shot of his inert body, a needle beside it. In the remaining scenes of the film inside the convent, high angle shots predominate. The viewer looks down on the confined lives of the nuns, 'imprisoned against the floor', as Almodóvar expresses it (Vidal 1988: 67). When Yolanda arrives at the convent, a long high angle shot of the darkened chapel (now with high contrast lighting which makes the darkness more impenetrable), reveals a sudden shaft of light at the rear as the doors open to reveal Yolanda bathed in celestial light. At dinner, a high angle establishing shot of the refectory is used rather than the standard medium shot for conversations. This enhances the symmetrical *mise-en-scène* of the top table (an allusion to the last supper) with the lesser side tables sym-metrically framing it. Some of these high angle shots self-consciously equate the viewer's high position with the omniscience of God: the Mother Superior addresses God after she has had a confrontation with Yolanda and she is filmed from high above, the high contrast image picking out her small figure among the shadows of the chapel. Her withdrawal from heroin is also filmed from a very high angle as we find her once again alone in the chapel, bathed in a white spotlight.

Extensive use is made of both panning and tracking shots. When the Mother Superior takes Yolanda to her room, a pan which is almost a full circle surveys the room like eyes taking it all in. To enable this circular pan, the camera begins by apparently passing through the wall. This shot clearly sacrifices a diegetically justified camera movement for the aesthetic value of a pan to allow full appreciation of the *mise-en-scène*. The décor, colour and iconography of this room are sumptuous in stark contrast to the rest of the convent. Another tracking shot through the 'jungle' of the convent's interior patio (complete with tiger), combines the tracking motion, suggesting something lurking in the undergrowth, with low key lighting and with the accompanying suspense music (from Miklós Rosza's music for *Providence* [Alan Resnais, 1976]), to create a genre-associated thriller effect. And when the nuns sit in the chapel listening to the lesson on kissing, a horizontal track establishes the similarity of all the nuns as well as their lack of mobility.

Point-of-view shots are also a feature in a film which focuses more on emotions than actions. Early in the film we see Yolanda's point of view of Jorge's diary as she asks him 'Have you written about me again?' Later, there is a point of view from Sister Manure as she looks through the keyhole at Sister Rat and Yolanda, immediately followed by an extreme close-up of Manure's spying eye, the light falling on it from inside the room. When Yolanda sings in response to the static Mother Superior, a complex combination of point-of-view shots, shot/reverse angles, and panning serves to enhance the equivocal proxemics between the two women. Yolanda appears to get closer to the Mother Superior, but finally a low angle longshot shows, metaphorically, how far apart they are, Yolanda's red blouse contrasting with the Mother Superior's habit. Almodóvar's use of editing here is similar to that in his previous films. Yolanda's journey on multiple buses is shown by editing (seven shots including one dissolve) and her recollection which motivates the flashback to when she met the nuns is signalled by a rather facile blurring and wobbling dissolve from Yolanda's point of view on the nuns' visiting card to their meeting. And the depiction of Yolanda's withdrawal symptoms uses many dissolves in a montage sequence, the nightmarish images of which combine shots of the convent, especially its iconography and its tiger, with an eerie blue lighting.

From *Dark Habits*, the more assured visual style of Almodóvar's films is determined much more by genre than by the unusual material and technical conditions of production. Just as Almodóvar's directorial style stems in part from his idiosyncratic rehabilitation of genres, so, too, his visual style is marked by genre iconography and *mise-en-scène*. Thus, the prevailing aesthetic mode of *What Have I Done* is grim social realism, combined with the garish poor taste of tacky décor. The optimistic and colourful visuals of *Women on the Verge* belong to what Almodóvar has called 'comedia wilderiana' (Billy Wilder being one of his influences; Vidal 1988: 266). *Kika*, on the other hand, is a black comedy about the deleterious power of the media. The satire of television's so-called 'reality shows' informs the visual style of the film, putting the very practice of filming and photographic reproduction on show. Almodóvar's camera follows the indiscretion of the hungry video camera, often imitating the home-movie style of poor colour quality and hand-held shakiness. Though in most films the viewer is privileged to see much more than any characters, in *Kika* the camera adopts all manner of angles to seek out the sensationalism in the interiors of society's homes and lives. After *Kika*, such self-consciousness and camera contortions become rarer.

Almodóvar's directorial peak is represented by *Flower*, *Live Flesh* and *All About My Mother*, all confident pieces of polished film-making. Almodóvar uses an artful and imaginative range of camera positions and *mise-en-scène*, but in such a way as to make each shot decision seem like the most natural of all possible choices. The perfect example of Almodóvar's capacity to mobilize exactly the right amount of technique and technology at his disposal in a perfect economy of directing, is the road accident of Manuela's son Esteban in *All About My Mother*. This scene is, to date, the most powerfully dramatic in all Almodóvar's work. The situation is not particularly original: an impressionable young man runs after his heroine in pursuit of an autograph; in the pouring rain he is hit by a car and left unconscious in the road, his mother witnessing it all then running to her son's side. A more conventional director, with a large special effects budget, might film this scene something like this: a close-up of the young man as he sees his chance, then cut to a full shot as he runs after the departing taxi; a longshot of another car going far too fast and then a cut to a close-up of the driver's shocked face as he slams on the brakes; slow motion begins as we see a choreographed crash (using at least two stuntmen) and the young man is thrown into the air and lands face down on the road; cut to a close-up of his mother raising her hands to her face with a terrified scream before a final full shot of the boy prostrate in the road. An expensive take, its exploitation of action-sequence conventions does not distinguish it from hundreds of like moments on film. Almodóvar's version is much more restrained, economic (both in showy technique and in financial terms): as Esteban sets off in pursuit of Huma, a fast tracking shot away from Manuela indicates the speed of her son's pursuit of the taxi (but the camera movement is also dramatic in itself); there is no shot of the other car but a very blurred longshot of the road indicates the poor visibility; the impact of the car hitting Esteban is heard, the only image being the broken glass of the windscreen which fills the frame in close-up; cut to a subjective shot, the camera, masterfully, appearing to take the point of view of the victim. We do not see the impact of the car hitting Esteban; indeed, we do not see Esteban at all. Instead, the camera appears to flail around as it falls towards the ground and remains in a dislocated roll position as the distant (and out-of-focus) Manuela runs in slow motion towards the camera, shouting 'My son' repeatedly. When she reaches her dying son, her face (still out of focus and blurred by the rain) comes right up against the camera in an extreme close-up as she continues to shout 'My son'. Finally, a small camera movement indicates an apparent fall to a resting place in an extreme close-up of the wet road, suggesting Esteban's loss of consciousness.

The road accident sequence appears some twelve minutes into the film, providing an early emotional hook which seizes the viewer for the remainder of the film. One of the characteristics of Almodóvar's facility in manipulating the viewer is the use of powerful and visually engaging openings in his films. Nowhere is this truer than in the first ten minutes of *Live Flesh*. The camera, *mise-en-scène*, editing and music are combined into a deliciously evocative sequence. Though these heights of visual pleasure are not quite sustained throughout the whole of the film, they represent – along with sequences in *All About My Mother* – the director's technique at its best. As the first of the opening credits flash up in luminous gold type, a crane shot pans to a close-up of Christmas decorative lights in the form of a star. Then another crane shot rises from ground level towards the window of Centro's bed-and-breakfast, before a cut to an interior. A close-up of a 1960s radio and a wig on a stand turns into a pan to reveal Doña Centro herself. This camera movement – close-up and pull back to pan – is very common in Almodóvar. A little later, a close-up of an angel statue which, to Isabel, looks as if it's going to fall, turns into a pan to Isabel herself inside the bus, and this is followed by a further close-up of Isabel's slippers as her waters break, forming a puddle on the floor of the bus. For the birth of Isabel's son (at Christmas) the bus is symmetrically framed in the middle of a street from a high crane shot, the star decoration above with its obvious Nativity connotations. (This same shot is used at the end of the film for the birth of Víctor's own son.) A gradual pan with the crane towards the bus ends with a medium shot through the bus windows, under which is written 'absolute precision' (for the bus clearly positions itself directly underneath Madrid's own nativity star). The birth itself is evoked in a longshot through the windows, showing only the heads of the three characters and with no blood. We hear Centro offer to cut the umbilical cord with her teeth, and only afterwards is there a close-up of Centro's bloody mouth. The transition from this 1970 sequence to twenty years later is sublime. Doña Centro holds the new-born Víctor up to show him outside the bus window and proclaims, 'Look, Víctor, Madrid!' A cut takes us to a circular tracking shot around the illuminated Puerta de Alcalá as the main title appears in gold. There then follows a second cut to a black and white cinema newsreel image (the frame masked off to suggest the interior of a film theatre). A delightful parody of the NoDo newsreel shows mother and baby celebrated by the media for the birth in the bus. Then, as the newsreader indicates that baby Víctor's lifetime bus pass represents for him 'a life on wheels', a fade to black and a dissolve into the dark streets under Víctor's motorcycle wheels transports the action to 1990. A pan reveals a grown-up Víctor in front of the same landmark as the titles '20 years later' appear. Next, a dissolve into a brilliant white image which, with a rapid zoom and pan out, is revealed as a police car headlamp; David and Sancho are lit in red; the view from the car is a lengthy tracking shot to show the low life of Madrid ending with Víctor as a pizza delivery boy. This long take is rendered more sustainable by the evocative song 'Mi perro'.

The visually captivating and the expositional are mutually beneficial. Almodóvar wants the viewer's absolute attention for narrative purposes, and the virtuoso display of camera and *mise-en-scène* techniques is conducive to this. The first three minutes of *Women on the Verge* is a good example of how character and narrative requirements are realized through visual style. After the shot of a model of Pepa's apartment building, we see chickens and other animals as Pepa's voice-over begins to narrate her story. The explanation – Pepa keeps animals on her roof terrace – does not prevent a moment of disorientation: no human plane has yet been established. Three extreme close-ups provide in-dicators of Pepa's situation: Iván's autographed dedication to Pepa on the sleeve of their favourite record, a slow pan across Pepa's bedside table showing an alarm clock and a photo of Iván, and an extreme close-up pan across the sleeping body of Pepa which ends with an extreme close-up of her head. This leads to a dissolve into the 'inside' of her head, Pepa's dream, described by Evans (1996: 33) as 'Fellini-esque'. Though dreams can often be bizarre and even stylized, Pepa's dream represents a comically facile interpretation of her predicament. Shot in black and white, it opens with a zoom out from a patterned hole in a wall to an extreme close-up of Iván's mouth as he uses a breath freshener. Then a long tracking shot of Iván walking past a parade of women plays out Pepa's fantasy of abandonment. This ends with a match shot of a red traffic light which dissolves into a sunset and gives way to another extreme close-up of Iván's mouth talking into a microphone. The dream flows seamlessly into Iván at work, without his ex-lover and colleague Pepa. With no explanation, there is a cut to the film *Johnny Guitar*, an image of Joan Crawford cut as if in a shot/reverse shot with Iván. But then a cut to Sterling Hayden shows that he is Crawford's reverse shot speaker. Iván is dubbing Sterling Hayden's voice in the film, but Joan Crawford's voice goes undubbed. Pepa is not in the sound studio but still asleep in bed. The next sequence of shots are alternating cuts between Iván, Crawford, Hayden and Pepa asleep. Finally, there is a shot of Iván in the foreground mimicking the actions of Hayden on the screen behind. As we reach the end of the reel, shots of the film number countdown are rapidly intercut with shots of Pepa's assortment of alarm clocks (she has an over-sleeping problem). This se-quence ends with a shot of Pepa asleep. The total length of the sequence this far is under three minutes, indicating the extent of editing needed to piece together such diverse visual elements. Only in *Matador* did Almodóvar take this editing further.

The five-minute opening of the film is densely orchestrated, the directing, *mise-en-scène* and editing combining to captivate the viewer. The montage of scenes from graphically violent films is revealed as a video watched by Diego. At first the television occupies the full frame with Diego's feet visible on either side (straddling the television as if in a sexual position), then a side angle full shot reveals exactly Diego's position: in the chair with his feet around the television masturbating to the screen images. The first shot of Diego giving the bullfighting class is pictorially composed with him to the right of the frame and a perfectly round technical drawing of the bullring occupying the left half of the frame. Diego's lesson is then intercut with alternating shots of María's literal execution of the theory, the victim not a bull but a human male. The climax to María's murder of her sexual partner is rapidly intercut with scenes of the bullfighting students practising their skills, fifty-two shots in just under three minutes. Lighting also adds to the darkness and mystery of María's sex murder: she seduces her victim in a room in semi-darkness, the light from the window casting strong shadows of the panes of glass on the walls. Also introduced in these expository sequences are items such as María's murderous hairpin, or the bullfighter's *capote*, which form an essential part of the film's iconography. A recurrent feature of Almodóvar's visual style is the importance attached to objects in the *mise-en-scène*.

The Importance of Objects

Objects tell us about characters, what they cherish, hate or fear. They can communicate information in simple denotative terms or, through connotation, convey even complex psychological aspects of the characters. The objects in films form part of the iconography of genres.[3] Melodrama, in particular, invests objects with a degree of connotative signification which compensates for what cannot be said directly. Though direct expression in Almodóvar is not limited by censorship or public moral taste, he none the less makes ample use of the associations of objects for his characters. Some are used in the same way in various films, such as close-ups of items thrown to the floor in anger: in *Dark Habits* the contents of Yolanda's bag by Jorge, in *Flower* a photoframe by Leo, and in *Live Flesh* kitchen items by David. The extreme close-up is a useful and frequent tool for singling out objects. Extreme close-ups are most frequent in the films which focus on the emotions of one central character, principally *All About My Mother* and *Flower*, and, to a lesser extent, *Women on the Verge*.[4]

The sequence that introduces Leo in *Flower* consists of a long pan with close-ups of objects which reveal much about her. A shot of the blinds of the apartment becomes a roving pan to open up the view outside the window: Leo lives in a community, though she is isolated within it. A cut to Leo then links her by means of a continued pan to the objects on her bedside table. The photographs, principally of her estranged husband Paco, reveal her emotional life, the books, her professional life. Then the wind blows open the windows fluttering the pages of a book to a page marked by a pen: the line 'defenceless against encroaching madness' is highlighted on the page, a literary allusion to her psychological state. A dissolve takes us into a close-up of Leo's desk, with notes and her typewriter where she has copied the quotation. Then there is a pan to the stickers which read 'pain' and 'life' which continues down to her boots which she cannot take off, for she is alone. Already we have learnt much about Leo. A subsequent scene begins with a close-up of a row of bottles in a restaurant which then pulls back to Leo and Betty at a table, the significance of the object explained by Leo herself: 'Except drinking, how difficult everything is for me!'

At other times, longshots best describe a character's relationship to something else: Leo's uncertainty about presenting her writing to the newspaper is depicted in a deep focus, low angle establishing shot of the *El País* offices before Leo appears, tiny, in the foreground at the bottom of the frame looking up at the company sign. Her disorientation after Paco has told her there is no hope for their relationship is conveyed by her physical dislocation amid the student protest outside her building. A dolly shot inside the mass of students discovers Leo lost in the crowds. A crane shot then pulls back out to a great height, the political flyers floating up into a blue sky. The camera follows them and for a long time remains fixed on this image, its beauty combining with the first strains of Bola de Nieve's evocative song 'Pain and Life', a song which sums up Leo's existence. The next sequence shows Leo waking up in Ángel's apartment. It begins with a close-up of the fabric of Ángel's black and white rug and a fast pan to the FNAC record store outside; a vertical pan reveals the poster advertising the Amanda Gris compilation, and the complex but unobtrusive pan continues inside Ángel's flat to reveal Leo asleep. In one take, we learn that Leo is waking up in Ángel's flat, and that her secret identity is revealed to him on the huge advertising hoarding of the FNAC.

Where in earlier films intimate, even scatological scenes have been filmed in uncomfortable close-up, here a discreet distance communicates the information without the shock value. A slow track towards her room – but still maintaining some distance – reveals Leo vomiting after she has taken an overdose of sleeping pills. Then there is a cut to a shot of her bath with the shower running; from inside comes Leo's wet hand to pull her up, the image looking like one from a horror film, and the shot ends with a scream, a sound bridge to the screaming contest which is on television in the next sequence, as if playing with the horror motif. Once out of danger, Leo is accompanied by Ángel to her village, a close-up of golden yellow fields panning up to a road to reveal Ángel's car. When they arrive, an establishing shot of the whitewashed houses (yellow for hope, white for purification) gives way to an interior, a golden bedside lamp filtered through the lace texture of a screen. The ancient lace acts as a filter for an older perspective – that of her mother – who then offers her interpretation of Leo's plight.

Almodóvar's camera in *All About My Mother* focuses almost obsessively on the objects which mark protagonist Manuela's existence in this film, both before and after the death of her son. The film begins with an unfocused extreme close-up of a hospital drip bag, followed by an extreme close-up pan down the clear tube to the falling drops of saline. The red titles which first appear superimposed on the plastic surface of the drip bag are also out of focus, as if filtered through the saline and plastic, and as each title appears it comes gradually into focus and then out again. After a dissolve into another extreme close-up of the monitoring apparatus of the intensive care unit, the camera finally tilts to bring Manuela into medium close-up; she is intimately linked to the medical and pastoral care of victims. The whole title sequence – apart from the main title of the film which comes after this prelude – is superimposed on to extreme close-ups, reflecting an obsessive attention to the minute details of life and death situations.

Extreme close-ups are used as a kind of shorthand, quickly expressing the relationship of characters to the world around them. As mother and son sit down to watch *All About Eve*, Esteban writes in his notebook the title of his next piece 'All About My Mother'. His relationship with words is as intense as his relationship with his mother; we see an extreme close-up of his pencil, followed by a reverse shot from the point of view of the notebook itself, the camera filming from underneath the translucent paper. When Esteban asks to see a photograph of his mother as an amateur actress, Manuela presents him with only half a photograph, the remainder torn off. An extreme close-up of Esteban's point of view on the photograph communicates visually what he subsequently writes in his notebook: this photograph symbolizes the half of Esteban which he feels is always missing – his father. Esteban's relationship to his writing and to the drama he loves is illustrated by an extreme close-up of the larger than life eyes of his heroine, actress Huma Rojo in a poster which occupies the whole theatre wall. (So magnified is this close-up that the photographic dots of the image are clearly visible.) This then dissolves very slowly, from red to blue, into a scene from the play *A Streetcar Named Desire*.

Many more extreme close-ups are used to redirect attention to Manuela's loss: one of Esteban's photos on Manuela's bedside cabinet as she sleeps, another of Esteban's notebook, the eyes from his portrait visible behind as Lola reads his son's last words. Extreme close-ups are also used to signal other characters: one of the theatre lights precedes a shot of Huma, and another of Huma's cigarette and a flame lighting it, reveals behind it a photo of Bette Davis smoking. Huma tells Manuela that she started smoking to imitate Bette Davis. And at the very end of the film, a close-up of Huma as she heads for the stage ('see you later') then cuts to an extreme close-up of the stage curtain's ornate but faded design for the film's dedication (to actresses of all kinds and to mothers of all kinds).

In contrast to these extreme close-ups, longshots situate characters in their larger environment, but their motivation is often principally aesthetic. When Manuela returns to Barcelona, her former home and the home of the father of her dead son, a beautiful panoramic helicopter shot over the mountains surrounding the city reveals the illuminated Catalan capital at night, before a cut to a pensive Manuela looking up at Gaudí's Sagrada Familia. As she rolls up the window of her taxi, the cathedral is reflected in the car window, the distortion making the already strange forms stranger still. When Manuela goes in search of her husband, transsexual Lola, the marketplace of these specialized prostitutes is portrayed in a long tracking shot reminiscent of the shot of low-life Madrid in *Live Flesh*. This distant viewpoint (long, tracking shot) is echoed again in a later shot when Manuela goes in search of drug addict Nina in another seedy Barcelona area: Manuela is in but not part of this seedy environment. A longshot inside the Hospital del Mar makes good use of the natural light of huge windows as Manuela and Rosa are filmed with their backs to the camera in silhouette, the blue sea behind them. As Manuela and Rosa leave the frame, the camera lingers on a beautiful longshot of the Mediterranean through the wall-height windows.

Even where the narrative concerns a group of characters, the objects which form part of their physical, emotional and symbolic world are picked out by the camera. In *Live Flesh*, these objects are diverse, and throughout the film the camera moves confidently in a range from extreme close-ups through to establishing shots. An extreme close-up shows Elena obsessively warming up a joint which characterizes her junkie phase. And when Clara sprays Sancho in the eyes we see only his eyes under the running tap water (a visual reference to an identical moment in *Women on the Verge*). Deep focus is also used effectively alongside the extreme close-up. A deep focus pan of the prison cell shows Víctor in the background, while in the foreground the bed shakes as his cellmate masturbates. Then a close-up pan over his possessions, photos and Elena's telephone number, reveals his preoccupations. Víctor's return to his mother's neglected house begins with a long panning shot of the imposing Torres Kío, which symbolize the relentless modernization of the city. This shot is then cut to Víctor's point of view (inside the house) and a zoom discovers one of his toy soldiers in extreme close-up as he recalls his childhood. And when David goes to see his wife at the shelter, a track through its corridors is filmed from David's wheelchair height. David's wheelchair is both the physical expression of his incapacity, and the symbol of his frustration. When he goes to challenge Víctor, a very low angle shot of David's feet and the wheels of his wheelchair is followed by a similar angle shot of Víctor doing press-ups.

In a film with five main characters, point of view becomes an issue in the narrative. Point of view can help to clarify and to dramatize relationships. As Víctor and Sancho struggle on the floor over possession of the gun, we see a point of view hand-held shot (from either Víctor or from Sancho – and this is critical though we don't yet know it); this shot includes a disorientating roll as camera and gun lunge about. The doubt about the holder of this point of view (the point of view of David's assailant and attempted murderer) is paralleled at the end of the film where Sancho's gun is shot in close-up pointing directly at the camera, but then, as Sancho points it back at himself, cuts to assume Sancho's point of view on his own suicide. While the extreme close-up of the gun corresponds to the iconography of crime genres, a magnified shot of the redial button on David's phone (which reveals to Elena who he has called) constitutes the magnified importance of telephones in melodrama. The telephone is similarly the dominant object in the iconography of *Women on the Verge*. We see Pepa framed under the telephone hood which forms a blue arc over her and the pink phone and her answering-machine also figure in countless extreme close-ups.

Just as iconography derives in part from genre (in the case of *Women on the Verge*, from comedy), so too décor and costume to a large extent follow genre expectations.

Décor and Costume

> Kitsch protects my modesty and so I'm very attached to it. (Strauss 1996: 42)

One of the most frequently expressed misconceptions about Almodóvar is that all his films are kitsch. Kitsch – the recuperation of a pretentious and bad taste aesthetic – may well have benefits in a referential, post-punk and postmodern society, but examples of it in Almodóvar's films represent isolated elements rather than a consistent aesthetic mode. Where there is an element of bad taste in the films (*Pepi, Luci, Bom* in particular has episodes reminiscent of John Waters's often repugnant *Pink Flamingos*), there is no pretence at all of any aesthetic beauty in the sordid or the plain. Most frequently, kitsch defines either a discrete location (domestic interiors in *What Have I Done* and the 1970 sequence in *Live Flesh*),[5] or a character. In *Women on the Verge*, two characters act as the locus for humorous kitsch. Pepa's faithful bleached blond taxi driver has named his vehicle 'mambo taxi' with good reason: it sports leopardskin seat covers and matching panda steering wheel. Candela, too, possesses a little piece of kitsch, in the form of a pair of coffee-pot earrings, which, for Varderi (1996: 204), signify her 'taking her house with her' as she flees from male treachery. They suggest the limited extent of Candela's domesticity. These discrete elements of kitsch paradoxically reflect a certain verisimilitude: some characters have a kitsch sensibility while others are naturally designer-conscious.

In *What Have I Done*, Almodóvar's depiction of the existence of different social groups provides an opportunity for a range of aesthetic styles in the interiors of the various dwellings. Gloria's flat is characterized by the lurid décor of cheap retro 1970s. This is an example of the verisimilitude of kitsch, as many poor households do have décor which is out of date and in bad taste: the striped pink and black cushions don't go with the pastel floral pattern of the sofa; the walls are covered with cheap reproduction paintings of the countryside and horses. A more optimistic kitsch lives next door in prostitute Cristal's flat. Painted shocking pink and blue, with black and white animal skin wallpaper, the

stylized boudoir features a padded white door and a heart-shaped blue
neon light. This is further contrasted by therapist Pedro's apartment
with modern art on the walls, and with the Berlin home of Ingrid
Muller, the rich textures and colours of wood and antiques indicating
a place far removed from the alternately sordid and modern Madrid.
The socio-economic significance of domestic interiors is reflected in
mise-en-scène and camera angles. Tight angles and high angle shots emphasize the smallness of the flat and of the characters respectively. An
example is the very high angle shot of Gloria sniffing glue on her sofa.
Only at the very end does the camera reveal exactly how the furniture
is placed, in a long almost full-circle pan around the flat, as Gloria
surveys her empty existence. An innovation (which subsequently appears
in other Almodóvar films) is the point of view shot from the perspective
of an object rather than a person. Instead of Gloria's point of view on
her washing machine we see a subjective shot of *her* from the point of
view of the washing machine and later from the oven. Such an anti-
illusionistic perspective suggests Gloria's relationship to domestic objects.
Kathleen Vernon (1995: 66) posits a social motivation for these shots:
'framed in this way, the image of the desiring female subject of consumer
society collapses into her own objectification'.

Almodóvar is perhaps most famous for the glossy, designer décor
which characterizes films from *Women on the Verge* to *Kika*. They reflect
a world of smart penthouses, stylish clothes and the confident, bold
colours of late-1980s and early-1990s Spain. The film titles for *Women
on the Verge* indicate a strong graphic design element, courtesy of Juan
Gatti, frequently Almodóvar's chosen designer. This style is mirrored in
the sets of the film itself. That much of the brash texture of this world
hides a shallow fragility is apparent from the very first shot of the film,
a scale model of Pepa's apartment building. Scale models are, of course,
often used in making films, but here there is no attempt to convince the
viewer that they are anything but hollow, a simulation. (Such scale models
of buildings become a feature of Almodóvar's films from here onwards.)[6] The studio setting – an industrial warehouse in Barajas – is
obvious (Boquerini 1989: 97). The film itself is equally unapologetic
about its fictionality: many directorial decisions about style are made
with a view to texture, visual pleasure and the witty *mise-en-scène* which
befits classic comedy. The same quality of superficial design characterizes
the décor of *Tie Me Up!* The look of this film is conditioned in part by
the flashy world of the film industry. The studio set for the filming of

Midnight Phantom suggests inauthenticity, and attention is drawn to the fragility of the stage décor and model buildings. It also provides for strong colours. Even the home of stage manager Pepe looks like a studio set with its mock classical arch for a doorway, its cast-iron bed, and window lights in the ceiling with remote-controlled curtains. The very first frame of the film is a painting of Christ repeated six times in Warhol superstar style, the iconography of religion offering a preview of the colours to come. The closed, saturated and florid interiors where Marina is imprisoned are contrasted with wide open location shots. Ricky is filmed on top of a castle with a lake in the background, the setting sun providing a shot of pure natural beauty. And at the end of the film, the shot of the car driving off into the distance evokes departures into the sunset typical of film endings.

In *Kika*, visual style similarly reflects the world of modern, stylish professionals. Ramón is a photographer (no accident given his voyeuristic tendencies) and a photo montage on his bedroom walls offers an insight into his preferred style: religious images and women. Ramón and Kika's flat is multi-coloured and modern, reflecting Ramón's visual sense and Kika's lively temperament. Kika herself – as the locus of a kind of comic optimism in the film – wears light, warm colours. Ramón's studio has the now ubiquitous scale models of Madrid's futuristic buildings, suggesting the inauthenticity of Ramón's obsession: just as his photography is a reproduction, his sexual appetite is for seeing rather than doing. Almodóvar refers to the look of the film as that of a 'plastic collage' (Cobos and Marías 1995: 111). Though the interiors offer a range of bright colours, red predominates as ever: Ramon's shirt, the television presenter's dress, Kika's fur coat, Ramon's bedspread, the red and black costume worn by Andrea in the first episode of *The Worst of the Day*, the empty red seats on the show's soundstage, Andrea's second red dress of rags, and the dress Kika is wearing when she is raped by Paul Bazzo. At the end of the film, however, the key colour becomes the golden yellow of the sunflowers, indicating optimism as, once again, a longshot of the car driving into the distance takes her away from the dangerous world of the indiscreet camera.

The monstrously voyeuristic camera also informs the costume in *Kika* through the personality of former psychologist-turned-television-presenter Andrea, famously dressed by exuberant designer Jean Paul Gaultier. According to Stella Bruzzi (1997:11): 'Andrea's costumes are not merely distancing devices but exaggerated, conventionalized mechan-

23. *Kika*. Andrea (Victoria Abril) in Jean-Paul
Gaultier's costume.

isms for making the female form into an objectified spectacle.' In the
first episode a long slow pan reveals a blood-red-edged train on a black
dress with red threads hanging like drops of blood from two openings
which correspond to the breasts [fig. 23]. The skin-coloured material
underneath suggests the breasts have been ripped off, their bleeding
edges dangling towards the floor. Unlike in the cases of most television
presenters (always impeccably dressed), here the presenter partakes in
the horrific spirit of her material. Bruzzi describes Andrea's appearance
in episode two of *The Worst of the Day* [see fig. 24]:

Andrea, deploying all the coquettish poise of the traditional tele-

24. *Kika*. Andrea (Victoria Abril) in episode two of
The Worst of the Day.

vision host, is dressed in parody evening wear: a tight, mutilated
red velvet dress over a loosely crocheted black vest, her hair
scraped back Flamenco style and her legs and arms (to the length
of extravagant evening gloves) swathed in surgical bandages which
offer a particularly gruesome and direct link with the ritual being
screened. (Bruzzi 1997: 11)

Andrea's outfit for episode three mixes black and red PVC and she
sports a mock artificial limb. This is part of a grotesque distancing
which completely dehumanizes the character. Bruzzi links Andrea's
costumes to a perverse deconstruction of femininity:

An anomaly suggested by the alienating way in which costumes function in *Kika* is that the more sensational clothes become, the less they signify the beauty and desirability of, in this instance, the female characters who wear them. This contravenes directly the traditional interpretation of adornment as something which accentuates and complements the feminine. (Bruzzi 1997: 13)

Andrea's on location outfit represents the ultimate in human-turned-machine: a rubber suit with a helmet which incorporates a mobile camera (making concrete the association between the voyeur's eyes and the camera lens); and breasts that have now become lights to illuminate interior scenes.[7]

Almodóvar's most remarkable costumes appear in the more stylized films such as *Kika*, *Matador* and *Women on the Verge*. In *Matador*, María's split personality is marked by costume.[8] As a lawyer, she wears a respectable black and white suit. As a murderer she dresses extravagantly. In the first scene she wears her hair up and a white shawl covering minimalist lingerie. For the scene on the viaduct she is wearing a long plait bound in red, a shimmering red and gold satin dress, and a yellow and black cape. In *Women on the Verge*, Pepa's dress sense is contrasted with the plainly-dressed housewife she plays in the washing powder advert. In even worse taste, Lucía lives in a time-warp, insisting on wearing only the most kitsch outfits from her youth. On her first outing she wears a leopardskin suit with matching tall hat, as well as copious amounts of grotesque make-up which only serve to emphasize her advanced age.[9] For the climactic scene, Lucía, the incongruous murderess, is clad in a baby-girl pink suit with white gloves.

Elsewhere, costume connotes social status or personal style. In *High Heels* mother and daughter are distinguished by their labels. Rebeca (Victoria Abril) is dressed by Chanel (the titles tell us this, and Becky remarks upon it immediately). Becky (Marisa Paredes) first appears in a stunning Armani red dress and wide-brim hat. Varderi (1996: 205) believes this 'fashion divide' is overdetermined: 'the Chanel–Armani dialogue obliterates, nevertheless, the discourse between the two women for the greater part of the film'. But costume is also used as a simple period element, as in the flashback sequence in the early 1970s, in which dress is marked by strong colours and flower patterns. In *What Have I Done*, costume reflects the differing social classes and values of the characters: the drab clothing of Gloria contrasts with the spectacular but cheap glamour of Cristal. Her first appearance is in leather mistress gear, to be followed by a white wedding dress comprising a revealing miniskirt. Later, there is a shot of Gloria in an old coat next to Cristal in a negligée to confirm their different fashion worlds.

Colour

Almodóvar's films are famous for their strong colours. It is true that his colour schemes are based on a unique personal style and not, usually, on verisimilitude: 'what doesn't interest me at all with colour is imitating reality' (Cobos and Marías 1995: 86). Lighting and colour can affect what Gianetti (1990: 72) refers to as the dominant – to what point in the frame our eye is first attracted. In Almodóvar, a splash of colour in a character's clothing or an item of the décor is the most frequent dominant and one of his films' most common visual motifs. Aside from the versatility of its many associations (blood, passion, anger), red is clearly Almodóvar's favourite colour in a purely aesthetic sense, and undoubtedly the dominant colour in all his films (excepting only *Pepi, Luci, Bom* where the sub-standard filmstock results in a vapid poverty of colour). In *Matador*, for example, the predominance of red is absolute.

Of all Almodóvar's films, *Matador* is the most abstract, less problematically an art film than his other more hybrid products. The composition of what appears in the frame is as much painterly as cinematic and there are many instances of tableaux *mise-en-scène* which emphasize immobility over action. Almodóvar wants us to look at the images as well as follow the action. *Mise-en-scène* is therefore more important even than camerawork. And colour is the most salient feature of the film. The titles are in red lettering and the associations of red with bullfighting are exploited throughout the film. Diego's home and bullfighting school echo the ring itself, the walls painted red up to waist height. The key meetings between the death-obsessed lovers Diego and María are especially colour-coded. The couple are strongly lit in red from the cinema screen when they chance upon the death of the two lovers in *Duel in the Sun*. When María takes Diego to her sanctuary to show him all the memorabilia she has collected, their mutual confession ends with a fade to red, rather than the usual black. The setting sun which coincides with the lovers' deaths also throws a rich red-orange light on the characters. And the film's final shot of the dead lovers is like a painting, the reds of the scattered roses and of the lighting over which appears the word

FIN (in red) before a fade to red for titles (yellow on red). Elsewhere red also dominates: in the casting session and in the *chotis* dancehall, in Eva's living room, and for Eva's last confrontation with Diego, where she dresses in bright red with a long red necktie.

In virtually every film, Almodóvar finds justification for the predominance of the colour red. In *High Heels*, red combines with black connoting the passion (and Becky's heart which is weak in both senses) and the crime elements of the narrative respectively. Letal's jacket, skirt, long gloves and shoes are red, signalling him as a point of impetuousness and danger. The curtains and décor of the Villa Rosa are also red. Manuel is wearing red pyjamas when he is murdered. And for the Judge's interrogation, both Rebeca and Becky are wearing red. Rebeca is still wearing this red outfit when she reads the news of her husband's death. In *Women on the Verge*, much of the action takes place in Pepa's apartment, a colourful, stylish late-1980s penthouse. The warm orange walls are complemented by red sofas and rich wooden floors. Reds and oranges predominate in the film as a whole. Pepa sleeps in bright pink pyjamas, the receptionist wears reds and oranges, and the counter is red. Pepa's telephone is red, and she wears a long red shirt and red slippers and a striped red jacket. Even her notepaper is red. At the very end of the film, both women are wearing red which stands out against the night sky behind. This scene is lit in classic Hollywood fashion with fill light and back lights to sharpen the edges of the actresses. It is perhaps the most artificial of all the film's scenes, the colours far from realistic.[10]

Colour also plays its part in the *mise-en-scène* of *Law of Desire*. Red dominates once again. At the start of the film, when Tina leaves Pablo's première, red curtains frame both her and the screen behind her. The stage curtains for *La voix humaine* are also red, as is the phone which Tina holds and even the poster for the play. The lighting in the bar where they celebrate the première casts a red glow on their faces. Pablo's bed and his shower curtain are red, as is Tina's hair, two of her dresses, Ada's blouse, and the envelope containing the script for his future film 'Laura P.' All the characters wear red at some point and Pablo drives a red car. When Tina is hosed down in the street, she is wearing a bright orange dress: a longshot of the dark street shows a stream of water coming from the hosepipe; a high angle shot reveals Tina, Ada and Pablo as they walk under the stream of water in the foreground, light glistening on its surface; Tina's orange dress is strongly lit against the dark blues of the night. Almodóvar cites US painter Edward Hopper as the visual referent of the film for both colour and framing (Vidal 1988: 244), and Hopper's hyperrealistic colours (oranges, blues, clay-colour and pastels) suit the equivocal tone of the film (thriller-melodrama), rather than the primary colours which characterize other films.[11]

Almodóvar has commented on the fact that *Law of Desire* was shot in summer (Vidal 1988: 194). Both the sense of open space and the strong Spanish sunlight are clearly felt in the film in which a number of exterior scenes are shot on location. For the first time in Almodóvar's work, the action leaves the Spanish capital for a number of scenes. When Antonio goes to visit Juan at a beach bar in the south, an extreme longshot of Antonio and Juan on the cliff's edge indicates the danger Juan is in moments before he is pushed to his death by Antonio. The next shot uses the natural light of the Andalusian summer in a startling contrast to the blue-filtered night scene before. The white walls reflect the sunlight and Pablo puts on his sunglasses. After his departure the policemen walk along the beach, and are seen at the very bottom of an extreme longshot with the clear blue sea behind them. Apart from the quality of natural light which is used extensively in the film, artificial lighting conveys the film's mood. In the pornographic film which opens *Law of Desire*, a directional strip of light falls on the young man and on the wall behind, picking him out from the semi-darkened room. And for the stage scene, a combination of frontal and back lighting highlights the edges of Ada's white communion dress. Then, for Tina's monologue over the phone, strong theatrical side lighting creates attached shadows on one side of Tina's face.

In *All About My Mother*, the ubiquitous almodovarian red is complemented by a rich array of blues. The titles are red and blue; Manuela stands in a long red coat in front of a theatre poster (also predominantly red); Huma wears a red shawl (matching her red hair) in the scene from *Yerma* which she is rehearsing with Lluís Pasqual near the end of the film; Manuela is wearing a red top as she sits next to her son to watch *All About Eve*; Esteban's bedroom is decorated in reds. But these reds (with all the usual connotations of warmth, blood, passion and desire) are contrasted with the blues which signal the stage production of *A Streetcar Named Desire*. The minimalist blue cyclorama behind Nina (as Stella with her baby [fig. 25]) is the strongest blue ever seen in an Almodóvar film. The performance also uses stylized lighting: as Blanche appears through a curtain, instant bright directional light falls on her, indicating a change of dramatic attention on stage. Where film more usually necessitates

25. *All About My Mother.* Nina (Candela Peña) performing *A Streetcar Named Desire.*

lighting and *mise-en-scène* which serve verisimilitude, Almodóvar takes advantage of the theatre's non-mimetic potential for metaphorical or purely aesthetic statement. A more varied and diegetically motivated colour spectrum is offered in the interiors of the various apartments. Most memorable is the somewhat kitsch 1970s décor of the apartment Manuela rents in Barcelona with its wallpaper of large brown and beige polka dots. This is rented décor and not Manuela's chosen style; her Madrid apartment is stylish in a contemporary fashion but not at all kitsch. Agrado's flat is a colourful mixture of styles reflecting her lifestyle and the fact that Lola has taken most of her things. Agrado admits to her retro style when she says that Lola has stolen her 1970s magazines from where she gets her inspiration. All this cheap and faded style is contrasted with the enduring stylishness of Rosa's parents' home in Barcelona's *eixample*: modernist wall decorations in reds and golds and a modernist chair. The tasteful extravagance of Catalan modernist architecture is filmed in a full shot of the building where Rosa's parents live, and in a detail of the multi-coloured columns of Palau de la Música from Agrado's window. And windows, as well as doors and other 'internal' frames (within the frame of the photographic image), are another feature of Almodóvar's visual style.

Framing and Mirrors

Framing choices can have a purely aesthetic motivation, the simple value of pleasurable looking. In *All About My Mother*, when Manuela takes Agrado to a pharmacy, they are framed behind the white metal shutters of the establishment in a shot which was also used extensively in the press.[12] And the theatre environment also provides interesting framing opportunities, as Almodóvar indulges his love for the frame of the proscenium arch. Kowalski's card game in *A Streetcar Named Desire* is played behind thin wire meshing, emulating a constructivist stage set. In an even more self-consciously artistic stroke of *mise-en-scène*, in *Women on the Verge*, the famously Picasso-like features of actress Rossy de Palma are reflected in the broken glass of Pepa's window making an even more cubist image.[13]

Textures fascinate Almodóvar (as they did the master of melodramatic *mise-en-scène*, Douglas Sirk).[14] In *Flower*, a shot of the phone ringing in the dance studio is revealed by a pan from behind a wrought-iron staircase; a two-shot of Ángel and Leo is filtered through the blinds of his office; Leo is also viewed from underneath her desk through its glass surface, through the woven backrest of a chair, or through the filter of lace curtains. Such images appear principally for their aesthetic qualities. Whenever possible, the environment dictated by the context concentrates this kind of framing within the *mise-en-scène*. A tracking shot in the book warehouse follows the editor and Leo: a longshot with deep focus shows them behind the stacks of books; then, as they walk along a row, a much closer shot (still tracking) shows them with the books in the foreground. The effect of this shot and many others is to relieve the potential immobility of a lengthy dialogue sequence.

At other times, framing is diegetically dictated (i.e. the story dictates a certain frame). In *Matador*, when Ángel spies on Eva, the frame is masked leaving a circular iris, imitating his point of view through the binoculars. The same keyhole effect in *Kika* suggests Ramón's point of view on his model through the screen at the photo session at the start of a film which is all about the (guilty) pleasures of looking without being seen. Framing can function as a kind of shorthand to convey information quickly. Near the end of *All About My Mother*, Manuela's

flight from Barcelona with the new Esteban (Rosa's baby son) is signalled
by an extreme close-up inside the theatre dressing-room rubbish bin of
all things, which fades to black and then dissolves into the tunnel of the
train indicating a return to Madrid. When she returns again to Barcelona,
an aerial shot of a train heading to the right (west to Madrid) dissolves
into the exact same shot but with the train heading to the left of the
frame (east back to Barcelona), over titles 'two years later' (a future
textbook example of economical editing and framing, no doubt).

Just as juxtaposed framing can direct attention to an important
element of the narrative, so too can a single shot. In *Women on the Verge*,
in order to show that Marisa has consumed the spiked gazpacho, the
frame covers only the half-empty jug and part of her elbow slumped on
a table, enough to tell us the gazpacho has put her to sleep. In the same
film, when Candela sees the news report about the Shiite terrorists on
television she realizes she could be accused of being an accomplice.
The camera remains static on the television set but Candela rushes back
and forth in and out of the frame; the viewer only needs to know she
is frantic, not what she is doing, hence the use of the open form; the
information on television is much more important. And towards the
comic climax of the film, a deep focus shot shows Iván in the foreground in the telephone booth, and then allows first Pepa into the
frame, and then Lucía who approaches from behind in the distance, the
ex-women of his life literally closing in on him. To heighten the comic
tension, the new lover, Paulina, is waiting in a nearby car and she sees
Pepa approaching through her wing mirror, hastily ducking to avoid
discovery. The over-populated frame is a metaphor for Iván's love life.

Equally, the relationships between characters in the narrative can be
effectively portrayed by framing. In *Flower*, as Betty tells Leo about her
affair with Paco they face away from each other in a side shot close-up,
Betty in the foreground facing to the left of the frame, Leo just behind
facing right (looking away in an attempt to deny what she is hearing).
The frame tells us how close they are and yet how far apart. Framing
can be used to link characters through blocking and proxemics.[15] In *All
About My Mother*, Manuela's relationship with her son is simply portrayed
in repeated medium close-ups of them as they wait for Huma outside
the theatre. Earlier, a medium close-up of Esteban looking at his mother
from inside a café opposite reveals him framed inside and behind the
window, the shot slightly out of focus (which has a softening, almost
romantic effect). This beautiful shot is used as a flashback later, as

Manuela's lasting memory of her son before his death. (This shot of Esteban sitting in the café and looking directly at the camera was used in publicity stills and magazine articles, largely for its visual pleasure.) A few moments later, Esteban is framed in close-up through the wet glass of the taxi window, and this image, too, is used for a flashback later when Huma recalls seeing the boy through the glass.

In contrast, framing can also serve to separate or even incarcerate characters. In *Dark Habits*, when Yolanda tells the Mother Superior they should both give up heroin, they are filmed in a longshot from outside two windows, separately, as if in a confessional. The windows reveal them in the same space but firmly kept apart. In the same film, a shot of the Mother Superior beside Sister Manure reveals the dark figures of the two nuns against the blue light of the background altar, the criss-cross shadows of the leaded windows cast over the back wall. The same criss-cross shadow is used for the first image in the convent, denoting the enclosed atmosphere aided by the side lighting which constantly casts shadows in the interior of the convent. The incarceration metaphor is taken further in *Tie Me Up!*, where the framing of many of the scenes strongly emphasizes restraint. Ricky's own captivity in the mental in-stitution at the start of the film seems to suggest to him the idea of the abduction and imprisonment of Marina. The first human figure (a patient at the sanatorium) is framed behind the bars of a door, and when Ricky is freed a fast pan shows him framed behind bars for the last time. When he looks at the heart-shaped box of chocolates through the shop window, he is framed in a reverse angle shot by the letter 'O' painted on the window. Later, when Ricky and Marina go to buy the drugs she needs, they are both framed behind the protective bars of the pharmacy. And near the end of the film, as Ricky ties Marina up for the last time, she is framed in a round hole in the wrought-iron bedstead. Similarly, in *Matador*, when Ángel first sees the lawyer María, only her eyes and the top of her head are visible, the rest of her face covered by the police cell bars. Their conversation is shot with close-ups tightly framed behind the bars, strongly suggesting incarceration.[16] Still more meta-phorical are two juxtaposed examples of framing in *Live Flesh*. When Víctor catches sight of Elena and David in the cemetery he is framed between two gravestones, echoing his chance encounter between two deaths (that of his mother and of Elena's father). A moment later, Clara is framed by a red flower wreath (a beautiful image used in almost all magazines and newspaper features) which foreshadows her own death.

Almodóvar is attracted to symmetry. Frequently, symmetry in visual style (*mise-en-scène*, framing, camera angles) is set against either disruptions in that symmetrical order, or other forms of stark disparity (in narrative, characterization, etc.). An example occurs in *Tie Me Up!*, where Marina and Ricky are sitting together occupying half the frame each while they eat and watch television. The symmetry of the frame contrasts sharply with their most unequal power relations as kidnapper and victim. Unsurprisingly, Almodóvar's most abstract film, *Matador*, makes the most use of symmetry. Both Ángel's conversation with his mother over dinner and the subsequent visit to church are framed in symmetrical longshots which connote rigidity and formality. As they sit at table, Berta is at one end of the frame and Ángel at the other, wall lights and religious figurines intervening and completing the symmetry. The architectural symmetry of the church is enhanced by a medium longshot of the altar, with the priest in the centre, and then a longshot of the whole nave.[17] A rare example of underlighting is used to illuminate the statues he passes as he leaves, giving them a ghostly appearance, though diegetically justified by rows of bright candles below. His arrival at the police station is also framed in symmetrical order – the double doors of the police station with its logo in the centre – and is followed by a cut to another symmetrically composed side angle shot of Ángel talking to the police receptionist. Deep focus reveals the Inspector behind, positioned in the exact centre of the frame. As they look at each other, a very successful (and economical) two-shot close-up reveals both their expressions at once: Ángel looking through the glass at the inspector, the inspector reflected in the glass. Both occupy half the frame in a shot which also serves to establish a link between them (the inspector's fascination for Ángel).[18] Reflecting surfaces hold a particular fascination for Almodóvar.[19] Principal among them are mirrors.

Mirrors, like framing devices, are used diegetically and metaphorically, as part of narrative or characterization, as well as for their purely aesthetic properties. Mirrors open up the frame with light and space. Small spaces such as dressing-rooms are made to look much larger. This is true for dressing-room mirrors in *Dark Habits*, *Tie Me Up!*, *High Heels*, *Flower* and *All About My Mother*, where performance is preceded by make-up [fig. 26]. Mirrors can also obviate the need for a camera to move by providing a perspective on something or someone else within a static shot. In *Flower*, a shot of Ángel opening the door to Leo at the end of the film is seen through a reflection in a round mirror. A more

26. *All About My Mother*. Huma (Marisa Paredes) and Manuela
(Cecilia Roth).

sophisticated version occurs in *Kika* where Juana is made-up by Kika
and looks at herself in a (masculine-coded) shaving mirror. The camera
frames her in the small round mirror as well as in the larger bathroom
mirror which also reveals Kika's reaction in the background, all without
moving the camera.[20] Sometimes the diegesis calls for a mirror, as in the
case in *Flower* in the dance studio where full wall mirrors reflect and
duplicate *bailaor* Joaquín Cortés. And in *Law of Desire*, there is a mirror
in the opening porn film which the director exploits for its associations
with auto-eroticism, directing the young man first to kiss himself, then
rub himself against it. Here, the mirror is like a window to a parallel,
fantasy existence where the young man is no longer alone but perfectly
complemented in a parody of narcissism.

Often an interesting aesthetic quality in mirrors is combined with a
metaphorical reference. In *Flower*, Leo is reflected in infinity in the parallel
mirrors of the *El País* bathroom, not only a visually engaging image,
but a reflection of her self-scrutiny prior to her interview. Similarly, in
Matador, Ángel gazes at himself in the bathroom mirror after his failed
attempt to rape Eva, seemingly searching for justification of his actions.
A possible answer to his psychological turmoil is confirmed in a shot

of his monstrous mother's silhouette seen through the opaque glass of the bathroom door. Almodóvar refers to mirrors as a means of communicating with oneself (Albaladejo et al. 1988: 79). Such use of mirrors for self-analysis is most sustained in *All About My Mother*. Manuela's journey from unbearable grief to emotional health and stability is marked by her sense of self-analysis. To look in the mirror is to communicate with herself, to assess how she looks and how she is doing in her efforts to appear strong and controlled for those around her. Manuela looks at herself in the mirror of the bathroom of the theatre to measure her strength after watching the play with such painful old and recent memories. She looks at herself again in the mirror of the dressing-room when Huma has offered her a job, pleased at her composure. Her new employer Huma is reflected in the same mirror, but the quadruple images symbolize her internal divisions and contradictions. In a nice comic stroke, the mirror also conveys Mario's shallow vanity: where others look to the mirror for some of kind of truth about themselves, he only looks to check that he is sufficiently attractive to deserve the oral attentions of Agrado as he prepares to receive a blow-job from her. Clearly, Almodóvar's men are not the experts of self-awareness that his women are.

Mirrors also serve as communicative interfaces between characters. Kika meets Nick as she makes him up and they talk through a mirror. In *Tie Me Up!*, Marina and Ricky talk to each other in the mirror as Ricky tells her how he likes the thought of them as husband and wife preparing to go out. They later look at each other in the mirror as Marina bathes his wounds and realizes she loves him [fig. 27]. They are again reflected in the two open mirror doors of the wardrobe, and when they finally make love they are reflected in multiple images on a ceiling mirror, the kaleidoscopic image suggesting multiple identities and the fracturing of hitherto passive–dominant power relations. And in *Matador*, Diego's first exchange with María is reflected in the mirror of the cinema bathroom; as they speak to each other facing the mirror she tells him 'don't trust appearances'. The manipulative effects of mirrors can also be given a metaphorical dimension. In *Flower*, Leo embraces Paco in their doorway and they are seen through the hall mirror, which is a composite of mirror tiles, an allusion to their fragmented relationship (Strauss 1996: 161). Later, in the bathroom, as Paco talks to Leo revealed in the main mirror, Leo's reaction is seen in a smaller shaving mirror, replicating her existence as subsidiary to Paco.

27. *Tie Me Up! Tie Me Down!* Marina (Victoria Abril) realizes she loves
Ricky (Antonio Banderas).

The alternation of closed framing and the more open frames of mirrors is used in *High Heels* to delineate the two principal characters. When Becky arrives at Rebeca's apartment, she greets her son-in-law (and former lover) and the two are reflected in the hall mirror. Here there is a cut to a flashback of Becky and Manuel running into each other's arms which is then matched in the next shot by the same position as they embrace for the first time in many years. Where Becky is often framed in mirrors (suggesting vanity and self-absorption), Rebeca is frequently framed in confined spaces or behind bars. When she is led out of the television studios by the policemen, there is a tracking shot from behind the partitions of the studio, the pipes and wires of technology visible, Rebeca's head squarely framed by the studio apparatus. She is later filmed behind the bars of the police car. At her husband's funeral, Rebeca is filmed from inside the grave throwing in flowers from outside and above, her figure framed by the edges of the grave. Here mirrors and frames are linked to performance. Becky's performative mode is the open platform of the stage (and her vanity is serviced by the reflection of her talent in the audience response). Rebeca is framed by the closed box of the television set which offers no opportunity for audience response.

Almodóvar's visual style makes no apologies for its intrinsic aesthetic pleasure. But this distinctive style, too often dismissed as superficial, marketable chic, plays a pivotal role in character, narrative and genre. Having complete control of the production affords the director a good deal of freedom. But after his early and sometimes ostentatious experimentation with the medium, his later films display an economy of direction, mobilizing just the right amount of technology and art. The visual balance between spectacular display and subtle minimalism perfectly accords with Almodóvar's unique equidistance between the excesses of Hollywood and the understatement of the European auteur tradition.

9

Music and Songs

Music

Almodóvar's choice of music for his films has evolved from the eclectic bricolage of the earlier films to the commissioned musical scores of the later ones. A feature of films up to *Tie Me Up!* is the recycling of songs and music featured in earlier films, an economy of incidental music, keeping rights permissions to a minimum. In *Labyrinth of Passions*, for example, the songs 'Gran ganga' and 'Suck It to Me' (composed by Almodóvar himself) are used for background music elsewhere in the film. The same is true for *Dark Habits* where the opening of the song 'Encadenados' is used as background music for the scene where the Mother Superior shows Yolanda to her 'suite' before it is featured in full later. Even where the music has been specially composed for the film, it is sometimes used elsewhere: the piece 'La soledad de Gloria' (Gloria's Solitude) at the end of *What Have I Done* becomes the second opening title music for *Law of Desire*. Wherever possible Almodóvar uses his own compositions as incidental music: in *Law of Desire* 'Voy a ser mamá' (I'm Going to be a Mother) and 'Satanassa', and in *Tie Me Up!* 'Susan Get Down' which is used as disco music in a Benidorm nightclub. In *Law of Desire* the introduction of 'Ne me quittes pas' is used well before the number appears in full and, more memorably still, the opening of 'Lo dudo' (I Doubt It) is used in rhythmic match with Pablo's typing. The repetition of music not only serves as an economy but also subtly links together often highly emotive moments in the films.

Almodóvar has recognized that the main reason for using classical pieces in his films is also an economic one, as the rights are either free or cheap to obtain: hence, the choice of Tchaikovsky for the 'Bragas Ponte' advert, and for the lesson on kisses in *Dark Habits*, Shostakovich's tenth symphony for the opening credits of *Law of Desire*, and Stravinsky's tango for Pablo's escape in his car in the same film. *Women on the Verge* similarly uses two pieces by Rimsky-Korsakov, the 'Capriccio espagnol' and 'The Sea and Sinbad's Ship' from *Scheherazade*. These economically expedient choices do not, of course, exclude artistic considerations. All these pieces are suited to the mood requirements of the scenes in which they appear. It is in the film *Kika* where Almodóvar's choice of music and songs creates the most coherent mood for a soundtrack made up of exclusively existing music. The title music is one of the most famous pieces of Spanish music, Granados' 'Danza española, 5'. Extensive use is made of the music of Pérez Prado (who is now widely known due to the discovery of his music's suitability in the world of advertising).[1] His 'Mamá yo quiero' and 'Guaglioni' provide perfect incidental music for this film, and his 'Concierto para bongo', which accompanies the transmission on television of Kika's rape, conveys the obsessive sexual staying power of rapist Paul Bazzo (see Chapter 4). Equally effective is the insistent rhythm of Kurt Weill's doleful 'Youkali tango habanera' for the build-up to the film's bloody climax. The more upbeat rhythm of 'La cumparsita' by Xavier Cugat (written by Matos Rodríguez) provides an optimistic mood for the conclusion as Kika rides into the distance with a new man.

The creation of a particular mood is the objective of much incidental music, and this can at times require musical pieces quite different from the tone of the rest of the film's score. In *Live Flesh*, Almodóvar chooses 'Whirl-y-Reel' by the Afro Celt Sound System, which is indeed a very different sound for Almodóvar but appropriate to the different environment of the disabled basketball team in training. Here, the rhythm of the music accompanies extensive use of cutting which adds to the impression of rapid action. In *All About My Mother*, Dino Saluzzi's 'Gorrión' (Sparrow) with its haunting stop-and-go bandoneón sound is used for Manuela and Esteban's wait for the boy's theatrical idol Huma outside the theatre, when the young man asks his mother to tell the difficult story of his father. In *Dark Habits*, it is the music which from the outset sets the much darker mood than in previous films as much as the visibly darkening skies over the Spanish capital.

The first example of an original score is that of *movida* figure Bernardo Bonezzi for *What Have I Done*. His pieces are composed specifically for scenes in the films as their titles convey: 'El lagarto' (The Lizard), 'La familia de Gloria' (Gloria's Family), 'Madrid–Berlin', 'La soledad de Gloria' (Gloria's Solitude) and 'What Have I Done to Deserve This?' The same is true for *Matador* where Bonezzi's pieces include 'Composición en rojo' (Composition in Red), the broody piano music for the opening sex murder and, later, the cacophonous 'Persecución telepática' (Telepathic Chase) for Ángel's hallucinations. By *Women on the Verge*, Bonezzi is more confident and varied. His 'Taxi mambo' contributes greatly to the genre-based comedy chase sequence (and it's a version of the main theme tune). His 'Hacia el aeropuerto' (To the Airport) accompanies Lucía's flying hair, reminiscent of the witch's flight in *The Wizard of Oz* (Victor Flemming, 1939). Almodóvar commissioned Ennio Morricone for the score of *Tie Me Up!* Much of the incidental music is typical of the thriller genre and sounds strangely foreign in Almodóvar. The director thought Morricone's music was far too conventional for *Tie Me Up!* (Strauss 1996: 119). The worrying opening theme, however, is perfect for the mental institution. The incidental music of Ryuichi Sakamoto in *High Heels* is fairly typical of melodrama and thriller genres. Here again, Almodóvar did not like much of Sakamoto's score for *High Heels* and a great deal of what appears on the released CD version does not feature in the film (Strauss 1996: 118). That Almodóvar's experiments with non-Spanish composers have left him unsatisfied attests to the cultural specificity of much of the scores in his films.

A new era in Almodóvar's film scores begins with the collaboration of Alberto Iglesias from *Flower* in 1995. The music by Iglesias is very cinematic and forms part of a much more professional and artistic package in Almodóvar's work. In *Live Flesh*, 'El flechazo' (for the slow motion sequence where Elena falls for the heroically calm David) is one of many excellent pieces in a film where the evocative integration of commissioned music and songs is at its best. Fernández (1999: 24) describes this score as 'full of Mediterranean resonances in its delicate orchestration of harmonica, mandolin, Portuguese guitar and strings'. And in *All About My Mother*, Iglesias's score is also prominent: examples include the opening credits 'Soy Manuela' with its deep piano tones following the movements of life-maintaining fluids through the tubes and cables of intensive care, or 'All About Eve' which has a dramatic orchestral sound befitting both melodrama and 'quality', 'art-house' cinema. The theme, 'Once Again Running Away without Saying Good-bye', marks Manuela's return to Barcelona, the rhythmic, percussive tones corresponding to the train travelling through the tunnels which convey her there. Another piece, 'Igualita que Eva Harrington' (Just Like Eve Harrington) is used for the meta-theatrical scene with Huma Rojo on stage playing Blanche Dubois, the title linking Tennessee Williams's character with Eve Harrington from *All About Eve* (Joseph L. Mankiewicz, 1950). The 'Dedicatoria', perhaps the most memorable theme from the soundtrack, is used as Almodóvar pays homage directly to all the actresses who have played actresses in films.

Sometimes music is chosen more for its specific, cultural or inter-textual associations rather than its quality or tone. Among such associations are those of national identity, religion, popular culture and other films. In the early films in particular, Almodóvar plays with questions of national identity in his choice of music. In *Pepi, Luci, Bom*, a number from the *zarzuela La verbena de la Paloma* is used for the attack on the policeman, suggesting a clash of urban cultures from different ages and providing an opportunity for irony but also a chance to pay homage to this type of music. A famous pasodoble is used for the policeman's attempted revenge, playfully suggesting a link between Spain's national police and its national music. And a Holy Week *paso* punctuates Bom and Luci's first meeting, and the infamous 'golden shower' scene, the juxtaposition of sexual transgression and religion contributing to the film's intentional debunking of previously sacrosanct national mythologies. Religious music is used with subtly ironic intent on occasions: in *Dark Habits*, to accompany Yolanda's withdrawal symptoms and nightmares, and in *Law of Desire*, where organ music and a religious song take Tina to her infancy, hinting at how the Church may have corrupted her childhood. In *Matador*, we hear an organ accompanying the traditional Madrid dance, the *chotis*. Spanish guitar is heard as Diego finds María on a video recording of his final bullfight. By *Flower*, the traditional Spanish form of the 'soleá' (the 'mother' of *cante jondo*) is heard in a distilled form by Gil Evans, for the dance performance of contemporary flamenco artists Joaquín Cortés and Manuela Vargas. On occasions, music from other films is used, as in *Labyrinth of Passions* where the music of Nino Rota is used to conjure up the spirit of Fellini (Vidal 1988: 62), or in *Dark Habits* where Miklós Rosza's music from *Providence* is used for the dramatic pan through the convent's patio jungle (Vidal 1988: 106; Albaladejo et al. 1988: 63). In *Kika*, 'The Car Lot, the

Package', from Bernard Herrmann's original score for *Psycho*, is used as incidental music, perfect for this film which borrows much from previous thrillers.[2] In *Labyrinth of Passions*, the music which accompanies the mothers in Doctor de la Peña's waiting-room is hyper-melodramatic, almost a parody of the genre, and reminiscent of the musical excess which characterizes some of Fassbinder's films. *Pepi, Luci, Bom*'s use of a tango to score the intertitles 'Pepi was hungry for revenge' is evocative of highly stylized pre-sound melodramas.

Songs

Songs are chosen for a variety of reasons including lyrics, mood, associations or, more frequently, for a combination of these reasons. A musical 'key' to a film or a sequence can be established by a song like 'Se nos rompió el amor' by Fernanda y Bernarda de Utrera which forms the soundtrack for almost five minutes at the start of *Kika*, or 'El rosario de mi madre' by El Duquende which is used in juxtaposition with images of La Ventilla and the Torres Kio in *Live Flesh*. A much less Spanish mood is evoked by the song 'Tajabone' by the Senegalese artist-songwriter Ismaël Lô, in *All About My Mother*. Its Dylanesque opening bars on the accordion are used for the presentation of Barcelona (the most exotic, cosmopolitan and least 'Spanish' of Spain's cities), images of the shining city spread out towards the sea, or the distinctive images of the towers of the Sagrada Familia reflected in the glass of Manuela's taxi. The melancholy voice of Lô himself provides the soundtrack for Manuela's search in the prostitute pick-up area, far from the modern tourist heart of the city. 'Tajabone' is a song for a Muslim celebration about the love of children, so it fits perfectly with a film all about motherhood.

A song may be inserted for a change of rhythm, as in *High Heels* where 'Pecadora' by Los Hermanos Rosario features in a prison yard dance sequence, or to create an air of improvisation as in *Tie Me Up!* where Lola's song and dance number in the post-filming party sounds like gypsies in a street performance with a tinny electric organ and trumpet. Or it may be there for its own sake as in the beautiful 'Tonada de luna llena' by Caetano Veloso for the final titles of *Flower*. As in the choice of music, association also has a part to play in song selection. In *Pepi, Luci, Bom* the opening pop song 'Do the Swim' by Little Nell, singing co-star of Jim Sharman's 1975 film, *The Rocky Horror Picture*

Show, not only connotes the cult movie, but the English lyrics testify to the popularity of Anglo-Saxon culture at the time. Kiti Manver's artiste sings flamenco-rock ('like a *tonadilla* but with a touch of the international'). However, by the end of the film, Bom's change of direction is indicated by the Latin song 'Estaba escrito' by Monna Bell. More sophisticated is the use of 'Ay mi perro' (Oh My Dog) by La Niña de Antequera in *Live Flesh*. The panning shot of the miserable street life of the city accompanied by the tune not only links to Sancho's remark, 'Dogs! That's how they treat us and that's what we are', but the song itself evokes affection, loss and a particularly Spanish sentimentality all at once. As a 'classic' number from Spain's folkloric past, it also serves to bridge the gap between the old regime, newsreel section narrating Víctor's birth on the city bus, and the contemporary 1990s section of the film.

Song lyrics are often used in ironic juxtaposition with the action or emotion of a sequence in Almodóvar's films. In *Tie Me Up!* the final song 'Resistiré' (I Will Survive) by El Dúo Dinámico not only suggests a happy ending, but points to Marina's submission to, rather than resistance of Ricky's unconventional courtship. The party scene of *Pepi, Luci, Bom* uses the song 'Tu loca juventud' (Your Crazy Youth) by Maleni Castro, not without irony: when this song first came out in the 1960s, Spain was far from 'crazy', but by 1978–79, the youth of Spain is finally catching up. *Dark Habits* uses the religious song 'Dueño de mi vida' (Lord of My Life) during the scene in which drug addict Yolanda arrives at the convent, the discordant voices of nuns offering a hymn to a woman who indeed becomes mistress of the Mother Superior's life. Yolanda herself sings – for the audience of nuns – the entirely inappropriate 'Salí porque salí' (I Left Because I Left) with lyrics which talk of 'amor prohibido' (forbidden love). And in *What Have I Done*, the Miguel de Molina song 'La bien pagá' (Well Paid) provides an ironic commentary on Gloria's life (see Chapter 4).

Parody is another rich area of exploitation for songs in Almodóvar. In *Labyrinth of Passions*, 'Gran ganga' by Almodóvar (with Los Pegamoides and Bonezzi) combines a somewhat middle-eastern 'exoticism' in the music with prosaic lyrics about bargains in the sex and drugs market. 'Suck It to Me' by Almodóvar and McNamara is sung in English, the numbers of the song corresponding to empty set phrases ('seven up', 'after eight', 'nine to five'), the ultimate in postmodern vacuity. In *Pepi, Luci, Bom*, Almodóvar adopts a punk style (though more aesthetically

28. *Pepi, Luci, Bom*. Bom (Alaska) sings 'Murciana marrana' with
Los Pegamoides.

than musically). 'Murciana marrana' was composed by Almodóvar and
Los Pegamoides and performed by Bomitony (alias Alaska and Los
Pegamoides) [fig. 28]. The lyrics of Alaska's 'Murciana marrana' (Dirty
Murcian) in *Pepi, Luci, Bom* are certainly not the stuff of the average
Spanish pop hit of the period, but neither are they as aggressive and
disturbing as some of the punk lyrics.

> I love you because you are dirty
> Disgusting whore and crawler
> The most obscene of all Murcia
> And entirely at my beck and call.
> All I think about is you, Murciana.
> Because you're a dirty pig.
> I stick my finger in your slit.
> I give you a couple of slaps
> I make you wank me
> I'm more violent than the GRAPO
> I'm like the ring on your finger
> With me you reach orgasms

> If I fart in your mouth
> You applaud me with enthusiasm
> You belong to me, Murciana
> Because I like it that way.[3]

These lyrics illustrate both a debt to punk and a departure from it. Almodóvar et al. took up the punk posture of parody and exploited it for humour rather than for subversive satire (Holguín 1999: 266–76). But Bom – rather like Almodóvar himself – subsequently abandons punk and turns to more Hispanic music.

At times a song can carry the full narrative weight of a sequence. This is the case in *Live Flesh* with Albert Plá's 'Sufre como yo' (Suffer Like Me). The eloquence of Plá's song in describing how Víctor feels is the perfect economy of emotion: no dialogue or voice-over is necessary:

> I want you to suffer like I suffer
> And I'll learn how to pray to achieve that
> I want you to feel as useless
> As an empty glass of whisky in your hands
> And for you to feel your heart in your chest
> Like it belonged to someone else
> I wish you death, wherever you are
> And I'll learn how to pray to achieve that.[4]

Almodóvar finds his most significant musical economy in the highly expressive *boleros* and other sentimental songs which enrich many of his films. The mobilization of the combined effects of voice, music and lyrics is one of the most prominent features of his film-making. In *Dark Habits*, Yolanda and the Mother Superior sing 'Encadenados' (Chained Together) by Lucho Gatica, the first in a long line of *boleros*. Their *raison d'être* is explained here by Yolanda: 'It's music which really speaks, which tells us about life' (and it's this song which marks the end of the film, perhaps the bleakest ending of any Almodóvar film). Where song lyrics can speak for the characters, Almodóvar allows them freely to do so, often with no voice-over or dialogue. Thus, just as in *Flower*, 'El el último trago' (The Last Drink) by Chavela Vargas expresses Leo's desire to drown her sorrows, 'Ay amor' by Bola de Nieve signals the start of her recovery from the edge of suicide. In *Live Flesh*, 'Somos' by Chavela Vargas not only speaks of the couple's desire to be one flesh, but it makes an otherwise over-lengthy love scene tolerable. The final love scene of *Matador*, carefully choreographed by the lovers themselves, is set to Mina's 'Espérame en el cielo' (Wait for Me in Heaven), its first bars of pure Spanish guitar perfect for the *corrida*-inspired tableau of yellow and red which is set before them. Almodóvar has commented that the song could have been made especially for his film (Vidal 1988: 172).

In *Women on the Verge*, the film opens and closes with songs which tell much of the essence of the plot. 'Soy infeliz' (I'm Unhappy) by Lola Beltrán provides the title music. Pepa has a record on which Iván has written 'I don't ever want to hear you say "I'm Unhappy"') and when Pepa hears the song later she loses her temper and throws the record out of the window. The closing song, 'Puro Teatro' by La Lupe, provides a characterization for Iván, the quintessential male liar:

> Just like on a stage
> You play out your cheap pain
> Your drama is unnecessary
> I already know that theatre
> Lying, how well you play that part
> After all it seems
> That is the way you are...[5]

Even where the lyrics are in a foreign language, the song is none the less integrated into the narrative. In *What Have I Done*, 'Nur nicht aus Liebe Weinen' (Don't Cry Over Lost Love) by Zarah Leander is pure nostalgia for taxi driver Antonio and a cause for jealousy and desperation for his wife Gloria, who associates the song with her husband's former German lover, and is excluded by its German lyrics.

In *Law of Desire*, two songs form the core of the emotions and relationships between the characters. Early in the film 'Ne me quittes pas' performed by Maisa Matarazzo indicates Pablo's love for Juan, when it is played during their last night together. Pablo later incorporates it into Tina's performance of Cocteau's *La voix humaine*. But the sentiment of the song also matches the emotions of both Tina and little Ada who also has a small part in the play, Tina because she has lost the love of Ada's mother, and Ada because she fears she will be taken away from Tina, her adopted parent. And the famous Los Panchos *bolero* 'Lo dudo' is given a dramatic twist in the film: Antonio's love for Pablo, while it is pure in intention, is neither heterosexual nor conventionally protective, rather it is dangerous and desperate. Antonio earnestly sings the song to Pablo in their last hour together, borrowing Los Panchos as a vehicle for 'performing' his emotions.

Apart from the many memorable songs which are used as counterpoint to the action or emotion of the films, there are also a number of songs and dance routines which are incorporated into the films as performances. These range from showcase performances (often inserted more for artistic than for narrative purposes) by real-life artists, to simulated performances, usually mimed and often parodies of an original song. Joaquín Cortés' and Manuela Vargas' dance performance of Gil Evans's 'Soleá' in *Flower*, though filmed for this film, is an event in its own right. Earlier we see Cortés at practice in the studio. Equally authentic is the appearance in *Labyrinth of Passions* of Almodóvar himself alongside Fabio McNamara performing 'Suck It to Me', a performance which is typical of their real-life activities in the early *movida madrileña*, the English lyrics and drugs theme authentically reflecting the times. Later in the same film, a real group plays 'Gran ganga', but Imanol Arias is miming (to the voice of Almodóvar). It is on stage that Sexi first encounters Riza; ironically, his time in Madrid is all performance as he is in disguise.

Elsewhere, performances are even more self-consciously staged. In *Pepi, Luci, Bom*, we see a rehearsal of the song 'Muy cerca de ti' (Very Close to You). Pop music was a feature of the *movida*, and live performances are also featured in Fernando Colomo's *¿Qué hace una chica como tú en un sitio como este?* (*What's a Girl Like You Doing in a Place Like This?*, 1978).[6] But despite the apparent authenticity of such scenes, whether they are actually staged for Almodóvar's camera or just captured by it only affects the nature of the performance not its performative status. In *Tie Me Up!* the post-filming party involves Lola singing, accompanied by amateur musicians and dancing family members (including Almodóvar's mother). This number serves to ease tension of the absent Marina's abduction and provides a break in the setting, much of which takes place in Marina's flat. But apart from this, it is indulgence on Almodóvar's part. He delights in what in Spanish is referred to as 'playback' – the miming of recorded songs. This may be simply a pragmatic decision: in *Dark Habits*, non-singing actress Cristina Pascual is dubbed by singer Sol Pilas for her cabaret performance of 'Dime' (Feelings). This translated and second-rate performance (she is distracted and forgets the lyrics) takes place in the mock-Andalusian Villa Rosa nightclub, the weakness of the performance drawing attention to itself.

29. *High Heels.* Letal (Miguel Bosé) with Rebeca (Victoria Abril).

Self-conscious theatricality also marks the last song in *Dark Habits*. Yolanda's performance of 'Salí porque salí' is very amateurish, and the song itself affirms 'life is a play'. A further irony is introduced in that the essential element of a performance – the audience, here made up of nuns – is not what is expected for this type of song.

More theatrical still, though with a melodramatic rather than comic purpose, are the performances within *High Heels*. Becky's performance of 'Piensa en mí' (Think of Me) in the María Guerrero theatre is fully integrated into the narrative. Becky kisses the stage and dedicates the song to her daughter who hears the song on the radio in prison. The lyrics are perfectly suited to the emotion of the scene: when Becky sings 'when you cry also think of me', her daughter is indeed both crying and thinking about her. Letal's repeat performance – an imitation of Becky – is low-key and has the air of a farewell about it [fig. 29]. Letal, another great performer with more roles than any other in Almodóvar's films, is reaching out to Rebeca. Letal's performance of 'Un año de amor' (A Year of Love) is a more complex sequence. Letal is a man performing as a woman, but the actor is the famous pop star Miguel Bosé, and his casting was a *cause célèbre* of the filming publicity.

The voice is that of another pop star, Luz Casal. More importantly, the performance also draws attention to the relationships of those watching: Becky is watching a parody of herself, a substitute for her in the eyes of Rebeca too, and an uncomfortable situation for narrow-minded Manuel; this imitation is then imitated by the drag-queen group Diabéticas Aceleradas, who copy the actions of Letal. This ritualizes Letal's performance; the fans engaged in a cult of stardom and of 'spirit and style', as Letal puts it.

What conclusions, then, can be drawn from the choices made by Almodóvar for the music and songs in his films? First, the importance he attaches to music (relative to other directors) and to the diverse cultural connotations of songs. The position of music and songs within the diegesis (i.e. integrated into the film rather than working as a counterpoint) is another important factor: many of the songs become performances within the film. Even where music is extra-diegetic, the connection with the narrative is often much more explicit than in many films. Perhaps the most important musical feature, though, is the recuperation of sentimental *boleros* and other once-embarrassing pieces of Latin popular musical heritage, leading to the pre-eminence of what Fernández (1999: 24) calls 'the pre-existing Hispanic musical canon'. The resurgence of popularity in such previously forgotten styles, and the consequent re-branding as 'camp but cool' of their former stars and songs, are largely the legacy of Almodóvar.[7]

Part Four
Conclusions

Postmodernism, Performance and Parody

> Cinema has nothing to do with life. In the cinema everything is false. (*Pepi, Luci, Bom*)

Ever since its invention, the cinema has sought to exploit its photographic advantage over earlier representational arts, and Hollywood made (a particular kind of) realism its conventional goal. Other cinemas, particularly European, stress auteurist values such as aesthetics or irony. Almodóvar's independence from the conventions and constraints of mainstream Hollywood films is matched by his manifest distance from the often abstract, hermetic or even solipsistic tendencies of much of European film. Thus, the originality of Almodóvar's cinema lies in its hybridity; it takes much from the world of Hollywood movies, but maintains a more intellectual, European scepticism, a distance marked by irony and self-reflexiveness. The free mixing of popular elements of mass culture such as Hollywood movies, advertising and television with the more artistic 'high culture' of auteurist, poetic cinemas has earned Almodóvar the label of postmodernist. Certainly, a number of characteristics of contemporary culture, often described as postmodern, can be usefully applied to Almodóvar's cinema. The breaking down of orthodox frontiers between mass and high culture, the opening up of media to new social groups, the tendency towards performance, simulation and parody, the absence of so-called 'grand narratives' and the weakening of historicity, are the double-edged swords of postmodernism. Some lament the contamination of high culture with commodified pop/trash/ kitsch, while others celebrate postmodernism's plurality and accessibility. The reflection and exploitation of these features of postmodernism in Almodóvar's films is, on balance though, to their benefit.

Almodóvar owes his career in part to opportunities opened up by a distinctly modern attitude to the production of culture. Unlike his predecessors who all came from the middle classes and attended film school, he acquired his own camera and began making films – spoof adverts – while working for the Spanish telephone company. His bricolage mode of production (see Chapter 1) gave an eclectic quality to his films: pop culture, advertising, narrative, intertextuality, music and kitsch décor were mixed with a substantial ironic and self-reflexive distance usually equated with 'high' culture.[1] From the beginning, Almodóvar turned the difficulties of producing his first film into playful self-reflexivity. Protagonist Pepi has a project for a film (to be shot on video, that most domestic of media), the story of Luci and Bom. As Pepi explains in the film, representation is all, to be natural is not sufficient.[2] Almodóvar's documentation of his contemporary reality (making films) is very different from the life-documentary style of Warhol. Where the American pop artist set the camera running and told the protagonists *not* to act, for Almodóvar, acting is all; the story of Luci and Bom must be *re-presented*. Pepi tells them, 'It's not just a matter of standing in front of the camera. Not only do you have to be yourselves but you have to represent your characters and representation is always artificial' [fig. 30]. And Pepi's justification for her film is also perfect for Almodóvar in his first full-length feature: 'At the end of the day it's only a game. If it doesn't come out right, there's no problem.' The concept of acting or performance colours much of Almodóvar's work.

Michel Benamou (1977: 3) describes performance as 'the unifying mode of the postmodern' and Steven Connor (1996: 109) affirms its importance in 'a culture that is so saturated with and fascinated by techniques of representation and reproduction, that it has become difficult for us to be sure where action ends and performance begins'. Almodóvar's work testifies to the performativity of human behaviour. To perform means to act, display certain skills, or even to dissimulate or pretend. The films are intrinsically performative in that they involve action simulated for the camera lens. Even where the action can be regarded as authentic, not simulated (as in the case of inserted performances which are merely recorded by the camera), the mode is still

30. *Pepi, Luci, Bom*. Pepi tells her friends that 'representation is always artificial'.

one of performativity, as actors (people who *do* things) know they have an audience. Almodóvar's characters are constantly dissimulating, taking on roles, false identities and shamelessly lying. Indeed, the very first action in Almodóvar's very first film is dissimulation: Pepi pretends not to be able to hear the policeman.

In true postmodern style, Almodóvar also shows how life itself becomes performance, how life imitates art. In *Matador*, the final death scene – set to music and with careful colour co-ordination – is a choreographed performance, though the spectators are Diego and María alone. The ending of *Women on the Verge* – expressed in the song 'Teatro' – is that Iván (and, by extension, all men) are performers. And in the first scene of *Flower*, the 'doubleness' of performance is explicitly acknowledged in the video recording of a simulated hospital scene. While it is clear that some kind of representation is taking place, it is not until after the scene that we are aware of the purpose behind it: the training of doctors to break the news of a family member's death and gently broach the subject of donating organs. The doctors perform their roles with clichés from film and television. The nurse Manuela simulates a grieving mother, her performance clearly identified as such;

she is at pains to distance herself from her role when the audience mistake her character's attitudes for her own. This simulation becomes the inspiration for *All About My Mother*, perhaps the film most concerned with investigating performance.

The title of Almodóvar's thirteenth film, *All About My Mother*, is a homage to Joseph L. Mankiewicz's 1950 classic, *All About Eve*. A scene from it is watched by the impressionable artist Esteban and his mother Manuela, and it inspires the young man to wait outside the theatre for his idol actress Huma Rojo just as Eve Harrington waits for Margo in *All About Eve*. But the relationship with *All About Eve* does not end there: Manuela, like Eve, becomes an assistant to the diva and then an understudy, though in the case of Manuela, without calculation. So when Almodóvar dedicates the film to all those actresses who have played actresses on the stage or in films, it is a dedication which colours the entire film and many of his other films. More than the obvious theatrical context, Manuela represents the actress in all women, a point made by Almodóvar in the Press Book of the film:

> My idea at first was to make a film about the acting abilities of certain people who aren't actors. As a child I remember seeing this quality among the women in my family. They pretended much better than the men. Through these lies they were able to avoid more than one tragedy.[3]

For Manuela, life dramatically imitates the simulation when her own adolescent son is killed and she enacts the grieving mother for real. Her son dies while chasing after actress Huma Rojo after a performance of Williams's *A Streetcar Named Desire*. Her obsession with the play which in her words 'has marked her life' is two-fold: she met her husband in a production of the play years before, and now she loses her son after another performance. Unable to keep away from the play, she encounters the actresses who play Blanche and Stella, and eventually stands in to play the role of Stella for the second time in her life. Manuela also has to 'perform' surrogate motherhood twice in the film and maintain the dissimulation of strength despite overwhelming grief for her lost son. In this film motherhood, and even gender, are equated with performance. Transsexual Agrado's impromptu performance on the Barcelona stage (which Almodóvar based on a real event),[4] asserts that authenticity – in her case womanhood – is achieved as much through desire as through actions.

The representation of identities (motherhood, gender) and other human activities as performance or simulation, invites the charge – levelled at postmodernism and at Almodóvar as a postmodern film-maker – of depthlessness, of what Baudrillard (1981) called 'simulacra', the copy without the original.[5] Jameson's (1991: 17–18) study of post-modernism critiques pastiche – defined as 'parody without a vocation [...] amputated of the satiric impulse' – for its cannibalization of dead styles, empty of any critical or satirical commentary. The same charge is brought against Almodóvar by critics who signal his 'irresponsible' pillaging of cultural traditions merely for their aesthetic qualities (Sánchez-Biosca 1989: 111–23). The prominence of glossy images and design in the films certainly corresponds to more general trends in contemporary culture and its marketing. But, as Yarza (1999: 35–7) points out, Almodóvar's recycling of cultural traditions is not only aesthetically motivated; there is a clear critical distance operating between the old and the new. I would go further: parody is Almodóvar's general mode of address. (And it features in every chapter of this book, almost on every page.) National identity, power and gender relations, sexuality, history, politics, cultural traditions, visual and musical choices are all mediated by a questioning, parodic distance. From the 'general erections' contest conflating the democratic process with the television gameshow format in his first film, to the almost nostalgic recuperation of the movie theatre newsreel format (the NoDo) in his twelfth, Almodóvar subjects cultural forms to variously light or savage parody.

Where Jameson (1991: 17) – concentrating on a US culture which, he argues, does not possess the critical edge of parody – affirms that pastiche (blank parody) is the determining code of the postmodern, others offer more positive evaluations of contemporary culture's parodic mode. Bakhtin's (1981: 76) definition of parody as 'an intentional dialog-ized hybrid' is particularly suitable for Almodóvar's reworking of filmic genres, visual motifs and even musical scores, all of which acquire new meanings when they are recontextualized. Such recuperated images, genres and references are not always reinscribed negatively or satirically as in Genette's (1982: 34, 36) definition of parody. There is much homage in Almodóvar (to other directors, other films, music or art). In this respect, Linda Hutcheon's broader definition of parody as 'one mode of coming to terms with that rich and intimidating legacy of the past'[6] is perhaps the most appropriate for Almodóvar's parodic stance. Almo-dóvar's films strategically recoil from reference to the past, symptomatic of the willed *desmemoria* which Spain (understandably) exhibits in relation to Franco's still recent dictatorship (see Chapter 2). Here, too, the films coincide with postmodernism's weakening of historicity, closely related to its lack of 'grand narratives' (big ideas). They reflect a nation which has seen both socialism and fascism fail, and which has achieved modernity, just in time to embrace postmodernity wholeheartedly (see Graham and Labanyi 1995: 396–406).[7] Nevertheless, in their forms and visual images, the films frequently refer to other texts (see Chapter 7) and self-consciously to themselves.

Throughout his work, Almodóvar makes particular use of certain cinematic techniques which are so self-consciously filmic as to border on parody. The director himself expressed the idea: 'In my films everything is on the verge of parody. It isn't just parody, it's also the line between the ridiculous and the grotesque, but it can easily fall across this divide.'[8] In many films, the film medium itself is parodied. Almodóvar rarely allows his audience complete absorption in the films as first-hand witnesses of a reality. We are constantly reminded that 'film is film', through distancing devices. These can be through the appearance on screen of Almodóvar himself (often in the role of the director, such as in *Pepi, Luci, Bom, Labyrinth of Passions* or *Matador*). Or they can take the form of film-within-film techniques, where the cinematic profession is shown exposed, stripped of its illusion. Almodóvar has said that 'there is nothing more authentic than artifice laid bare'.[9] A number of the films foreground the film medium, among them *Tie Me Up!* (see Chapter 4), *Law of Desire* and *Women on the Verge*. In the latter film, it is immediately apparent that this film is to have a strong element of self-reference. The final title drawing to accompany the credit which reads 'Script and direction, Pedro Almodóvar', shows three women being filmed with silhouetted cameras in the foreground and a microphone above. The main character, Pepa, works in the film and television industry and her dreams are also taken from that area. When we see Pepa at work in the (real-life) sound studios EXA,[10] we see the recording studio through viewing booths with all the film technology in full view. A subsequent gag perfectly illustrates the film's self-conscious cinematic pose: when Pepa is pursuing Iván's ex-wife Lucía, she gets into a cab and orders, 'Follow that taxi.' The driver responds, 'I thought that only happened in films.'

Where in *Women on the Verge* meta-cinematic conceit is a comic device, *Law of Desire* adopts a more interrogative perspective and goes even further in the inclusion of film within film. The opening titles are typewritten on to crumpled pieces of paper, and light is cast on them in the shape of an eye. In shorthand, Almodóvar already reveals two of the themes of his film: the typewriter, which is scriptwriter Pablo's medium of expression (and which also betrays him) and the voyeuristic eye of the camera, which represents both the seduction and the danger of the film-maker's art. The opening scene is a film-within-a-film, though at first this is not apparent. The foregrounding of the scene as meta-cinema 'makes strange' the pro-filmic event, destroying the illusion of the cinema of being an 'invisible guest'. Kaja Silverman (1986: 220), in her notes on suture, refers to the importance of the shot/reverse shot in cinema 'because it demonstrates so lucidly the way in which cinema operates to reduplicate the history of the subject'. The need for the viewer to be included in the film fiction ('imaginary plenitude') is confounded by the opening of *Law of Desire*, where an off-screen voice immediately points the viewer to an Other. Where classic cinema attempts to conceal the passivity of the viewer, to include her/him inside the fiction by denying the existence of anything outside it, here, the viewer's faith in the integrity of the fictional world of the frame is destroyed from the outset.

In many ways, *Law of Desire* exemplifies Almodóvar's parodic mode and his cinema as a whole: the representation of gender identity – so long the mainstay of film theory – is knowingly articulated as a theme itself; religious iconography is reinscribed as both a naive spirituality and an aesthetic; and the *bolero* is transcontextualized as contemporary and non-heterosexual. What Almodóvar has achieved in twenty years is to shift the frame of reference for Spanish cinema (and culture more generally). The cultural myths and stereotypes of high passion, religious fervour, death-obsession, machismo and backwardness are all still in the frame, but they are decentred. The marginal (punks, transvestites, lesbians, gays, drug addicts, criminals) become the mainstream, pathos becomes comedy, outmoded musical heritage is reclaimed, and minority subcultures become mainstream, Oscar-winning products. The films appeal to mainstream audiences in Spain, and elsewhere they are in-creasingly moving beyond their (particularly loyal) niche audiences. And yet there remains a localized national quality about them, what we might call a particularly Spanish form of irony or the grotesque. A line can be traced back from Almodóvar through Buñuel, Valle-Inclán, Picasso and Goya to Cervantes.[11] Paradoxically, Buñuel's versions of this grotesque found little favour in his native Spain and much of his *oeuvre*, though the work of a Spaniard, has been forcibly integrated into a universal canon of international film art. At the beginning of the twenty-first century, Almodóvar has it both ways: in his own country, he has arguably more freedom than any of his contemporaries; and abroad, he has been chosen as the chief embodiment of the new, postmodern Spain.

Notes

Preface and Acknowledgements

1. Lauren Bacall, interviewed by Mark Cousins in *Scene by Scene*, BBC2, 5 August 2000.

2. Hollywood has made Almodóvar various directing offers, including the scripts of *To Wong Foo* and *Sister Act* (Cobos and Marías 1995: 109).

Introduction: Almodóvar – the *Auteur* of a Free Spain

1. Brenan (1943).

2. The origins of the name Almodóvar are taken from Covarrubias' 1611 volume *Tesoro de la Lengua Castellana o Española* (1943: 99).

3. Almodóvar has sometimes given small acting parts to his team, including his brother Agustín who is the only actor to appear in all thirteen films. His fondness for his production director Esther García inspired the production manager in *Tie Me Up!* played by Loles León (Strauss 1996: 68). In *Flower*, Leo's pseudonym in *El País* is Paz Sufrategui, the real name of El Deseo's press officer, and, according to Almodóvar, 'a writer's name'.

4. Boquerini (1989: 34) includes some of Almodóvar's projected backstories and continuations of characters from *Pepi, Luci, Bom*.

1. Cultural Context

1. Candela Peña, writing in the Press Book of *All About My Mother*.

2. Almodóvar's production manager Esther García in an interview with the author.

3. Ibid.

4. For an account of the financing of Spanish films, see Peter Besas (1997: 241–59).

5. Esther García, interview with the author.

6. For an account of youth culture in Spain, see Allinson (2000: 265–73).

7. Jordan and Morgan (1998: 115) make the point that Almodóvar was as much a product of the so-called 'comedia madrileña' (localized comedy of 1970s and 1980s) and *esperpento* as of the *movida*.

8. For an account of punk as subcultural style see Hebdige (1979).

9. These were later published under the title *Patty Diphusa y otros textos* (1991).

10. Lévi-Strauss, *The Savage Mind* (1966) and *Totemism* (1969), cited by John Clarke (1976: 177).

11. In 1981, Almodóvar published a short novel *Fuego en las entrañas* (*Fire in the Entrails*) with illustrations by the now world-famous Catalan designer Javier Mariscal (Boquerini 1989: 26).

12. For a more detailed account of the political exploitation of the *movida* see Allinson 2000: 268–70.

13. Almodóvar in Strauss (1996: 161).

14. Interviewed by Iñaki Gabilondo for TVE1's *Gente de Primera*, 26 October 1993.

2. National Identity

1. Carlos Saura, for example, has a trilogy of films based on the Spanish tradition of flamenco. The last of the series, simply entitled *Flamenco* (1995), is almost a documentary of this performance. Almodóvar, on the other hand, began his own, much more melodramatic story, about a lame flamenco singer, supposedly burned to death in a house fire. The idea – originally given the title *High Heels*, until that title was borrowed for a completely different film – remains unfilmed (Strauss 1996: 104).

2. See Higginbotham (1988: 1–2).

3. Elsewhere in Almodóvar's work, death figures not as a national institution but as an inevitable part of life. In *What Have I Done* the grandmother's favourite subject is death, as she speaks with an old friend about who has died lately in their village. In *All About My Mother* both the death of Manuela's son Esteban and that of Sister Rosa give rise to an emotional study of coping with a loss which is universal rather than idiosyncratically Hispanic. In most other films, death means murder, its associations not nationally specific to Spain, and, indeed, often borrowed from American genres.

4. Of course, '*corrida*' is also a play on the Spanish word *correrse*, which means to come in the sexual sense.

5. In fact, Almodóvar remarks that the character of María is so masculine that her relationship with Diego could almost be described as homosexual (Strauss 1996: 57).

6. This relates to the need to position the arms in such a way as to force the bull's head down, directing any possible injuries away from the chest. Thus, if the rule is not followed, death is a very real risk.

7. The civilization of Minoan Crete with its symbolic investment in the bull, or the rituals of the Roman arena, provide parallels in other cultures. In Spain, the bull has associations of sexual magic, and was probably an element of fertility rites (Álvarez de Miranda 1979).

8. Even here, though, Spain may differ only by degree in relation to other Western nations. Jonathan Dollimore (citing Denis de Rougement's *Love in the Western World* [1956]), explains that 'From the twelfth century on [...] sex and religion had become fatally crossed, and the history of passionate love in all great literature [...] is the history of the secularization of this crossing, of the tragic and more and more desperate attempts of Eros to take the place of mystical transcendence by means of emotional intensity' (Dollimore 1996: 379).

9. Franco maintained this privileged position of the Catholic Church in return for the right to appoint bishops himself rather than have them chosen by the Vatican. After Franco's death, the new Spanish constitution barely mentions the Church, and Spain has no official religion. For a brief survey of the role of institutionalized religion in contemporary Spain see Hooper 1995: 126–45.

10. '*Hostias*' means the Host – see p. 44.

11. Edwards (1995: 168) suggests that 'the reasons for Ángel's sexually arrested development have clear Buñuelian echoes'.

12. See Graham and Labanyi (1995: 423) or Hooper (1995: 140).

13. The altar which appears in *Law of Desire* is a reworking of a version from Almodóvar's 1975 short film *Homenaje* (Albaladejo et al. 1988: 69).

14. 'What interests me, fascinates me and moves me most in religion is both its ability to create communication between people, even between two lovers, and its theatricality' (Strauss 1996: 37).

15. María Donapetry (1999: 71) also identifies Julia's (Carmen Maura) cradling of Ángel (Antonio Banderas) in *Matador* as a visual reference to Michelangelo's *Pietà*.

16. 'Kitsch exists in all my films and it's inseparable from religion' (Strauss 1996: 36).

17. For Yarza (1999: 17) Almodóvar's liberation and reappropriation of Spanish iconography makes him a political film-maker.

18. The other is in *High Heels*, when little Rebeca and an aunt (Eva Siva) watch the television news of the girl's stepfather's sudden death. The newsreader ends the broadcast with a reference to the excellent health of the head of state (General Franco).

19. Almodóvar has stated that his main motivation for this sequence with the medical students was their white coats which help to highlight Leo's colour within the crowd (Strauss 1996: 160).

20. Elsewhere Germans are not treated so respectfully. In *Law of Desire* Antonio says of his mother, 'My mother is German and she likes to spy.'

3. Social Structures

1. From the dialogue of *Matador*, the character of costume designer Francis Montesinos (played by Almodóvar himself), explaining the theme of his fashion show to a reporter.

2. Shaw, in an unpublished article, 'Men in High Heels: The Feminine Man and Performances of Femininity in *Tacones lejanos* by Pedro Almodóvar', 7.

3. On Almodóvar's casting of Javier Bardem (associated with particularly hyper-masculinist roles in many films) in the role of disabled David, see Conway (2000: 256).

4. See Longhurst (2000: 19).

5. Only the British watch more television. See Hooper (1995: 307).

6. Almodóvar interviewed for *La Luna de Madrid*, 43, October 1987.

7. In 1985, Almodóvar directed an advert for the Volkswagen Polo which was then rejected by the producers. See Boquerini (1989: 73).

8. D'Lugo (1991: 49) points to the irony of Almodóvar's mobilization of religion to depict gay love (the visual reference to the *pietà*) at end of *Law of Desire* as well as to the police presence and tacit acceptance of the scene.

9. According to Hooper (1995: 210), reported crime in Spain is less than a third of reported crime in England and Wales.

10. In Pepi's script, lesbian couple Luci and Bom are given a boy recently released from a mental institution as a wedding present, excising the father figure altogether.

11. Almodóvar particularly likes friendship between women. See Vidal 1988: 33.

4. Gender

1. These are *Pepi, Luci, Bom, Dark Habits, Women on the Verge* and *All About My Mother*.

2. Kaplan explains how Lacan's idea of a girl's Oedipal crisis throws light on this tendency for women to position themselves in passive roles: the girl is forced to turn away from her mother and finds a role in the linguistic world as an object not a subject; her sexual pleasure can thus only be constructed around objectification (Kaplan 1983: 26).

3. Kaplan (1983: 28), summarizing Doane's essay 'The "Woman's Film": Possession and Address' (Doane 1984: 67–82).

4. Almodóvar recounts that this sequence was in fact made up of three fixed camera shots but editing and the actresses' movement suggests a tracking shot (Vidal 1988: 122).

5. A reference to the character Máximo Estrella, famous destitute, blind poet and fictionalized creator of the *esperpento*, a new Spanish form of the grotesque, written by Ramón del Valle-Inclán.

6. Lacan describes the moment when the child recognizes his own image in the mirror as crucial for the constitution of the ego. As the screen is like a mirror (it frames a person in surroundings), it permits a temporary loss of the ego while simultaneously reinforcing it – the idea of forgetting who and where one is. For an explanation of this aspect of Lacan's theory see Bowie (1991: 21–6).

7. For Peter Evans, 'Almodovarian men, capable of all the sins of their fathers, are also epitomized by extremes of emotion, sexual desire for one another, unmanly intuition, gentleness, weakness and resistance to conformist stereotype' (Evans 1993: 331).

8. This anticipates Almodóvar's next film, *Law of Desire*, where the first scene

is a self-conscious challenge to the established order, a new take on the male gaze (see Chapter 5).

9. Fiercely self-sufficient, the Andalusian singer (played by Kiti Manver) reacts against being used by men and is hypersensitive to any male interest. She spends all her time aggressively affirming, 'I'm a model and a singer, not a whore ... You men are all the same.'

10. Shaw, in an unpublished article, 'Men in High Heels: The Feminine Man and Performances of Femininity in *Tacones lejanos* by Pedro Almodóvar', 4.

11. In the Press Book of *Law of Desire*.

12. Almodóvar borrowed this phrase from his own discussion about women, colour and literature in the Press Book of *Flower*.

5. Sexuality

1. Almodóvar makes a further distinction between the two films: 'I deal with sex in *Matador*, which is something very concrete, in a very abstract, metaphorical way, whereas in *Law of Desire*, I deal with desire, which is very abstract, in a very concrete, realist way' (Strauss 1996: 64).

2. Smith (1992: 178) makes the point that 'if lesbian love is taken wholly for granted, then its specific relationship to social reality will be erased'.

3. Smith (1992: 182) questions whether the viewer should take this scene as 'a subversion of Catholic dogma' or as 'a secularization of divine love'.

4. Another less compromising and somewhat stereotyped lesbian appears in *High Heels*. Bibi Anderson plays a lesbian who commits a crime just to be with her girlfriend already in prison.

5. The scene where Toraya ventures into a public toilet is excised from the filmed version, as Smith points out (1994: 27).

6. Quoted in Waugh (2000: 49).

7. Arroyo draws on Bordwell's idea of the 'primacy effect' here (Bordwell et al. 1985: 37).

8. An attempt at a more comprehensive definition of queer theory is made by Ellis Hanson, who writes: 'queer theory submits the various social codes and rhetorics of sexuality to a close reading and rigorous analysis that reveal their incoherence, instability, and artificiality, such that sexual pleasure or desire, popularly conceived as a force of nature that transcends any cultural framework, becomes instead a performative effect of language, politics, and the endless perversity and paradox of symbolic (which is also to say historical and cultural) meaning' (Hanson 1999: 4).

9. This theory originated in the work of Mary McIntosh and is cited in Penn (1995: 27).

6. Madrid: Cinematic and Socio-cultural Space

1. Almodóvar in the Press Book of *Law of Desire*.

2. Statistics are taken from *España 1995*: 33–4.

3. See Vernon (1995: 64–5).

4. This metro diagram was drawn by Spanish pop artist Dis Berlin.

5. Almodóvar uses Barcelona to much the same effect in *All About My Mother*, showing both the middle-class homes of Rosa's mother, and the much less up-market areas populated by prostitutes and drug addicts.

7. Genre

1. The history of authorship both in Europe and the USA is charted by Pam Cook (1985: 114–206).

2. Cook (1985: 116). The most celebrated authorial presence within a corpus of film is that of Alfred Hitchcock, who was ever-present even in those films where he did put in a token appearance.

3. See Lapsley and Westlake (1988: 112).

4. See Cook (1985: 189).

5. On authorship and the *Cahiers du Cinéma*'s role in the rehabilitation of the 'great' Hollywood directors, see Cook (1985: 114–36).

6. David Bordwell (1985) gives a comprehensive account of how narrative structuring operates in mainstream films.

7. In fact, happy endings are common to most genre films, but, as pointed out by Neale and Krutnik (1990: 30), in comedy the happy ending can be through chance, while in other genres it tends to be the result of causality.

8. For a discussion of black humour see Gehring (1988: 167–87).

9. Unpublished script, p. 8.

10. Ibid., p. 2.

11. Much of Spain's strongest dramatic tradition in its Golden Age (the seventeenth century) depends on the honour codes which affected all relationships, but in particular it depends on the precariousness of female honour and its potential also to shame the women's closest male relatives.

12. For a discussion on the use of scatological or sexual bad language in Almodóvar's films, see Chapter 2.

13. Almodóvar's appearance in the *fotonovela* scene of *Labyrinth of Passions* was prompted by the necessity of properly directing Fabio (Vidal 1988: 51). He later told Frédéric Strauss, 'I was almost holding him on a leash' (Strauss 1996: 21).

14. Almodóvar recalls that his appearance on stage with Fabio in *Labyrinth of Passions* was also pure chance, because original choice Popocho failed to appear. The same is true for his role in *Matador* as Francis Montesinos (Vidal 1988: 55).

15. Almodóvar in *La Luna de Madrid*, 43, October 1987.

16. Susan Martín-Márquez (1999: 30) believes that the displacement of the violation as the central focus of the scene is more troubling than the comic tone.

17. Gypsies are associated in Spain with a cheap kind of false gold. Note that this type of racist comment is still accepted in Spain.

18. Almodóvar has commented that such toilet scenes reflect his desire to portray people at their most intimate moments (Vidal 1988: 20).

19. Almodóvar likens Leo to the women in the melodramas of Tennessee Williams (Cobos and Marías 1995: 101).

20. The inaccuracy of the English translation of the title once again affects the reception of the film, as the English 'High Heels' suggests stylish comedy, where the Spanish 'Distant Heels' reflects the sentimentality of family melodrama. (The Spanish title relates to Rebeca's childhood recollection of her mother's approaching footsteps.)

21. Kinder (1993: 257) compares this sacrificial gesture with that attempted by Mildred Pierce in the eponymous 1945 Michael Curtiz film.

22. Buckland (1998: 81) affirms that 'historically, melodrama has replaced religion as a way of thinking through moral issues and conflicts'. This film can be seen as representing the tension between the rigorous certainties of religious faith and the doubts aired in melodrama.

23. See Vidal (1988: 293) and Cobos and Marías (1995: 134). In the latter interview Almodóvar recognizes that all the elements outside the Barrio de la Concepción building do not really work.

24. For Celestino Deleyto (1995: 59), drag 'in its excess and artificiality, [becomes] another case of transcontextualisation', taking popular performance out of context and thus parodying it.

25. Potentially the most surreal sequence, which involved Vanesa appearing in a circus, using her mother as a knife-throwing target, was dropped from *What Have I Done* (Albaladejo et al. 1988: 77).

26. Almodóvar remarked that the only person to recognize these obscure clips was Quentin Tarantino (Cobos and Marías 1995: 113).

27. 'When I insert an extract from a film, it isn't a homage but outright theft' (Strauss 1996: 47).

8. Visual Style

1. See note 1 to Chapter 1 for Candela Peña's description of Almodóvar's improvising of script parts in pre-rehearsals.

2. See note 10 to Chapter 1.

3. For a discussion of the importance of objects in classic melodramas such as those of Douglas Sirk, see Chapter 7.

4. Throughout *Women on the Verge*, the camera obsessively homes in on the smallest details which reveal the sentiments or preoccupations of the characters. Almodóvar believes that the extreme close-up is uncommon in comedy and suggests the director's parallel interest in the emotional and the melodramatic. The extreme close-up of Iván's lips as he prepares to dub *Johnny Guitar* sets a melodramatic tone for this scene, though much of the rest of the film is comic (Strauss 1996: 84). Extreme close-ups of the answering-machine, of the tomatoes and gazpacho, of the burning matches on the bed, of the wet carpet after Pepa has hosed it down to put out the fire, all indicate Pepa's state of mind. An extreme close-up at ground level of Pepa's pacing feet pans back and forth as she paces. And at the end of the film, a close-up of Lucía's hair flying horizontally (with the force of the speeding motorbike) and then another of her head travelling horizontally along a conveyor belt (as if severed from her body) serve to suggest her madness. Subjective point-of-view shots (though anti-verisimilitude) also express deeper sentiments, such as the subjective shot of Pepa from inside the wardrobe

where Iván's clothes hang, or the point of view from inside her answering-machine looking up at Pepa's anxious face above.

5. The 1970 sequence affords Almodóvar an opportunity to indulge in the visual nostalgia of Centro's fake fur coat and wig, the bus conductor's uniform and the garish colours of early-1970s interiors.

6. The inspiration may have been the cardboard cut-out models of Madrid buildings which were a feature of the *movida* magazine *La Luna* (see Chapter 1).

7. Bruzzi (1997: 11) suggests Gaultier's robot costume for Andrea is a reference to Lang's *Metropolis*.

8. The costumes in *Matador* were designed by José María de Cossío (a frequent collaborator) and by Francis Montesinos, Ángeles Boada, Ángela Arregui and Antonio Alvarado.

9. Lucía's flat is similarly outmoded with 1970s coloured patterned curtains.

10. Evans (1996: 29) links this unreal quality with the transformation through the narrative: 'the city now seems all the more fantastic and magical; it has at some level mutated from a place governed by patriarchal orthodoxies to one ruled by alternative measures, susceptible to infinite transformations'.

11. Holguín (1999: 160) picks out a scene in *Law of Desire* where Pablo, Tina and Ada eat in the Madrid restaurant Manila, as Almodóvar's particular homage to Hopper's famous painting *Nighthawks* (1942) in the film, although in Hopper's scene green dominates, while Almodóvar's scene is a mixture of blues and oranges.

12. This framed image is very similar to one in *Tie Me Up!* when Ricky and Marina also communicate with a defensive pharmacist through the protective bars of the shutters.

13. Framing is even used at one point to make a reference to another film (Hitchcock's *Rear Window*, 1954) when Pepa waits outside Lucía's home to catch Iván.

14. See Elsaesser (1987: 62) on 'the contrasting emotional qualities of textures and materials' in melodrama. Waugh (2000: 51) lists among the elements borrowed from Sirkian melodrama by Fassbinder, railings, grilles, foreground frames and mirrors, all elements which Almodóvar too has borrowed.

15. Camerawork combines with *mise-en-scène* to suggest the relationships between certain characters. Deep focus is used when Antonio is talking to Lotte Von Mossel on the telephone; Gloria is in the foreground, on a different plane from her husband. We see her reaction to the conversation which she cannot even understand. Then a split screen is used for Antonio and Lotte Von Mossel's conversation, the divided frame placing Antonio and his former lover much closer together.

16. In *Kika*, Andrea and Nick's confrontation takes place through the bars of the windows of the house, and Víctor in *Live Flesh* views Elena's flat through the railings, looking in but kept outside.

17. This religious form is interestingly copied later in another longshot of the set for Eva's casting session, which is dominated by a central image of a Gaudí-like church. In *Dark Habits*, a shot of the convent dormitory is also composed in perfect symmetry with the door in the centre and a bed with a crucifix above on each side, once again imitating the architectural form of the church.

18. When the inspector questions Ángel's mother, they are filmed through the blinds of the police station office, the traffic outside reflected in the windows, but

here they are separate, the intervening blinds indicating their lack of mutual understanding.

19. Other reflective surfaces are exploited for the variety of their textures: when Ángel talks to Leo over the phone, Leo is reflected in the shiny black lampshade of her desk, which contrasts with the close-up of Ángel, its deep focus revealing a busy Gran Vía at night below. And on Leo's second meeting with Ángel she is reflected in triplicate in the glass door of his office while he is seen through the glass. And in *Kika*, when Andrea comes to the house she and Nick are reflected in a garden pond, and this is paralleled at the end when Kika enters the silent house and is reflected in a pool of Nick and Andrea's blood.

20. In this world of stolen intimate images, mirrors play an even larger role than is usual in Almodóvar. Rapist Paul Bazzo is reflected in a round mirror as he returns to Kika's bedroom.

9. Music and Songs

1. In UK adverts for Guinness and for the Post Office.

2. Rather than borrowing, Almodóvar claims that he actually stole two pieces from George Fenton's score for *Dangerous Liaisons* (Stephen Frears, 1988): Rebeca leaving prison and returning to prison in the van (Strauss 1996: 118).

3. Te quiero porque eres sucia
   Guarra puta y lisonjera
   La más obscena de Murcia
   Y a mi disposición entera
   Sólo pienso en ti, Murciana
   Porque eres una marrana
   Te meto el dedo en la raja
   Te arreo un par de sopapos
   Te obligo a hacerme una paja
   Soy más violenta que el GRAPO
   Te voy como anillo al dedo
   Conmigo tienes orgasmos
   Si en la boca te echo un pedo
   Me aplaudes con entusiasmo
   Me perteneces, Murciana
   Porque a mí me da la gana

4. Yo quiero que tú sufras lo que yo sufro
   Y aprenderé a rezar para lograrlo
   Yo quiero que te sientas tan inútil
   Como un vaso sin whisky entre las manos
   Y que sientas en tu pecho el corazón
   Como si fuera el de otro y te doliera
   Yo te deseo la muerte donde tu estés
   Y aprenderé a rezar para lograrlo

5. Igual que en un escenario
   finges tu dolor barato

Tu drama no es necesario
ya conozco ese teatro
mintiendo qué bien te queda el papel
después de todo parece
que ese es tu forma de ser…

6. Almodóvar is among the audience in this scene from Colomo's film, one year before he was to make his own full-length feature debut.

7. Three compilations of *bolero* singer La Lupe have been released with the titles, *Laberinto de pasiones* (*Labyrinth of Passions*), *La ley del deseo* (*Law of Desire*) and *Mujeres al borde de un ataque de nervios* (*Women on the Verge of a Nervous Breakdown*).

Postmodernism, Performance and Parody

1. Irony and self-reflexivity were salient features of Modernism, the zenith of avant-garde high culture at the start of the twentieth century, and the context and aspiration of much intellectual, auteurist cinema since.

2. It transpires that Pepi's script is, in fact, the story of the film, as we see when Pepi starts to write it down: 'The guy says to her, "I want Luci to suck me off" and Bom replies, "Come on, eat up before it gets cold".' The dialogue is taken from the 'general erections' scene. Pepi also intends to include the scene where she makes Bom urinate on Luci, knowing it will please her masochistic side.

3. From the Press Book of *All About My Mother*.

4. This event, involving the famous Spanish theatre actress Lola Membrives, is related by Almodóvar in the Press Book of *All About My Mother*.

5. Baudrillard's ideas on postmodern culture and simulacra are summarized by Selden et al. (1997: 205).

6. Hutcheon (1985: 4), borrowing a phrase from W. Jackson Bate's *The Burden of the Past and the English Poet*. Cambridge, MA: Belknap Press/Harvard University Press, 1970.

7. In his explanation of why such 'meta-narratives' are no longer valid, Jean-François Lyotard (1979) mentions some of the social and political disasters of the modern period. Twentieth-century Spanish history provides a good example of the leap from pre- to post-modern.

8. Interview in *Film Quarterly*, 17 November 1987.

9. From the Press Book of *Tie Me Up!*

10. The sassy receptionist played by Loles León even makes an announcement for Señor Salcedo, the name of Almodóvar's real-life film editor.

11. See Fuentes (1995: 157–8) for a discussion of the carnivalesque/grotesque inheritance in Almodóvar.

Appendix 1
Glossary of Spanish Terms

AVE   Alta Velocidad Española – Spain's high-speed train.

bacalao al pil-pil   Cod in sauce (a notoriously difficult dish).

bailaor   A male flamenco dancer.

beatas   Older religious women for whom the Church – in particular the administration of its outward trappings – is the main focus of life.

bolero   Sentimental song or ballad originating in Latin America and increasingly popular in Spain (largely as a result of an Almodóvar-inspired revival of interest).

cante jondo   Deep song – the vocal interpretation of flamenco.

capote   Pink and yellow cape in bullfighting.

castizo   Traditionally Spanish, but with particular associations with Castile and even more with Madrid.

cava   Spanish version of champagne.

chorizo   Spicy sausage (*choricillo* in diminutive form, little *chorizo*).

chotis   Traditional Madrid dance.

chulaponas   Female version of *chulo*.

chulo   A typical madrilenian male costume, but also used to refer to Madrid types much in the same way as 'Cockney' is used for a certain locally-identified Londoner.

cilicio   A spiked chain worn on the upper thigh to inflict pain while keeping the scars from view; it is meant to cause suffering in the self-mortification tradition of excessive Catholicism.

corrida Bullfight: literally – 'running' of bulls.

Cruz de Mayo A local or domestic shrine set up in honour of a particular saint.

desmemoria The collective tendency wilfully to forget Spain's past, either because it is too painful, or because it is politically expedient (given that so many of Franco's men remained in the political sphere after the end of his regime).

destape Literally 'uncovering' – the rush to make the most of the much-relaxed censorship laws following the death of Franco, by offering spectacles based on nudity, titillation or outright pornography.

eixample The nineteenth-century grid system of streets which spread out from Barcelona's old quarter. The area, which includes much of Gaudí's most famous architectural work, is now distinctly bourgeois.

esperpento A term coined by the highly influential Spanish dramatist Ramón del Valle-Inclán (1866–1936) to denote a typically Spanish form of grotesque manipulation in literature and art.

estocada In bullfighting, a sword thrust.

faena The stage of a bullfight from where the *picadores* finish and the *matador* takes up the *muleta* (red cape) until the end of the *corrida*.

Falange Spain's fascist party, created in 1933.

fotonovela Comic narrative using photographs rather than drawings.

gazpacho Famous Spanish cold tomato soup.

GRAPO Grupos de Resistencia Antifacista Primero de Octubre (First of October Anti-fascist Terrorist Groups), based in Catalunya.

Guardia Civil Rural police force introduced to combat banditry in the nineteenth century. It was unpopular during the Franco regime.

machista Male chauvinist.

maricón Queer (often used indiscriminately as an insult).

matador Bullfighter who actually kills the bull.

movida The explosion of music and pop culture after the death of Franco especially in the years 1977–84. Based in Madrid, this cultural renaissance soon expanded to include plastic art, design and film.

muleta Red cape in bullfighting.

NoDo The Franco regime's obligatory movie theatre newsreels, which functioned from 1942 to 1976.

Opus Dei   Ultra-conservative lay Catholic organization founded in Spain in 1928. Its members were influential in Franco's governments until 1973.

paso   The religious music which accompanies a float in Holy Week processions.

pasota/pasotismo   An apathetic attitude among the young, often associated with a particular style of speech from Madrid.

PSOE   Partido Socialista Obrero Español. Spanish Socialist Party in government from 1982 to 1996.

soleá   One of the major and more serious styles of *cante jondo*.

tonadilla   Light-hearted song originally part of theatrical performances.

torero   Bullfighter.

traje de luces   Suit of lights.

UCD   Unión del Centro Democrático. Centre-right Spanish party in government from 1977 to 1982.

zarzuela   Spanish operetta.

Appendix 2
Filmography and Plot Summaries

Pepi, Luci, Bom and Other Girls on the Heap [Pepi, Luci, Bom y otras chicas del montón] (1980)

Pepi is visited by a policeman who has spotted her marijuana plants from his flat across the street. She buys his silence with an offer of oral sex, but the policeman rapes her, ruining her hopes of selling her virginity to the highest bidder. Desperate for revenge, Pepi arranges for a group of her friends to beat up the policeman. But they attack his twin brother by mistake, and Pepi has to look for another means of getting even. She befriends the policeman's docile wife Luci and soon introduces her to a young punk girl, Bom. Luci's masochism and Bom's aggression quickly lead to the two women becoming lovers. Pepi, meanwhile, is forced to find work as her father decides to stop her income. She sets up her own publicity company, designing adverts for multi-purpose underwear and sweating, menstruating dolls. She also begins to write a script which will be the story of lesbian lovers Luci and Bom. The policeman traps his wayward wife and abducts her, determined to make her pay for her behaviour. His brutality is what Luci has always wanted, and, bruised and bandaged in her hospital bed, she tells Bom she is returning to him for a life of abuse. Bom is lost without Luci and laments that pop is also out of fashion. Pepi has the solution to both problems. Bom should move in with Pepi as her bodyguard and start singing *boleros*.

Production Company: Figaro Films
Producer: Pepón Corominas
Script: Pedro Almodóvar
Executive Producer: Félix Rotaeta
Director of Photography: Paco Femenia
Editor: José Salcedo

Cast

Carmen Maura	Pepi
Félix Rotaeta	policeman
Alaska (Olvido Gara)	Bom
Eva Siva	Luci
Kiti Manver	flamenco rock artiste
Julieta Serrano	actress
Fabio de Miguel (McNamara)	Roxy

Labyrinth of Passions [*Laberinto de pasiones*] (1982)

Nymphomaniac rock singer Sexi and gay sex addict Riza shop around the Rastro market for sexual partners, though as yet they don't know each other. Riza is the son of the Emperor of Tiran and is in Madrid *incognito*. By chance, his stepmother is also in town, receiving fertility treatment from Sexi's father, and hopeful of tracking down her stepson as a means of regaining favour with her ex-husband, Riza's father. Riza goes to a gig and finds himself replacing the lead singer who has broken his leg. Sexi sees Riza on stage and instantly falls in love. Meanwhile, poor Queti is suffering sexual abuse by her father who wilfully mistakes her for his absent wife. In search of consolation, Queti, who works in a dry-cleaning store, dresses up in the clothes of her role model Sexi. One day Sexi spots Queti in the street wearing one of her outfits and confronts her. They become friends. Queti tells Sexi about the problem with her father and Sexi confesses she can't stop thinking about Riza. When Riza and Sexi finally meet, their mutual adoration 'cures' Riza's compulsive homosexuality and Sexi's nymphomania. Queti and Sexi hatch a plan: they agree to swap identities so that Queti can escape her dry-cleaning and take on the role of Sexi for real. This would also allow Sexi to escape with her lover Riza. But Riza's stepmother finds him and seduces him. Discovered by Sexi, Riza tries to convince her that sex with the other women was only practice for the real thing with her, but Sexi is distraught. Queti has plastic surgery to make her look like Sexi and persuades Sexi to give Riza another chance. But by now, Riza has been discovered by Tiranian terrorists and must flee the country.

After a chase to the airport, the two depart, their love noisily consummated on board.

Production Company: Alphaville
Script: Pedro Almodóvar
Production Manager: Andrés Santana
Director of Photography: Ángel Luis Fernández
Editor: José Salcedo

Cast

Cecilia Roth	Sexi
Imanol Arias	Riza
Marta Fernández Muro	Queti
Fernando Vivanco	doctor
Helga Liné	Toraya
Ofelia Angélica	Susana
Antonio Banderas	Sadec
Luis Ciges	dry-cleaner

Dark Habits [*Entre tinieblas*] (1983)

Cabaret singer Yolanda brings heroin to her lover only to witness him drop dead after taking it. Desperate to escape the police, she recalls a visit by nuns from a local convent who claimed to be admirers. She arrives at the convent and is rapturously greeted by the Mother Superior. The mission of the order, called the Humiliated Redeemers, is to offer shelter and redemption to fallen women. On arrival, Yolanda is their only guest. The nuns, Sister Manure, Sister Damned, Sister Snake and Sister Rat of the Sewers make her welcome, but the Mother Superior quickly becomes obsessed with Yolanda. Together they consume heroin until Yolanda decides both should come off the drug. Withdrawal for Yolanda is like a painful catharsis, but for the Mother Superior it confirms her very sinful nature. Lusting after girls and drugs, she has become worse than the girls she is supposed to redeem. Yolanda puts her life back together again in a convent which is falling apart and threatened with closure. The Mother Superior prepares to resort to drug trafficking to maintain the independence of her convent, but as most of the nuns leave, she discovers that Yolanda has also departed.

Production Company: Tesauro
Script: Pedro Almodóvar
Producer: Luis Calvo

Director of Photography: Ángel Luis Fernández
Editor: José Salcedo
Costume: Teresa Nieto Morán, Francis Montesinos

Cast

Cristina Pascual	Yolanda
Julieta Serrano	Mother Superior
Marisa Paredes	Sister Manure
Chus Lampreave	Sister Rat
Carmen Maura	Sister Damned
Lina Canalejas	Sister Snake
Mari Carrillo	Marquesa

What Have I Done to Deserve This? [¿Qué he hecho yo para merecer esto?] (1984)

Housewife Gloria struggles to make ends meet with cleaning jobs apart from her housework in a tiny flat by the Madrid orbital motorway. She lives with her taxi driver husband, his mother and their two sons. Her *machista* husband Antonio worked in Germany and longs for his former employer and mistress Ingrid Muller. His services for her had included forging a copy of letters she had allegedly received from Hitler. Antonio casually mentions this to a client, Lucas, who has the idea of forging Hitler diaries for profit. Gloria is increasingly desperate to find extra money to pay the bills and she is addicted to sedatives. Her sons have learnt their own survival strategies. The elder son, Juan, deals in drugs while the younger son, Miguel, sleeps with older men. Gloria eventually agrees to 'sell' Miguel to a dentist with an unhealthy interest in young boys and Miguel agrees, subject to certain material conditions. When Ingrid Muller decides to pay her former employee a visit in Madrid, it is the last straw for Gloria. Refused sedatives by a pharmacist, she returns home to find her husband preparing to take his ex-mistress out for drive. They argue and when Antonio slaps Gloria, she hits him on the head with a leg of ham. He hits his neck on the sink and dies instantly. Police investigations do not discover Gloria's guilt and she finds herself alone when her elder son leaves with his grandmother for her village. Gloria moves through her empty flat and leans over the balcony as if contemplating suicide. But just then her younger son, Miguel, returns, bored with the dentist and proclaiming, 'This house needs a man.'

Production Company: Tesauro
Script: Pedro Almodóvar
Production Manager: Luis Briales

Director of Photography: Ángel Luis Fernández
Music: Bernardo Bonezzi
Editor: José Salcedo
Costume: Cecilia Roth

Cast

Carmen Maura	Gloria
Ángel de Andrés López	Antonio
Chus Lampreave	grandmother
Verónica Forqué	Cristal
Kiti Manver	Juani
Juan Martínez	Toni
Miguel Ángel Herranz	Miguel
Katia Loritz	Ingrid Muller
Gonzalo Suárez	Lucas
Emilio Gutiérrez Caba	Pedro
Amparo Soler Leal	Patricia

Matador (1986)

Ex-bullfighter Diego harbours disturbing longings for blood and violence, years after a goring in the ring ended his career. Now he teaches bullfighting. We hear him give a lesson while an unknown woman lures and kills a young man apparently following exactly Diego's instructions on killing the bull. One of Diego's pupils is Ángel, an introvert who asks Diego for advice on how to treat women. Diego tells him to treat girls like bulls. Surprised that the young man has never been with a girl, Diego asks Ángel if he's gay. Ángel swears he will prove he's not a queer and subsequently tries to rape a neighbour, Eva, to prove himself. Not by coincidence Eva is Diego's girlfriend. Ángel, torn by guilt, confesses at a police station. While being interrogated by the inspector (who is gay and attracted to the young man), Ángel confesses to several murders. In custody he is visited by a lawyer, María. This woman is none other than the murderer of the opening scene, and representing Ángel is her means of coming into contact with his teacher, Diego, with whom she is obsessed. Eventually, Diego and María meet and she wastes no time in trying to kill him with her hairpin in the back of the neck (a bullfighting move she uses on all her victims). Diego prevents her, but they soon fall in love. Despite his confession the inspector does not believe Ángel committed the murders and increasingly suspects Diego. María and Diego, both equally obsessed with death, plan to kill each other in one ecstatic moment. Diego's girlfriend, Eva, overhears them plan their escape and each confess to the murders. Eva goes to the police and they pursue the lovers to their country retreat. But when they arrive, the two have already realized their dream of the ultimate erotic death.

Production Company: Iberoamericana (and TVE)
Script: Pedro Almodóvar & Jesús Ferrero
Executive Producer: Andrés Vicente Gómez
Director of Photography: Ángel Luis Fernández
Music: Bernardo Bonezzi
Editor: José Salcedo
Costume: José María Cossío

Cast

Assumpta Serna	María
Nacho Martínez	Diego
Antonio Banderas	Ángel
Eva Cobo	Eva
Julieta Serrano	Berta
Chus Lampreave	Pilar
Carmen Maura	Julia
Eusebio Poncela	inspector

Law of Desire [*La ley del deseo*] (1987)

Film director Pablo Quintero says goodbye to his lover Juan who is off to work for the summer in the south. Antonio, a closet gay with a dangerously homophobic attitude, becomes obsessed with Pablo and eventually they have sex. What for Pablo is a one-night stand is taken as a relationship by Antonio, who is jealous and manipulative. When Antonio finds out about Juan he travels south and murders him. Pablo drives down to see his dead lover and confronts Antonio about the murder. They fight and Pablo drives off pursued by the police before crashing his car and injuring his head. Pablo wakes up in hospital suffering from acute amnesia. His sister, Tina, visits him and has to fill in their life stories. Tina had once been a boy, and had undergone a sex change after running away with their father. After their incestuous relationship finished, Tina had returned to Madrid, co-inciding with the death of their mother, and had been reunited with Pablo. With Pablo in hospital, Antonio starts to see Tina as a way of getting closer to his obsession. Once Pablo regains his memory he discovers that Antonio is with his sister and, worried that he may harm her, he sets off with the police in pursuit. Antonio takes Tina hostage, but agrees to let her go if Pablo will talk with him. They spend an hour together, their last, for Antonio shoots himself.

Production Company: El Deseo SA
Script: Pedro Almodóvar
Executive Producer: Miguel A. Pérez Campos
Production Manager: Esther García
Director of Photography: Ángel Luis Fernández
Editor: José Salcedo
Costume: José María Cossío

Cast

Eusebio Poncela	Pablo
Carmen Maura	Tina
Antonio Banderas	Antonio
Miguel Molina	Juan
Manuela Velasco	Ada
Bibi Anderson	Ada's mother
Fernando Guillén	inspector
Fernando G. Cuervo	detective
Nacho Martínez	doctor
Helga Liné	Antonio's mother

Women on the Verge of a Nervous Breakdown [Mujeres al borde de un ataque de nervios] (1988)

Actress Pepa is abandoned by her lover Iván just as she discovers she is pregnant. She spends twenty-four hours trying to get in touch with him to let him know, but events in her household divert her attention. She spikes some gazpacho with sleeping pills in the vain hope that Iván will appear and she will force him to stay. Her friend Candela arrives, worried because she has discovered that a man she was sleeping with is a terrorist planning to hijack a flight to Stockholm. A young couple – Carlos and Marisa – arrive to view the apartment (which Pepa has decided to rent) and it transpires that the man is none other than Iván's son. When the hysterical Candela tries to throw herself off the roof in desperation, Carlos helps to save her, and Marisa, traumatized by the near-tragedy, goes to the kitchen and drinks a large quantity of the gazpacho. She then falls asleep for most of the rest of the day. Pepa goes to a lawyer to seek representation for Candela. Carlos recommends a female lawyer, who had been his mother's in a lawsuit against Iván, but she turns out to be Iván's new lover. They are planning to go away together *to Stockholm*. Carlos – informed by Candela of the impending hijack – rings the police and they soon arrive in pursuit of the terrorists. Pepa knows nothing of the hijacking but she finally works out who Iván's new lover is. Carlos' mother (Iván's ex-wife Lucía) arrives in search of Iván whom she has decided to kill. The police represent little threat because they have accepted an offer of some gazpacho and soon fall asleep. Lucía hijacks a motorcycle and departs for the airport, Pepa in hot pursuit in a taxi. Pepa arrives just in time to save Iván's life though by now with no hope of reconciliation. She returns home and tells Marisa of her pregnancy.

Production Company: El Deseo SA
Script: Pedro Almodóvar
Executive Producer: Agustín Almodóvar
Production Manager: Esther García
Director of Photography: José Luis Alcaine
Editor: José Salcedo
Music: Bernardo Bonezzi
Costume: José María Cossío

Cast

Carmen Maura	Pepa
Fernando Guillén	Iván
Julieta Serrano	Lucía
Antonio Banderas	Carlos
Rossy de Palma	Marisa
María Barranco	Candela
Kiti Manver	Paulina
Chus Lampreave	doorwoman
Loles León	receptionist
Willy Montesinos	taxi driver

Tie Me Up! Tie Me Down! [¡Átame!] (1990)

Mental patient Ricky is released from an asylum intent on marrying his obsession, Marina, a former porn actress whom he once slept with during an escape from the asylum. He turns up at the studio where Marina is filming a horror film. The ageing director Máximo Estrella is sexually attracted to Marina and is enjoying what could be his last experience of directing a sexy female lead. After filming the last scene, Marina goes home to change for the post-shoot party. She answers the door to Ricky, who forces his way in and brutally knocks her to the floor when she screams. Marina wakes with terrible toothache which normal painkillers do not counter, as she is addicted to stronger drugs. Ricky explains that he has entrapped her so that when she gets to know him better she will fall in love and they will get married and have children. Marina is shocked and in pain and eventually persuades Ricky to take her to a doctor for her necessary drugs. Ricky barely leaves her alone with the doctor and she is unable to communicate her plight. Unable to get the drugs in the pharmacy, Ricky goes off to get them on the black market. But rather than paying the street price, he attacks the dealer to get the tablets. Marina's family and friends miss her and her sister visits the apartment and leaves a note. In the street again, Ricky is spotted by the dealer whom he had attacked and he is beaten and left unconscious. When he returns to Marina, she bathes his wounds and is suddenly struck by his devotion to her. They make love at length and Ricky seems to be on the verge of achieving his aim. But Marina's sister discovers her tied up and rescues her. Marina informs her sister that she loves her attacker. In the end it is Marina who goes after Ricky and they drive off into the distance.

Production Company: El Deseo SA
Script: Pedro Almodóvar
Executive Producer: Agustín Almodóvar
Production Manager: Esther García
Director of Photography: José Luis Alcaine
Editor: José Salcedo
Music: Ennio Morricone
Costume: José María Cossío

Cast

Victoria Abril	Marina
Antonio Banderas	Ricky
Loles León	Lola
Julieta Serrano	Alma
María Barranco	doctor
Rossy de Palma	drug dealer
Francisco Rabal	Máximo Espejo

High Heels [Tacones lejanos] (1991)

Television presenter Rebeca anxiously awaits the arrival of her mother whom she has not seen since she was a child. Her singing star mother Becky is just as anxious to rescue their relationship because she has an incurable heart condition. Desperate to emulate her, Rebeca has even married one of her mother's old lovers, Manuel, who no longer loves

Rebeca and foolishly attempts to restart the affair with Becky. Rebeca, meanwhile, has impromptu sex with a transvestite Letal whose act involves impersonating Rebeca's famous mother, Becky. A month later Manuel is found dead, and mother and daughter are both questioned. Becky reveals that she had been having an affair with her son-in-law. Rebeca does not confess to the Judge, but prefers to confess to the whole nation when she reads the news of her husband's death. She is immediately imprisoned but the investigating Judge seems desperate to prove her innocence despite all the evidence. Becky makes her return to the Madrid stage while Rebeca spends her first night in prison. The Judge arranges for Becky to see her daughter, and Rebeca now denies the murder of Manuel but confesses to her mother to the murder of Becky's second husband. As a child (we witness these scenes in flashback), Rebeca had overheard her stepfather deny Becky the right to go to Mexico to film. She had swapped his pills over so that he would overdose and leave his wife free to live her life. Rebeca's confession of the limitlessness of her adoration is too much for Becky's heart and her condition worsens. Back in prison, Rebeca discovers she is pregnant – carrying Letal's child. At once the Judge releases her from prison but without any fresh evidence. Rebeca goes to see Letal's final drag performance and in the dressing-room discovers that he is the Judge, Letal being one of the Judge's disguises. He explains that his dressing up was no more than an investigative strategy and, knowing about her pregnancy, asks her to marry him. As Rebeca struggles to take this in, they see a TV broadcast relating Becky's sudden heart attack. They rush to the hospital. Rebeca confesses to her mother the murder of Manuel, and Becky decides to take the blame in order for her daughter to go free. Soon after this sacrifice, Becky dies.

Production Company: El Deseo SA, Ciby 2000
Script: Pedro Almodóvar
Executive Producer: Agustín Almodóvar
Production Manager: Esther García
Director of Photography: Alfredo Mayo
Editor: José Salcedo
Music: Ryuichi Sakamoto
Costume: José María Cossío, Giorgio Armani, Chanel

Cast

Victoria Abril	Rebeca
Marisa Paredes	Becky
Miguel Bosé	Letal/Judge Domínguez
Feodor Atkine	Manuel

Pedro Díez del Corral	Alberto
Ana Lizarán	Margarita
Miriam Díaz Aroca	Isabel
Mayrata O'Wisiedo	Judge's mother

Kika (1993)

Photographer Ramón arrives at his mother's home in time to hear gunfire as she apparently kills herself, wounding her husband Nick (Ramón's US stepfather) in the process. Some years later beautician Kika explains how she had met Nick when she made him up before a TV interview. Subsequently, Nick had called Kika to his home to make up the dead body of Ramón who had died of a heart attack. But when Kika makes him up he awakes – not dead after all. Several years later Nick returns to Madrid after a period abroad and is met at the station by Ramón and Kika, now a couple. Relations between stepfather and son are cool. Ramón asks Kika to marry him, but she has her doubts, among them the fact that she has been sleeping with Nick. She is also concerned about Ramón's voyeur fetish. Meanwhile, Nick is approached by Ramón's former analyst (and former lover though this is not yet clear). Andrea now works in TV, presenting the morbid reality show *The Worst of the Day*. One of the episodes relates the story of rapist and prison escapee Paul Bazzo. Paul is the brother of Kika and Ramón's maid, Juana. His first call is on his sister. Once inside the flat he rapes Kika, unaware that he is being filmed by a voyeur (none other than Ramón who admits later that he likes to spy on his own girlfriend). Kika is less traumatized by the rape than by its subsequent transmission on Andrea's TV show. She decides to leave Ramón and – inspired by the film *The Prowler* – he starts to suspect that his stepfather had murdered his mother. He goes to confront Nick but has an attack. Nick assumes he's dead, but he is not out of trouble yet. Andrea has also worked out that Nick is a murderer and when she challenges him they end up killing each other. Kika arrives at this bloody scene, but she is able to revive Ramón. As he sets off in an ambulance, Kika follows in the car. But she breaks down and is rescued by a handsome bachelor and agrees to go with him to a party.

Production Company: El Deseo SA, Ciby 2000
Script: Pedro Almodóvar
Executive Producer: Agustín Almodóvar
Production Manager: Esther García
Director of Photography: Alfredo Mayo
Editor: José Salcedo

Costume: Jean-Paul Gaultier, Gianni Versace, José María Cossío

Cast

Verónica Forqué	Kika
Peter Coyote	Nick
Victoria Abril	Andrea
Alex Casanovas	Ramón
Rossy de Palma	Juana
Santiago Lajusticia	Paul Bazzo
Anabel Alonso	Amparo
Bibi Anderson	Susana
Charo López	Ramón's mother

The Flower of My Secret [*La flor de mi secreto*] (1995)

Novelist Leo is having problems with her husband Paco, a soldier on service in Bosnia. She confides in her psychologist friend Betty who tells her to keep occupied and suggests she get in touch with a publishing friend, Ángel, who works for the daily *El País*. She is commissioned to write on literature for the newspaper and telephones Paco to let him know. He cuts her short, attributing her contentment to alcohol. (Leo does have a drink problem.) Apart from her 'serious' unpublished work, Leo writes pulp romantic novels under a pseudonym. Her editors are shocked and angry when she departs from the sugar-sweet storylines. Soon after, Paco calls to tell her he has a day's leave. Leo, overjoyed, prepares for the day, but they are both very nervous. Paco soon tells her that the shift has been changed and that he only has two hours. They argue and Leo finally asks him if their marriage has any future. Paco replies that it doesn't. Leo takes a bottle of pills. She wakes to the voice of her mother leaving a message on the answer-phone, throws up the pills and goes out into the street in search of a coffee. She runs into Ángel who takes her back to his flat to recover. The next day he reveals that she has told him her secret – that she is the famous writer of romantic fiction whom no one has ever seen in public. When Ángel takes her home they discover Betty, who is distraught, thinking that Leo has killed herself with the pills. She confesses that she and Paco have been having an affair. Leo decides to go with her mother to their village to recover. Without her knowing, Ángel completes her contract. Freed from this obligation, Leo can now start to rebuild her life without Paco.

Production Company: El Deseo SA, Ciby 2000
Script: Pedro Almodóvar
Executive Producer: Agustín Almodóvar

Production Manager: Esther García
Director of Photography: Affonso Beato
Editor: José Salcedo
Music: Alberto Iglesias
Costume: Hugo Mezcua

Cast

Marisa Paredes	Leo
Juan Echanove	Ángel
Carmen Elías	Betty
Rossy de Palma	Rosa
Chus Lampreave	Leo's mother
Kiti Manver	Manuela
Joaquín Cortés	Antonio
Manuela Vargas	Blanca
Imanol Arias	Paco

Live Flesh [*Carne trémula*] (1997)

Víctor is born on a Madrid bus at Christmas in 1970 during a national state of emergency. His mother is a prostitute. Twenty years later he is a pizza delivery boy excited about his first date with Elena. But when he calls her she says she has other plans. He manages to get into her apartment and they argue. Elena pulls out a gun and a shot is fired but no one is injured. Nevertheless the police arrive and Víctor panics, taking Elena hostage. Sancho, the elder of the policemen, is a drunkard and impetuously tries to grab the gun. In the confusion another shot is fired, this time injuring David, the younger policeman. Víctor is imprisoned for the shooting and David, now paralysed, becomes a member of the paralympic basketball team. Elena and David have married since the shooting. Víctor is released from prison intent on revenge against David and Elena. He works as a volunteer in the shelter for homeless children which Elena runs. David, disturbed by Víctor's stalking of his wife, threatens him. Meanwhile, Víctor meets Sancho's mistreated wife Clara and they start an affair. Eventually, Clara tells Víctor that in the struggle which led to David's shooting it had been Sancho who pulled the trigger because David was having an affair with Clara, and Sancho wanted to shoot him. Elena is shocked and feels responsible for Víctor's false imprisonment. Strongly attracted to Víctor they sleep together and she admits it to David. Angry and hurt, David resolves to tell the violently jealous Sancho. Clara flees her violent husband but he tracks her down and they end up shooting and killing each other.

Elena and Víctor stay together and at the end of the film they are about to have a child, also on the streets of Madrid like Víctor's birth, but in very different circumstances.

Production Company: El Deseo SA, Ciby 2000, France 3
Script: Pedro Almodóvar (with Ray Loriga and Jorge Guerricaechevarría)
Executive Producer: Agustín Almodóvar
Production Manager: Esther García
Director of Photography: Affonso Beato
Editor: José Salcedo
Music: Alberto Iglesias
Costume: José María de Cossío

Cast

Francesca Neri	Elena
Liberto Rabal	Víctor
Javier Bardem	David
Ángela Molina	Clara
Pepe Sancho	Sancho
Pilar Bardem	Doña Centro
Penélope Cruz	Isabel

All About My Mother [Todo sobre mi madre] (1999)

Manuela works as an intensive-care nurse and liaison officer with the national centre for organ transplants. She acts as a grieving wife or mother in simulations designed to train doctors how to deal with transplant donors' families. A single mother, she takes her eighteen-year-old son Esteban to see Tennessee Williams's *A Streetcar Named Desire*. Esteban loves to write and wants an autograph from actress Huma. After the show they wait outside the theatre. Esteban tells his mother he wants to hear the whole story of his absent father and she promises to tell him when they get home. But running after Huma's taxi in pursuit of the autograph, Esteban is hit by a car and fatally injured. Manuela signs the organ donor form she has seen so many times, this time for her own son. She decides to travel to Barcelona in search of Esteban's father to tell him about his son. He is now a half-operated transsexual. Once in Barcelona, she meets Agrado, an old friend and also a transsexual, but Agrado tells Manuela her estranged husband Esteban (now called Lola) has disappeared. They visit a social worker nun, Rosa, who tells them she had helped Lola to detox. Later, Rosa confesses that she is pregnant and that Esteban-Lola is the father. Manuela is furious with her husband but does not tell Rosa. She goes to see the same version of *Streetcar* she had seen in Madrid with her son. There she meets actress Huma who is in love with fellow actress Nina. Drug addict Nina has run off so Manuela drives Huma to a drug-market street and they find her. The next day, Huma offers Manuela a job as her personal assistant. One night Nina is too drugged to perform and Manuela offers to play her role. She does it very well and Nina is furious. Manuela has to explain to them why *Streetcar* has marked her life. Rosa is HIV-positive, the virus picked up from drug addict Esteban-Lola, and her pregnancy is a difficult one. Manuela soon gives up the job with Huma to look after her constantly. Rosa tells her she is going to call the baby Esteban if it's a boy, in memory of Manuela's dead son. But Rosa dies in childbirth and Manuela is left to look after the baby who has the HIV virus. Rejected by the baby's grandmother, Manuela leaves with her adopted son for Madrid. But three years later she is back for a medical conference, her little Esteban one of the first babies to completely eliminate the virus.

Production Company: El Deseo SA, Renn Productions, France 2 Cinéma
Script: Pedro Almodóvar
Executive Producer: Agustín Almodóvar
Production Manager: Esther García
Director of Photography: Affonso Beato
Editor: José Salcedo
Music: Alberto Iglesias
Costume: José María de Cossío

Cast

Cecilia Roth	Manuela
Marisa Paredes	Huma Rojo
Candela Peña	Nina
Antonia San Juan	La Agrado
Penélope Cruz	Hermana Rosa
Rosa María Sardá	Rosa's mother
Fernando Fernán Gómez	Rosa's father
Fernando Guillén	Doctor
Toni Cantó	Lola
Eloy Azorín	Esteban
Carlos Lozano	Mario
Lluís Pasqual	*as himself*

Appendix 3
Video and DVD Availability

Pepi, Luci, Bom and Other Girls on the Heap   UK: Tartan (VHS); USA: Cinevista Video (VHS)

Labyrinth of Passions   UK: Tartan (VHS); USA: Cinevista Video (VHS)

Dark Habits   UK: Tartan (VHS); USA: Cinevista Video (VHS)

What Have I Done to Deserve This?   UK: Tartan (VHS); USA: Cinevista Video (VHS)

Matador   UK: Tartan (VHS); USA: Cinevista Video (VHS)

Law of Desire   UK: Tartan (VHS); USA: Cinevista Video (VHS)

Women on the Verge of a Nervous Breakdown   UK: Polygram Video (VHS); USA: MGM Home Entertainment (VHS)

Tie Me Up! Tie Me Down!   UK: Enterprise (VHS); USA: Anchor Bay Entertainment (DVD/VHS)

High Heels   UK: Columbia Tristar Home Video (VHS); USA: Paramount Home Video (VHS)

Kika   UK: Polygram Video (VHS); USA: Image Entertainment Ltd (DVD), Trimark Home Video (VHS).

The Flower of My Secret   UK: Polygram Video (VHS); USA: Columbia Tristar Home Video (VHS)

Live Flesh   UK: Twentieth Century Fox Entertainment (DVD/VHS); USA: MGM Home Entertainment (VHS)

All About My Mother   UK: Polygram Video (DVD/VHS); USA: Columbia Tristar Home Entertainment (DVD/VHS)

Bibliography

Almodóvar

Albaladejo, Miguel et al. (1988) *Los fantasmas del deseo. A Propósito de Pedro Almodóvar*. Madrid: Aula 7.

Almodóvar, Pedro (1991) *Patty Diphusa y otros textos*. Barcelona: Anagrama.

— (1997) *Carne trémula. El guión*. Barcelona: Plaza y Janés.

Arroyo, José (1992) '*La ley del deseo*: A Gay Seduction', in Richard Dyer and Ginette Vincendeau (eds), *Popular European Cinema*. London: Routledge, pp. 31–46.

Boquerini (1989) *Pedro Almodóvar*. Madrid: Ediciones JC.

Cobos, Juan and Miguel Marías (1995) 'Almodóvar Secreto', *Nickel Odeon* 1, 74–149.

Deleyto, Celestino (1995) 'Postmodernism and Parody in Pedro Almodóvar's *Mujeres al borde de un ataque de nervios* (1988)', *Forum for Modern Language Studies*, XXXI, 49–63.

D'Lugo, Marvin (1991) 'Almodóvar's City of Desire', *Quarterly Review of Film and Video*, 13(4), 47–65.

Donapetry, María (1999) 'Once a Catholic … : Almodóvar's Religious Reflections', *Bulletin of Hispanic Studies*, LXXVI, 67–75.

Escudero, Javier (1998) 'Rosa Montero y Pedro Almodóvar: miseria y estilización de *la movida* madrileña', *Arizona Journal of Hispanic Cultural Studies*, 2, 147–61.

Evans, Peter (1993) 'Almodóvar's *Matador*: Genre, Subjectivity and Desire', *Bulletin of Hispanic Studies*, LXX, 325–35.

— (1996) *Women on the Verge of a Nervous Breakdown*. London: BFI.

Fernández, Agustín (1999) 'Almodóvar y el patetismo musical latino', *Manantial*, 24, University of Newcastle.

Fuentes, Víctor (1995) 'Almodóvar's Postmodern Cinema: A Work in Progress…' in Kathleen M. Vernon and Barbara Morris (eds), *Post-Franco, Postmodern. The Films of Pedro Almodóvar*. Westport CT: Greenwood Press, pp. 155–70.

García de León, María Antonia and Teresa Maldonado (1989) *Pedro Almodóvar, la otra España cañí*. Ciudad Real: Biblioteca de Autores y temas Manchegos.

Holguín, Antonio (1999) *Pedro Almodóvar*, 2nd edn, Madrid: Cátedra.

Nandorfy, Martha J (1993) '*Tie Me Up! Tie Me Down!*: Subverting the Glazed Gaze of American Melodrama and Film Theory', *Cineaction*, 31 (spring–summer), 50–61.

Navajas, Gonzalo (1991) 'Lo antisublime posmoderno y el imperativo ético en *¡Átame!* de Pedro Almodóvar', *España Contemporánea*, 4(1), 65–83.

Prout, Ryan (1999) 'Kicking the Habit? Cinema, Gender, and the Ethics of Care in Almodóvar's *Entre tinieblas*', *Bulletin of Hispanic Studies*, LXXVI, 53–66.

Sánchez-Biosca, Vicente (1989) 'El elixir aromático de la postmodernidad o la comedia según Pedro Almodóvar', in José A Hurtado and Francisco M. Picó (eds), *Escritos sobre el cine español 1973–1987*. Valencia: Ediciones Textos Filmoteca, pp. 111–23.

Smith, Paul Julian (1994) *Desire Unlimited*. London: Verso.

— (1996) *Vision Machines*. London: Verso.

Strauss, Frédéric (1996) (ed.), *Almodóvar on Almodóvar*, trans. Yves Baignières. London: Faber and Faber.

Triana Toribio, Nuria (1996) 'Almodóvar's Melodramatic Mise-en-scène: Madrid as a Setting for Melodrama', *Bulletin of Hispanic Studies*, LXXIII, 179–89.

Varderi, Alejandro (1996) *Severo Sarduy y Pedro Almodóvar. Del barroco al kitsch en la narrativa y el cine postmodernos*. Madrid: Pliegos.

Vernon, Kathleen M. (1995) 'Melodrama Against Itself: Pedro Almodóvar's *What Have I Done to Deserve This?*' in Kathleen M. Vernon and Barbara Morris (eds), *Post-Franco, Postmodern. The Films of Pedro Almodóvar*. Westport CT: Greenwood Press, pp. 59–73.

Vernon, Kathleen M. and Barbara Morris (eds) (1995) *Post-Franco, Postmodern. The Films of Pedro Almodóvar*. Westport CT: Greenwood Press.

Vidal, Nuria (1988) *El cine de Pedro Almodóvar*. Barcelona: Destino.

Vidal-Beneyto, José (1999) 'Almodóvar polítcamente correcto', *El País*, 3 November, 17.

Yarza, Alejandro (1999) *Un caníbal en Madrid. La sensibilidad camp y el reciclaje de la historia en el cine de Pedro Almodóvar*. Madrid: Libertarias.

Spain and Spanish Cinema

Allinson, Mark (2000) 'The Construction of Youth in Spain in the 1980s and 1990s', in Barry Jordan and Rikki Morgan-Tamosunas (eds), *Contemporary Spanish Cultural Studies*. London: Edward Arnold, pp. 265–73.

Álvarez de Miranda, Ángel (1979) *Ritos y juegos del toro*. Madrid: Taurus.

Besas, Peter (1997) 'The Financial Structure of Spanish Cinema', in M. Kinder (ed.), *Refiguring Spain. Cinema/Media/Representation*. Durham, NC and London: Duke University Press, pp. 241–59.

Brenan, Gerald (1943) *The Spanish Labyrinth. An Account of the Social and Political Background of the Spanish Civil War*. Cambridge: Cambridge University Press.

Conway, Madeline (2000) 'The Politics and Representation of Disability in Contemporary Spain', in Barry Jordan and Rikki Morgan-Tamosunas (eds), *Contemporary Spanish Cultural Studies*. London: Edward Arnold, pp. 251–9.

Covarrubias (1943) *Tesoro de la Lengua Castellana o Española* (1611), ed. Martín de Riquer. Barcelona: Horta.

Edwards, Gwynne (1995) *Indecent Exposures*. London: Marion Boyars.

Elms, Robert (1992) *Spain. A Portrait After the General*. London: Mandarin.

España 1995 (1995) Madrid: Secretaría General del Portavoz del Gobierno.

Evans, Peter (1995) 'Back to the Future: Cinema and Democracy', in Helen Graham and Jo Labanyi (eds), *Spanish Cultural Studies. An Introduction*. Oxford: Oxford University Press, pp. 326–31.

Gallero, José Luis (ed.) (1991) *Sólo se vive una vez. Esplendor y ruina de la movida madrileña*. Madrid: Ardor.

García Lorca, Federico (1960) 'Teoría y juego del duende', trans. J. L. Gili, in *Lorca. Penguin Poets*. London: Penguin.

Graham, Helen and Jo Labanyi (eds) (1995) *Spanish Cultural Studies. An Introduction*. Oxford: Oxford University Press.

Gubern, Román et al. (1995) *Historia del cine español*. Madrid: Cátedra.

Higginbotham, Virginia (1988) *Spanish Film Under Franco*. Austin, TX: University of Texas Press.

Hooper, John (1995) *The New Spaniards*. London: Penguin.

Hopewell, John (1986) *Out of the Past. Spanish Cinema After Franco*. London: BFI.

Hurtado, José A. and Francisco M. Picó (eds) (1989) *Escritos sobre el cine español 1973–1987*. Valencia: Ediciones Textos Filmoteca.

Jordan, Barry and Rikki Morgan-Tamosunas (eds) (1998) *Contemporary Spanish Cinema*. Manchester: Manchester University Press.

— (eds) (2000) *Contemporary Spanish Cultural Studies*. London: Edward Arnold.

Kattán-Ibarra, Juan (1989) *Perspectivas culturales de España*. Lincolnwood, IL: National Textbook Company.

Kinder, Marsha (1993) *Blood Cinema*. Berkeley, CA: University of California Press.

— (ed.) (1997) *Refiguring Spain. Cinema/Media/Representation*. Durham, NC and London: Duke University Press.

Lawlor, Teresa and Mike Rigby (1998) *Contemporary Spain*. London: Longman.

Longhurst, Alex (2000) 'Culture and Development: the Impact of 1960s "desarrollismo"' in Barry Jordan and Rikki Morgan-Tamosunas (eds), *Contemporary Spanish Cultural Studies*. London: Edward Arnold, pp. 17–28.

Martín Márquez, Susan (1999) *Feminist Discourses and Spanish Cinema*. Oxford: Oxford University Press.

Montero, Rosa (1995) 'The Silent Revolution: The Social and Cultural Advances of Women in Democratic Spain', in Helen Graham and Jo Labanyi (eds), *Spanish Cultural Studies. An Introduction*. Oxford: Oxford University Press, pp. 381–5.

Moreiras, Cristina (2000) 'Spectacle, Trauma and Violence in Contemporary Spain', in Barry Jordan and Rikki Morgan-Tamosunas (eds), *Contemporary Spanish Cultural Studies*. London: Edward Arnold, pp. 134–42.

Shubert, Adrian (1990) *A Social History of Modern Spain*. London and New York: Routledge.

Smith, Paul Julian (1992) *Laws of Desire*. Oxford: Oxford University Press.

Stanton, Edward F. (1999) *Handbook of Spanish Popular Culture*. Westport, CT: Greenwood Press.

Torres, Augusto M. (1995) 'The Film Industry: Under Pressure from the State and Television' in Helen Graham and Jo Labanyi (eds), *Spanish Cultural Studies. An Introduction*. Oxford: Oxford University Press, pp. 369–73.

Triana Toribio, Nuria (2000) 'A Punk Called Pedro: *la movida* in the films of Pedro Almodóvar', in Barry Jordan and Rikki Morgan-Tamosunas (eds), *Contemporary Spanish Cultural Studies*. London: Edward Arnold, pp. 264–82.

Truscott, Sandra and María García (1998) *A Dictionary of Contemporary Spain*. London: Hodder and Stoughton.

Vallina, Isabel (1984) 'La movida madrileña representada en la exposición "Madrid, Madrid"' *Garbo*, 16 July, 31.

Film and Theory

Anderson, Benedict (1991) *Imagined Communities*, 2nd edn. London: Verso.

Bakhtin, Mikhail (1981) *The Dialogic Imagination*, trans. Caryl Emerson and Michael Holquist, ed. Michael Holquist. Austin, TX: University of Texas Press.

Bataille, Georges (1962) *Eroticism*, trans. Mary Dalwood. London: Calder and Boyars.

Baudrillard, Jean (1981) *Simulacra and Simulation*, trans. Sheila Faria Glaser. Ann Arbor: University of Michigan Press.

— (1990) *Seduction*, trans. Brian Singer. London: Macmillan.

Benamou, Michel and Charles Caramello (1977) *Performance in Postmodern Culture*. Milwaukee: Centre for Twentieth Century Studies.

BFI Companion to Crime (1997) ed. Phil Hardy. London: Cassel.

Birken, Lawrence (1988) *Consuming Desire: Sexual Science and the Emergence of a Culture of Abundance, 1871–1914*. Ithaca, NY: Cornell University Press.

Bordwell, David (1985) *Narration in the Fiction Film*. London: Methuen.

Bordwell, David, Janet Staiger and Kristin Thompson (1985) *The Classical Hollywood Cinema*. New York: Columbia University Press.

Bourget, Jean-Loup (1977) 'Social Implications in the Hollywood Genres', in Barry K. Grant (ed.), *Film Genre: Theory and Criticism*. Metuchen, NJ: Scarecrow Press, pp. 62–72.

Bowie, Malcolm (1991) *Lacan*. London: Fontana.

Bristow, Joseph (1997) *Sexuality*. London and New York: Routledge.

Bruzzi, Stella (1997) *Undressing Cinema*. London: Routledge.

Buckland, Warren (1998) *Film Studies*. London: Hodder and Stoughton.

Burston, Paul (1995) *What are You Looking at? Queer Sex, Style and Cinema*. London: Cassell.

Buscombe, Edward (1977) 'The Idea of Genre in the American Cinema', in Barry K. Grant (ed.), *Film Genre: Theory and Criticism*. Metuchen, NJ: Scarecrow Press, pp. 24–38.

Butler, Judith (1990) *Gender Trouble*. London: Routledge.

Clarke, John (1976) 'The Creation of Style' in Stuart Hall and Tony Jefferson (eds), *Resistance Through Rituals*. Birmingham: Centre for Contemporary Cultural Studies, University of Birmingham, 1975; reprinted London: Hutchinson, 1976.

Cohan, Steve and Ina Rae Hark (eds) (1993) *Screening the Male*. London: Routledge.

Connor, Steven (1996) 'Postmodern Performance' in Patrick Campbell (ed.), *Analysing Performance: A Critical Reader*. Manchester: Manchester University Press.

Cook, Pam (1985) *The Cinema Book*. London: BFI.

Crofts, Stephen (2000) 'Concepts of National Cinema', in John Hill and Pamela Church Gibson (eds), *World Cinema. Critical Approaches*. Oxford: Oxford University Press, pp. 1–10.

Doane, Mary Ann (1984) 'The "Woman's Film": Possession and Address', in Mary Ann Doane, Patricia Mellencamp and Linda Williams (eds), *Re-Vision. Essays in Feminist Film Criticism*. Los Angeles: University Publications of America, pp. 67–82.

Dollimore, Jonathan (1996) 'Desire is Death', Margreta de Grazia, Maureen Quilligan and Peter Stallybrass (eds), in *Subject and Object in Renaissance Culture*. Cambridge: Cambridge University Press, pp. 379–86.

Dyer, Richard (1990) *Now You See It: Studies on Lesbian and Gay Film*. London: Routledge.

— (1992) *Only Entertainment*. London: Routledge.

Eaton, Mick (1981) 'Laughter in the Dark', *Screen*, 22(2), 21–8.

Ellis, John (1981) *Visible Fictions: Cinema, Television, Video*. London: Routledge.

Elsaesser, Thomas (1987) 'Tales of Sound and Fury: Observations on the Family Melodrama', in Christine Gledhill (ed.), *Home is Where the Heart is: Studies in Melodrama and the Woman's Film*. London: BFI, 1987, pp. 43–69.

Finney, Angus (1996) *The State of European Cinema*. London: Cassell.

Foucault, Michel (1978) *The History of Sexuality, Vol. 1: An Introduction*, trans. Robert Hurley. New York: Random House.

Gehring, Wes D. (1988) *Handbook of American Film Genres*. New York: Greenwood Press.

Genette, Gérard (1982) *Palimpsestes*. Paris: Seuil.

Giannetti, Louis (1990) *Understanding Movies*, 5th edn. Englewood Cliffs, NJ: Prentice-Hall.

Hanson, Ellis (1999) *Out Takes. Essays on Queer Theory and Film*. Durham, NC: Duke University Press.

Hebdige, Dick (1979) *Subculture: The Meaning of Style*. London: Routledge.

Hutcheon, Linda (1985) *A Theory of Parody*. New York and London: Methuen.

Jameson, Fredric (1991) *Postmodernism or the Cultural Logic of Late Capitalism*. London: Verso.

Kaplan, E. Ann (1983) *Women and Film. Both Sides of the Camera*. London: Routledge.

Katz, Steven (1991) *Film Directing: Shot by Shot*. Los Angeles, CA: Michael Weise.

Lapsley, Robert and Michael Westlake (1988) *Film Theory: An Introduction*. Manchester: Manchester University Press.

Lehman, Peter (1993) *Running Scared. Masculinity and the Representation of the Male Body*. Philadelphia: Temple University Press.

Lyotard, Jean-François (1979) *The Postmodern Condition*, trans. G. Bennington and B. Massumi. Manchester: Manchester University Press.

McConnel, Frank D. (1977) 'Leopards and History: The Problem of Film Genre', in Barry K. Grant (ed.), *Film Genre: Theory and Criticism*. Metuchen, NJ: Scarecrow Press, pp. 7–15.

McNair, Brian (1996) *Mediated Sex. Pornography and Postmodern Culture*. London: Edward Arnold.

Maule, Rosanna (1998) 'De-Authorizing the Auteur. Postmodern Politics of Interpellation in Contemporary European Cinema' in Cristina Degli-Esposti (ed.), *Postmodernism in the Cinema*. New York and London: Berghahn Books, pp. 113–30.

Mulvey, Laura (1989) *Visual and Other Pleasures*. London: Macmillan.

Neale, Stephen (1980) *Genre*. London: BFI.

— (1993) 'Masculinity as Spectacle. Reflections on Men and Mainstream Cinema', in Steve Cohan and Ina Rae Hark (eds), *Screening the Male*. London: Routledge.

Neale, Steve and Frank Krutnik (1990) *Popular Film and Television Comedy*. London: Routledge.

Nowell-Smith, Geoffrey (1977) 'Minelli and Melodrama', *Screen*, 18(2), 113–18.

Palmer, Jerry (1987) *The Logic of the Absurd. On Film and Television Comedy*. London: BFI.

Penn, Donna (1995) 'Queer: Theorizing Politics and History', *Radical History Review*, 62 (spring), 24–42.

Riviere, Joan (1986) 'Womanliness as Masquerade', in Victor Burgin, James Donald and Cora Kaplan (eds), *Formations of Fantasy*. London: Methuen.

Sedgwick Kosofsky, Eve (1990) *Epistemology of the Closet*. Berkeley, CA: University of California Press.

Selden, Raman, Peter Widdowson and Peter Brooker (1997) *A Reader's Guide to Contemporary Literary Theory*. London: Prentice Hall/Harvester Wheatsheaf.

Silverman, Kaja (1986) 'Suture', in Philip Rosen (ed.), *Narrative, Apparatus, Ideology. A Film Reader*. New York: Columbia University Press, pp. 219–36.

Smith, Anthony D. (1991) *National Identity*. London: Penguin.

Waugh, Thomas (2000) *The Fruit Machine*. Durham, NC: Duke University Press.

Weeks, Jeffrey (1995) *Invented Moralities: Sexual Values in an Age of Uncertainty*. Cambridge: Polity Press.

Index

('i' refers to illustration page number)